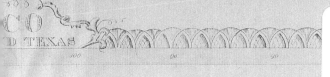

Ehrenberg

GOLIAD SURVIVOR, OLD WEST EXPLORER

A BIOGRAPHY
BY NATALIE ORNISH

With the first complete scholarly translation of

THE FIGHT FOR FREEDOM IN TEXAS IN THE YEAR 1836

BY HERMAN EHRENBERG

Translated by Peter Mollenhauer
With annotations by Natalie Ornish

TEXAS
Heritage
PRESS

Published by Texas Heritage Press
P.O. Box 12765
Dallas, Texas 75225

Library of Congress Cataloging-in-Publication Data

Ornish, Natalie
    Ehrenberg: Goliad survivor. Old West explorer / by Natalie Ornish.
        p.   cm.
    Includes bibliographical references and index.
    Includes a translation of Ehrenberg's memoir published in 1844: Der
Freiheitskampf in Texas im Jahre 1836.

    ISBN 0-9620755-1-5 (alk. paper)

    1. Ehrenberg, Herman. 1816–1866. 2. Goliad Massacre, Goliad, Tex.,
1836. 3. Texas–History–Revolution, 1835–1836. 4. Explorers–West
(U.S.)–Biography. 5. German Americans–West (U.S.)–Biography. 6. West
(U.S.)–Discovery and exploration.
I. Ehrenberg, Herman, 1816–1866. Freiheitskampf in Texas im Jahre 1836.
English. II. Title.
F390.E365075   1997
978'.02'092–dc21
[B]   97–23996
                                                                      CIP

FIRST EDITION

Printed in the United States of America

CONTENTS

The Fannin Monument
The sculpture shows the Goddess of Liberty
lifting a fallen soldier in chains.

We have inserted illustrations showing what the characters in this true story looked like to enhance the tale and make it more vivid. Also, these can be helpful should a motion picture or video production be made of this story. The purpose of this book is not to glorify Ehrenberg, nor Milam, Houston, De Zavala, Travis, Crockett or any of the men and women who struggled for Texas independence. Rather, it is to tell the story that freedom comes at an exceedingly high price. It needs to be cherished and protected at all times.

Although we have focused here on rebels on the run, we also salute nesters, without whom there would be no future generations to enjoy the freedoms won so dearly.

"Nation shall not lift up sword against nation;
nor shall they learn war any more."

Dedicated to all survivors,
who lived through
the Inquisition,
the Holocaust, and other
oppressions, and who found
within themselves the strength
to survive battles and struggles
with those who rob human
beings of their lives, resources,
dignity, and nobility of purpose.

Acknowledgments

My deep and heartfelt appreciation goes to everyone who contributed so much to make this book possible.

Much information that was fragmented has now been collected for the first time. Originally I planned to make available to a wide audience a fine translation of Ehrenberg's Goliad account. I am tremendously indebted to Dr. Peter Mollenhauer who, with grace and patience, spent almost an entire summer translating the account from a tiny book with very difficult typography, as I wrote furiously. Dr. Mollenhauer received his Ph.D. in German Literature from the University of Texas at Austin in 1965, and besides being a translator he is also a college professor and author.

After the translation was completed, Kim Hinnrichs did an expert job as typist. I then decided to accompany the Goliad story with a substantive account of "Who was Ehrenberg?" I had as a nucleus much data on Ehrenberg I had assembled for a previous (1989) book I had written on pioneer Texans, which featured Ehrenberg the soldier.

Working chronologically, I collected hundreds of little pieces of information like parts in a jigsaw puzzle. City directories, census records, old magazines, newspapers, journals, and other primary records in archives all were surveyed. I seldom traveled to any city that I did not take a taxi to its finest library to see what the special collections contained. The joy of discovering something new on Ehrenberg served to keep the momentum going for five more years.

Finally I had all the pieces of the puzzle together except two. The only blank left is a two-year period – from when he was honorably discharged from the Texian army in 1836 – until he was recorded as a passenger sailing from Galveston to New Orleans in 1838. During one set of years unaccounted for, I finally discovered that Ehrenberg had left his mining exploration to go to New York to raise funding, which he received from Samuel Colt, the Connecticut armsmaker. Some writers have said Ehrenberg "disappeared for years," but I discovered that perseverance and superb cooperation of librarians solved these mysteries.

At the University of California (Berkeley) Bancroft Library, most valuable were Peter E. Hanff, Bonnie Hardwick (Curator of the Bancroft Collection), and Larry Burnett (researcher).

Libraries include The Huntington (San Marino, California) and others throughout the United States and abroad. I researched in the Center for American History and the Harry Ransom Humanities Research Center, both on the campus of the University of Texas (Austin). At the Huntington Library I became indebted to Frances Rouse, Virginia J. Renner, Lisa Ann Libby (Rare Book Stacks Supervisor), Alan Jutzi (Curator of Rare Books), David S. Zeidberg (Director of the library), and Peter Blodgett (Curator of Western American History).

I am very appreciative of Gary Kurutz (Principal Librarian, Special Collections Branch) of the California State Library (Sacramento), and editor of the Book Club of California (San Francisco).

I would like to thank David, Marsha, and Elliot Karpeles of the Karpeles Manuscript Library and Museum (Santa Barbara, California), for their granting us the right to copy on our inside cover the antique (1856 Edward Edmonds, Sydenham School) illustrated map of California preserved in their museum. A very similar map (listed in a catalog as 1850) includes the vignettes such as the gold washing in California. The map is engraved: "J. & P. Tallis, London, Edinburgh & Dublin. The Map Drawn & Engraved by J. Rapkin. The Illustrations by H. Warren."

At the Southwest Museum (Los Angeles), which includes the Munk Library of Arizoniana and the Braun Research Library, my contacts were Kim Walters and Michael Wagner. Ms. Walters (Director of the Braun Research Library) furnished extensive computer print-outs of large sections of the more than 4,000 images in their collection of photo archives. From these extensive lists I discovered the antique pictures of the Mohave children and a reservation. The many hours she devoted to this project are priceless.

Other sources of information from California include: Sutro Library (San Francisco), Clyde Janes (Director), Frank Glover (Assistant Director), and Richard Terry (supervisor of the California section). Also Mary Inglis Sims (Sacramento), specialist in California genealogical research. San Francisco, Honolulu, Tucson, and San Diego, were all part of the trail. I appreciate all of the many researchers and scholars who became part of an international team.

For sources of explorer Ehrenberg's adventures in the Pacific, I worked with numerous enthusiastic researchers. At the Hawaii and the Pacific Section of the Hawaii State Library (Honolulu), those who helped me include Dr. Chieko Tachihata (curator of the Hawaii and Pacific Collection), and reference librarians Neil Hatayama and Ms. Jaya R. Poepoe. Also archivist Gina Bautista and Della Kuaana of the Historical Records Branch of the Hawaii State Archives. I appreciate help from the University of Hawaii (Manoa), Hamilton Library, Special Collections (Honolulu). Gordon Frazier (Honolulu) proved a help in my research as well as Katherine Knight, a volunteer librarian at the Hawaiian Historical Society (Honolulu). I am grateful to the State Archives for Ships in the Hawaii State Archives on the Iolini Palace grounds (Honolulu), the Hawaii Historical Society, and the Genealogical Society in the Bishop Museum.

To inquire about Ehrenberg's adventures in French Polynesia I worked with the Musee de Tahiti et des Iles (Papeete, Tahiti). In 1992 excellent material on Queen Pomare IV was sent to me by Madame Veronique Mu-Lupmann (conservateur), Musee de Tahiti (Punaauia, Tahiti).

During the more than five years spent researching and writing this book, much time was spent in the Arizona Historical Foundation Special Collection, Hayden Library, Arizona State University (Tempe). Senator Barry Goldwater was president of the Arizona Historical Foundation for more than thirty-five years. I am grateful to the senator, whose letters to me in 1991 were very supportive, and also to Doris Berry, his assistant, and to his wife Mrs.

Susan Goldwater.

In Arizona I worked extensively with Anita Abbott, Susie Sato, Dr. John Goff, the collection of Benjamin Sacks, M.D., Dick Lynch, Dean Smith, Nan Bowers, Esther Fireman, and Marilyn Wurzberger, and later Ed Oetting and Laurie Hochhalter. I would like to recognize Dr. Evelyn Cooper (Director of the Arizona Historical Foundation) and James Allen II (Library Supervisor).

When I researched in the Arizona state archives in the state capitol (Phoenix), known officially as the State of Arizona Department of Library, Archives and Public Records, especially helpful were Director Arlene Bansal and Ray Tevis (Director of Research Division), Cathy Griffin (State Documents Librarian, Research Division), Donald H. Langlois and Adrienne Sander (reference librarians in the Research Division), and Linda S. McCleary (Genealogy Librarian). Also helpful was Jerry Franklin of the Arizona Office of Tourism (Phoenix).

In 1986 I researched in the special collections of the University of Arizona library (Tucson). In that city I met Mildred Chanin and Abraham S. Chanin. He is Director and Research Professor of the Leona G. and David Bloom Southwest Jewish Archives at the University of Arizona. His historic programs are of national interest. From the Arizona Historical Society (Tucson) I recall Kim Frontz and Joan M. Metzger. Also I thank Mark Santiago at the Arizona Historical Society museum (Yuma), and also the Maricopa County Historical Society's Desert Caballeros Western Museum (Wickenburg, Arizona).

Librarian Kathryn Kujawa (Prescott) came to my aid. From the Bisbee Mining & Historical Museum (Bisbee, Arizona), Boyd Nickoll (photo curator) sent historic mining photos. I am indebted to Riva Dean (Library/Archives Co-manager) of the Arizona Historical Society, Southern Arizona Division (Tucson), for locating illustrations of surveyors instruments. Especially acting above the call of duty was Brad Bennett of the Grand Canyon National Park, who took the stunning photograph of Ehrenberg Point, reproduced on the cover.

I am grateful to Ron Tyler, director of the Texas State Historical Association and editor-in-chief of *The New Handbook of Texas*, for the opportunity to write the entry on Herman Ehrenberg, the subject of this book, for the 1996 edition of that encyclopedia of notable Texans. Appreciation also goes to managing editor Douglas Barnett, editor Roy Barkley, and associate editors Penelope C. Anderson and Mark S. Odintz for their patience over a decade, while I contributed approximately sixty other biographies.

At The Center for American History – formerly The Barker Texas History Center – at the University of Texas (Austin), Don Carleton, Kate Adams, Alison Beck, and Ralph Elder are but a few of the staff who guided me through the years. As I list librarians par excellence, I remember my friend Dr. Chester Kielman (Austin), who gave stature to the word *librarian*.

The Texas State Library and Archives (Austin), the Bexar Archives (San Antonio), the Rosenberg Library (Galveston), the DeGolyer Library on the campus of Southern Methodist University (Dallas), and other Texas libraries were consulted for decades.

At the Texas State Library and Archives, I am indebted to the staff there when I researched: William Gooch (State Librarian until 1996 when he retired and Dr. Robert Martin became State Librarian), and Raymond Hitt (Assistant State Librarian). Also Christopher LaPlante (Staff Archivist who later became State Archivist), David Richards and Marsha Evans (research assistants), and Laura Saegert (Archivist). Especially helpful was Donaly E. Brice (Reference Specialist who later became Supervisor of Archival Reference).

In later years my contacts at the Texas State Library included John Anderson (Preservation Officer), Wendy Clark (Supervisor of the Genealogy Collection), and (Ms.) Eddie Williams (Reference Assistant), all in Archives and Information Services in the Lorenzo de Zavala State Archives and Library building. John M. Molleston (Research Specialist) in the Archives and Records Division has been a long-time contact for me in the Texas General Land Office (Austin).

Casey Greene and Nancy Milnor of the historic Rosenberg Library (Galveston) have been dependable friends through the years, as have officers and staff of the Galveston Historical Foundation, in recent years Christy Benson.

In Dallas I appreciate Maurine Pastine (Director of Central Libraries of Southern Methodist University, including The Fondren), Marcella Stark (Head of Reference Services), and the many reference technicians, especially Carolyn Heizer. On the same campus, Dr. David Farmer (Director, The DeGolyer Library) has been helpful and cordial, as well as his stellar staff – especially Kay Bost, Cammie Vitale, and Duane Harbin. At the Bridwell Library of SMU, I appreciated the professionalism of Valerie Hotchkiss (Director), Page A. Thomas (Special Collections) and Laura H. Randall (the Reference Librarian).

The archives of the Dallas Historical Society have proved valuable, and I acknowledge the help from the staff, both scholarly help while preparing manuscripts, and support afterwards. Andrew Wolber has proved a great director, whose team includes Gaylon Polatti (Librarian and Archivist), talented David Newell (Custom Curator), and Mary Ellen Holt (Collections Manager).

I acknowledge the abundance of materials in the Dallas Public Library, especially the Texas/Dallas History branch headed by Marvin Stone, Carol Roark, and Jim Foster.

At the University of Texas (Arlington), Gerald Saxon (Director of Special Collections) and Kit Goodwin (Director of Cartography Department) were helpful. At the Sam Houston Memorial Museum (Huntsville), Mac Woodward (Curator of Collections), was of assistance with pictures of Old Sam, as was Derek Birdsall (Curator of Education), and Dr. Patrick Nolan (Director). At the Peabody Library at Sam Houston State University, I appreciate Paul M. Culp, Jr.

It has been a pleasure working through the years with Tom Shelton (Photo Archivist), University of Texas Institute of Texan

Cultures (San Antonio), as well as Steven Green (Librarian), Rex Ball (Director), Janet Weber and Walter Fein. Thanks also to Cathy Herpich (Director), Martha Utterback (Assistant Director), and Warren Stricker (Archivist) of The Daughters of the Republic of Texas Library at the Alamo (San Antonio).

Kevin Young, consultant on Goliad (Presidio La Bahia, where the subject of this book was held captive and now a museum), was a good correspondent during my early research, and Newton Warzecha (Director of Presidio La Bahia), and (Goliad) mayor A. (Buddy) Zavesky, made memorable my visit there in spring of 1997 to research and to attend an annual re-enactment of the battles and massacre. Thanks also to Elaine Noland (Goliad County Library Board chair), (the Director of the Goliad Public Library) Mary Ann Welch, (the Manager of the Chamber of Commerce) Linette Lancaster, Sue Miller (of the Goliad County Historical Commission), Dolores Clark, and Dennis Riedesel, Ph.D., University of Houston (Victoria branch).

Ever since the signing of the Texas Declaration of Independence March 2, 1836, the history made there has been well preserved (at Washington-on-the Brazos, Texas, near Brenham, where my mother spent her childhood). At the Star of the Republic Museum, (Curator of Education) Lisa Kalmus and (Director) Houston McGaugh were generous with information. Thanks also to Brian Butcher of the San Jacinto Museum of History (Houston).

As the book reached its post-partum stage, my helpers included Deveril (Dee) Gaines (editorial assistant), and Zaliza Zaini-Stevens (computers).

For sharing their expertise, I thank Joann and James Long, historian Jackie McElhaney, Evelyn Oppenheimer, Patrick Murphy, Dorothy Sloan, Paula Bosse, Mindy Auerbach, Kay Connelly, Julie Arthur Sherman, Karen Perea, Susanna Nawrocki, Shannon Landry, Marc L. Raphael, Hasia Diner, Norton B. Stern, Ruth Kelson Rafael, Charlotte and Gould Whaley, Bill Mercer, Dr. Elizabeth Gunter, Rebecca Sinkler, Marian Heiskell, and Stanley Marcus.

I would like to take this medium to thank four Texans who have long encouraged my work as a historian. The late Wayne Gard, fellow Northwestern University alumnus, historian of the frontier West, and author of *The Chisolm Trail* and many other books, long served as a mentor and editor of my work. John Edward Weems, whom I met in 1976, has been supportive of my writings through the years. A. C. Greene has long been an inspiring mentor and good friend. In 1977 I first met with Dr. William Goetzmann at The University of Texas (Austin). He is author of several books on the American West and is a Pulitzer Prize historian. I regret I did not join his program in American Studies then and follow his plan for me to add to the many credits I had left over from the master's degree and receive the Ph.D. degree under his guidance. However, his support had long range benefit and I often recall the last line of one of his letters which said, "Above all, do not become discouraged."

I also thank my husband Edwin and our adult children and spouses – Laurel, Dean, Steven, Kathy, Martha, and John – for being patient when my workload crossed over into their lives. I also treasure Molly Blackwell and my adult god-children, Gail L. Marsh and Mitzi Krockover and their families. Also Andre and Miles, wishing for them a better world.

I hope this public statement will help those I cherish know how very much they are appreciated.

THE TRAVELS OF HERMAN EHRENBERG:
A CHRONOLOGY OF SIGNIFICANT EVENTS

1850   On September 28, 1850 he informed the census taker in Union Town (now Arcata near Eureka), California that he was 28.

1854   In San Francisco. Listed in *San Francisco City Directory 1854* as "lithographer. 152 Washington, 2d floor."

1854   "In Sonora with one of the filibustering expeditions."

1854   Made official map of the Gadsden Purchase of land from Mexico.

1858   Visited New York to sell capitalists on the idea of investing in silver mining in northern Mexico. Invested in mining enterprises in Arizona and became pathfinder for new roads to mines in Arizona.

1860   Told Eighth U.S. Census taker at Tubac, Arizona, in September, 1860, that he was 39 years old.

1863   Wrote about the mining districts along the lower Colorado River for the *Alta California* newspaper published in San Francisco.

1863   Stayed in San Francisco at the Tehama House, corner California & Sansome streets, and the Globe Hotel.

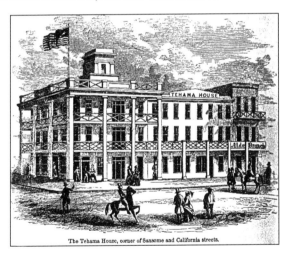

The Tehama House, corner of Sansome and California streets.

1864   Lived in San Francisco on NW corner, Jackson at DuPont (now Grant Street). Civil engineer.

1864   Lived and explored in LaPaz (now Yuma), Arizona.

1864   Served as Indian Agent for American Indians in Mohave Desert.

1865   Stayed at 1024 Stockton Avenue, San Francisco.

1866   Was murdered October 9, near present-day Palm Springs, California.

xix

Foreword

By the Honorable Barry Goldwater

*Former United States Senator and former president of
the Arizona Historical Foundation*

HERMAN EHRENBERG WAS A CLOSE FRIEND of my grandfather Mike. There was a great feeling of friendship between the two that resulted in Mike in 1867 giving the name Ehrenberg to a town in Arizona.

In 1866 my grandfather and my uncle Morris had been traveling by buckboard from Los Angeles east to the Colorado River. They stopped to spend the night at a trading post near Dos Palmas or "Two Palms" near present-day Palm Springs, California. There they discovered the body of their friend Herman. The storekeeper told the story that Herman had been murdered by Indians. Neither my grandfather nor my uncle believed this. They honestly felt that the storekeeper murdered him because he might have been carrying a large sum of money, which he often did.

There isn't a lot known about Herman Ehrenberg because up until now no one has taken the trouble to write a book about his very colorful and full life. Ehrenberg migrated from Germany, worked his way to the United States, and later landed in New Orleans. The Texas War for Independence was on, and he enlisted in the New Orleans Greys. He fought in several battles and was imprisoned at Goliad with Fannin and his men. He was one of the few men to escape this massacre in 1836. He went back to Germany but returned and crossed the continent to Oregon. From there he went to Honolulu, and from there eventually made his way to Arizona.

I personally am happy that Natalie Ornish is finally taking on the job of writing about his life. The Arizona Historical Foundation has had thousands of notecards collected on this man that were just waiting for someone to take on the task. This outstanding Westerner's history was long overdue. He was well-educated and widely known. This is a very, very important book because it describes in detail the life of a man who contributed so much not only to the making of the American West but also the future of the United States.

Scottsdale, Arizona

Book I

The Amazing Life of Herman Ehrenberg, A Biography

A Rebel on the Run

~

HERMAN EHRENBERG, whose story of surviving the Goliad Massacre is one of the most important documents on the Texas Revolution, continued to be a major contributor to the developing culture of the American Old West. He was also a world explorer, had unbelievable adventures in the South Seas — he became an island queen's lover — and met his death in a strange and tragic episode just as he was becoming an important figure in California and Arizona history.

Ehrenberg was an international traveler. He had an amazing life that covered two-thirds of the globe. He was at home in Leipzig and New Orleans as well as the then frontier towns of San Antonio, San Francisco, San Diego, Honolulu, Papeete, Valparaiso, and Tucson. In an era in which it took several weeks to cross the Atlantic, he made three crossings, the first in 1835. His journeys on horseback overland were many, covering the areas from New York to Texas, from the Atlantic to the Pacific coasts, and from Oregon to Mexico. He explored northern California years before the Gold Rush.

When *sailing* literally meant sailboats dependent on the wind for power, he crossed the vast Pacific Ocean in 1845 in a

journey to Honolulu that took over three weeks. Ehrenberg drew
the first map of the town of Honolulu. Those today who complain
about the long jet flight from California to Hawaii should com-
pare their air conditioned plight to that of this sturdy pioneer.

From the North Pacific Ocean he sailed to the South Pacific
and visited a number of islands, including the Marquesas,
Samoa, and Tahiti in French Polynesia. In Tahiti he met and
became the lover of the young queen of the island nation.

When Ehrenberg left the South Pacific, he traveled east to
Valparaiso (on the coast of Chile) in South America. He often
traveled along the coast of Mexico's Baja California. Later he
explored the Grand Canyon, where a point is named in his honor
in the Grand Canyon National Park. His interests in gold, copper, and silver mining motivated frequent travels between San
Francisco and Arizona. In 1854 Ehrenberg made the first official
map of the Gadsden Purchase, in which the United States purchased the town of Tucson and more than 45,000 square miles of
Mexican land in what is present day Arizona and New Mexico.

His final resting place is near present-day Palm Springs, California, southeast of Los Angeles. If he had any roots at all, it was
in Arizona along the lower Colorado River, where today sprawling ranches meet the colorful canyons. Senator Barry Goldwater
is probably the only living person at this writing (1997) whose
family had first-hand knowledge of this fascinating man.

I believed that secondary sources also were limited, until I
began research on Ehrenberg's life. After several years it became
clear that while there was much information, it was conflicting.
Only the date he was murdered is exact. He was born in Germany around 1816, but the date of his birth, his parentage,
where and when he was at times, and even his religion have various versions.[1] This book's main focus is on his spirit of adventure, his loyalty to America, and his love of the land.

What happened to Ehrenberg during his adventurous life?
The travels of Marco Polo, Christopher Columbus, and Captain
James Cook have been documented and historians regularly

study them, as well Balboa, Cabeza de Vaca, and Oñate. Ehrenberg traveled the routes of many of these earlier explorers seeking the same things to which they aspired — land and minerals. Like Francisco Vasquez Coronado who searched for gold, Herman Ehrenberg sought El Dorado, the legendary nude man covered in gold dust. El Dorado, the Seven Cities of Cibola, and the Fountain of Youth represented a multitude of tales pointing the way to untold wealth.

When Coronado made his first search for the wondrous Cities in the 1500s, Coronado did not find cities with gates of gold that flashed in the sun. Instead he found among the Zuñis—in what is now Arizona—walls of mud and naked burrows in barren cliffs. Coronado rode on, a thousand miles across unknown mountains and plains, but besides Indians, he found only buffalos. As Texas writer J. Frank Dobie pointed out, for hundreds of years conquistadors and later the adventurers rode on, searching for El Dorado.

The public has long been fascinated with the mystique of the men on horseback who sought for gold in vain. How much more, then, should we focus on the men who not only rode on horseback and sought for gold, but also discovered it!

This is significant in the light of economists who do not agree with the theory that for one person to gain, someone has to lose. Instead, they believe that real wealth comes when people work to explore the natural resources of the earth and thereby discover hidden resources waiting to be utilized. The discovery of gold in California, silver in Nevada and Colorado, and copper and silver in Arizona added to the traditional belief of wealth to be discovered on the American frontier. Herman Ehrenberg was part of that group of explorers.

If he was not in the category of these explorers for gold and silver, then surely he was in the company of John Fremont and Christopher (Kit) Carson in the American West and Daniel Boone in the East. Ehrenberg covered the whole nation from north to south and from east to west. He was a pathfinder and a path marker.

Ehrenberg came to America only fourteen years after Spain gave up its approximately three-hundred-year control over Mexico-Texas in 1821. The unending Spanish sovereignty was accompanied by the grim shadows of the Inquisition which began in Spain and crossed the Atlantic into the New World and included burning heretics at the stake in Mexico City. Included among these are the noted conquistador and writer, Luís de Carvajal el Mozo (The Younger).

From the 1300s, even prior to Ferdinand and Isabella, until 1834, the Inquisition was present in Spain; and from the 1500s until 1821 (the year of Mexico's independence from Spain) the Inquisition brought terror in the Americas.

In Mexico, the roots of dissatisfaction with its rulers ran deep. When Napoleon invaded Spain in 1808, factions in the colonies prepared for independence from Spain. One of the first events in the quest of the people in Mexico for independence was the revolt September 16, 1810 of Father Miguel Hidalgo y Costilla. The day that his movement began has been celebrated as Mexico's Independence Day. Father Hidalgo risked his life many times and was fatally shot in 1811. Ten years later the revolt begun by Father Hidalgo finally succeeded, and Mexico won its independence from Spain. The town of Goliad, Texas was named to memorialize

Doña Mariana de Carvajal as Inquisitors set fire to her in Mexico City in 1601.
From El Libro Rojo, 1520-1867 *by Vicente Riva Palacio and Rafael Payno, 1870. De Golyer Library, Southern Methodist University, Dallas.*

Hidalgo. The Congress of Coahuila and Texas declared the La Bahía presidio a town in 1829 and changed its name to Goliad, an anagram of (H)idalgo (Hidalgo spelled virtually backwards). It was outside this town that the historic Goliad massacre of approximately three hundred Texans took place.

In his book *The Fight for Freedom*, Herman Ehrenberg gives a brief background of these early factors. He also explains in his writings how free-

Father Hidalgo, "Liberator of Mexico."
From Mexico, A Través de los Siglos *by Vicente Riva Palacio, 1887. Institute of Texan Cultures.*

doms won in the favored Constitution of 1824 covering Mexico and Texas were overturned by the dictator Santa Anna. In the Declaration of Independence of March 2, 1836, the "delegates of the people of Texas" wrote they were forced "either to abandon our homes, acquired by so many privations, or submit to the most intolerable of all tyranny, the combined despotism of the sword and the priesthood." The delegates also wrote, "It incarcerated in a dungeon, for a long time, one of our citizens [Stephen F. Austin] for no other cause but a zealous endeavour to procure the acceptance of our constitution."

Ehrenberg's book about his experiences in Texas had three printings in Germany but has never before been published unabridged outside of Germany. (The titles of the three editions of Ehrenberg's book are listed in the bibliography at the end of this book.)

We have included herewith a complete translation of his book. In other words, we have here a book within a book. This translation was made by Dr. Peter Mollenhauer, Associate Professor of German at Southern Methodist University, Dallas, Texas. Dr. Mollenhauer was Chair, Department of Foreign Languages and Literature (1967-1972) and since 1976 has served as director of the "SMU-in-Austria" summer program. He has written extensive articles published internationally, lectured widely, co-authored one book, and made scholarly translations of three books.[2]

A master's thesis at the University of Texas by Edgar Bartholomae (1925) made a primary translation, but the Mollenhauer translation is a new, complete, and separate project. A condensed version of Ehrenberg's Goliad account was published in 1935, with a preface by Dr. Herbert P. Gambrell, an SMU history professor who wrote of Ehrenberg:

"He came to Texas from a radically different environment, and recorded what he saw and felt in more graphic and detached fashion, perhaps, than a citizen of the United States could have done. . . The book is a valuable source for the period it covers."

Herman Ehrenberg is, in this passage of his life, a historian. He accompanies his eyewitness experiences in Texas with a narration of the historic events going on in other parts of the state at the same time. His glowing descriptions of the beauty of the flora and fauna of Texas were a factor in interesting many Europeans to leave their homeland and settle in the American Southwest.

This is despite the fact that he wrote chiefly about one of the lowest points in his life, his incarceration near the town of Goliad in an old fort in south Texas called La Bahía, which became a concentration camp after the defeat of Texas military leader Colonel James W. Fannin. The events at Goliad are second only to the Alamo in their significance in the decades-long struggles for Texas independence.

Herman Ehrenberg's account of the Goliad Massacre preserved in eyewitness form one of the most significant events in Texas history. The bloody massacre was the catalyst that gave rise to the battle cry, "Remember the Alamo; remember Goliad!"

This bloodbath angered the Texans to the point that they rallied an unorganized group of young men into a fighting army. This remnant of rebel forces consisted of an eclectic collection of men from all parts of the United States and Mexico.

Numerous men of Hispanic origin, Tejanos, were for freedom and separation from the dictator. The Erasmo Seguín family made their ranch a supply station for Texas troops. Other Tejano leaders include Juan M. Veramendi, governor of San Antonio (whose daughter married James Bowie), José M. J. Carbajal, and Lorenzo de Zavala, who became vice president of the Republic of Texas.

Anglos on the Mexican side include Colonel Juan Davis Bradburn, commander of 150 Mexican forces at Anahuac. There were lines of nationality but they were not clear-cut, and Ehrenberg vividly wrote about Colonel Juan Holsinger, a German engineer in the Mexican service.

Here at Goliad the volunteers had been joined by additional troops in the form of the "Red Rovers," some 70 men recruited from Alabama, and five smaller companies from Tennessee, Mississippi, and Texas. Through a long and bloody afternoon, three hundred inexperienced Texans fought the thousand seasoned veterans of the Mexican army which encircled them at Coleto Creek in South Texas.

Following the battle, the Texans surrendered

Stephen F. Austin, 1821, colonizer who became "Father of Texas.,"
Engraving by Charles K. Burt. Courtesy San Jacinto Museum of History, Houston, Texas

and the victorious Mexican generals herded Fannin and his men into the presidio La Bahía del Espíritu Santo (Bay of the Holy Spirit) at nearby Goliad. Here the prisoners of war were told they were to be marched to the coast of the Gulf of Mexico.

However, eventually the captives were lined up and faced a firing squad. Incredibly, the bullet intended for Ehrenberg missed him and, in the smoke that followed, he was one of the handful who fled. Records state that Col. Fannin and 342 men were executed at Goliad on March 27, 1836. Herman, one of the youngest, was one of 28 who escaped.

Herman had left his home in Germany at about the age of 17 and sailed to New York from Bremen. Ships records show a Herman Ehrenberg arrived in America from Bremen on board a Dutch merchant sailing ship, the galliot *Ludwig*. He was the only cabin-class passenger. The vessel arrived in New York on August 11, 1834. Ehrenberg was listed as an 18 year-old merchant from Leipzig.[3]

Herman made his way to New Orleans, where he was employed a short time in the manufacture of "loco focos," matches capable of being ignited by friction, according to Charles D. Poston[4], who knew Ehrenberg later in Arizona. In October of 1835 there was a rally in New Orleans to raise men and money to help the Texans in their struggle for independence from Mexico. A resident of Texas for many years, Nicholas Adolphus Sterne had traveled to New Orleans to give his personal and financial support to the rally.

Sterne fought for Texas' freedom ten years before the major battles of 1836. Sterne participated in the Fredonian Rebellion for Texas independence in 1826. He was arrested, imprisoned, and a Mexican military court sentenced him to be shot. However he was released on parole. He was "an historical character of much complexity. He was an urbane, sophisticated man of the world who was a mover and a shaker in the early period of Texas history."[5]

Sterne had been a Texan for more than six years before Sam Houston arrived in Texas (in December 1832) after resigning as governor of Tennessee. The two had been friends in Tennessee and Houston came to Texas at Sterne's encouragement, living for a time in Sterne's home. "Sam Houston became a permanent guest of Adolfo Sterne and won the affection of every member of the family. This assured his position socially as well as politically."[6] Sterne lived in Nacogdoches, an important town at that time, and he had become its *alcalde* or mayor.

Sam Houston in 1830, two years before he came to Texas. At the time he served as ambassador of the Cherokee Nation of American Indians.

Adolphus Sterne, who came to Texas around 1826.
Institute of Texan Cultures, San Antonio

Even after Houston became general of the Texan army and also in the republic era, their friendship stayed bonded, and on December 10, 1840 in Austin, Sterne saved Sam Houston's life. Sterne wrote in his diary, "On this evening Ge'l [General] Houston was attacked by Col [S. W.] Jordan of the late Federal army, and had it not been for my interference Jordan would have killed him with an axe."[7] In 1847 Sterne won election to the House of Representatives of the State of Texas and in 1851 advanced to the Senate. He died in 1852 in New Orleans.

Sterne had made many notable friends in Louisiana. Ehrenberg's book reveals that a member of Santa Anna's army told Ehrenberg that they planned to burn the town of New Orleans in punishment for the help given by the Jewish merchants there. This refers to Sterne and his friends.[8] Had there been a Mexican victory at the Battle of San Jacinto in 1836, history would have witnessed a second Battle of New Orleans.

Sam Houston Memorial Museum, Huntsville, Texas

Excitement permeated New Orleans as Sterne stepped on the platform at Bank's Arcade October 13, 1835. Sterne felt at home in New Orleans, having lived there in his twenties, working as a clerk and law student. He made it known that Texas wanted men as well as money and that, as a Texan agent, he had that day purchased fifty muskets to be given to those who would go with him to Texas. When Sterne recruited troops for the new Texan army, young Herman was the third man to volunteer. Two companies were raised. The Texan committee dressed the volunteers in gray uniforms and, called the New Orleans Greys, they departed for the theatre of war.[9]

Most of the brave "men of Texas" who fought in its battles for independence were scarcely men and were newly-arrived in Texas. These 118 men in New Orleans came from twelve states and six foreign countries. They were in reality youths — many of them mere teen-age boys — from Cincinnati, Ohio; New Orleans, Louisiana; Charleston, South Carolina; Philadelphia, Pennsylvania; as well as Alabama; New York; and Tennessee. In his narrative Ehrenberg names buddies who have wide geographic representation.

T. C. Richardson wrote that "Adolphus Sterne spent $820 to buy rifles for the first fifty recruits from the United States, and the rifles were claimed by the New Orleans Greys. . . Some of the horses and money for the equipment of the New Orleans

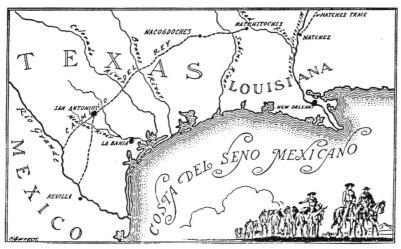

Route of the Volunteers, New Orleans to San Antonio.
Map by José Cisneros.

company were furnished by the most wealthy of the Mexicans in Nacogdoches."[10] Ehrenberg wrote about the sumptuous banquet given in honor of the troops in Nacogdoches on the eve of their departure for the front. Sterne paid toward the transportation of the Greys to Texas.[11]

From Nacogdoches, Ehrenberg rode with the Greys to San Antonio, then called Bexar (pronounced *Bear*). Here he took part in The Storming of Bexar in December 1835. This was guerrilla warfare, in which Texan troops went from house to house until they took the city of San Antonio. During this battle, the Greys also stormed the Alamo, attacking the outside of the old mission which the Mexican soldiers had fortified. This is the opposite location of the troops in the later battle, in which the Texans were on the inside.

Soldier Ehrenberg wrote of his experiences there, where on the sixth day "The fire of the enemy had died down... The humble white flag of submission was waving from the ruins of the Alamo... The Mexicans were to be allowed to march away unmolested. As a protection against the Comanches they were allowed 150 guns..." This is in stark contrast to the treatment the Mexican generals later inflicted on their prisoners of war.

Soon after the departure of the enemy troops, a little detachment of nine men, including Ehrenberg, set up living quarters in the Alamo, a retreat offering protection against the cold and storm of the winter of 1835. While living in the Alamo, Ehrenberg served the Texas army by scouting the area and obtaining much needed corn and other provisions in enemy areas, often risking his life.

In addition to the most famous battle at the Alamo in 1836 dramatized in the movie "The Alamo," and the Storming of Bexar two and a half months earlier in which Ehrenberg directly participated, there had been other battles at the Alamo. It was the site of battles for Texas independence as early as 1813, when Mexico-Texas was still under Spanish rule. Samuel Noah, a West Point graduate, and his men, as part of the ill-fated

Led by a Mexican lieutenant, the Texans, including Ehrenberg, attacked the Mexican army inside the Alamo in 1835, winning a six-day war. The victorious Texans let the Mexicans go free, after which Ehrenberg and others lived in the Alamo until spring.

Noah-Gutierrez-Magee Expedition, marched into the Alamo in 1813 and released seventeen of their fellow revolutionaries.

Twenty-two years after this Spanish defeat at the Alamo, there occurred the December 1835 defeat of Mexican force at the Alamo. Few persons outside of Texas have ever heard of these other battles at the Alamo that were victories for the Texans, their being overshadowed by the thirteen-day seige and overwhelming fall of the Alamo on March 6, 1836, and the deaths of all remaining soldiers, including the colorful David Crockett. Before the fall of the Alamo, the Mexicans had offered the Texans a chance to surrender; however, their fate likely would not have been improved, judging from what occurred at Goliad.

Crockett had been a member of the U. S. congress from Tennessee, and when defeated for re-election in 1834 he reportedly said his constituents could go to hell and he would go to Texas.[12] He reached Nacogdoches, home of Adolphus Sterne, on January 5, 1836 and attended a banquet there for two high Mexican officials sympathetic with the Texan principles, before marching on to war. This was similar to the feast Ehrenberg attended two months earlier, described in detail in his memoirs, that citizens of Nacogdoches hosted for the New Orleans Greys in 1835.

After the Storming of Bexar in 1835 and after wintering in the Alamo, when the grass

Tennessee's David Crockett.

Art by John G. Chapman, Harry Ransom Humanities
Research Center, University of Texas at Austin.

began to turn green, Ehrenberg and a number of men in the Greys set out from San Antonio towards Goliad. It was their goal to march eventually to Matamoros. However, the group ended up staying under Colonel James W. Fannin's leadership. Ehrenberg wrote vividly of Fannin and the subsequent battle of Coleto Creek, where the Texan forces surrendered to Gen. José de Urrea. After the surrender near Coleto Creek, the men were herded like cattle into the fort known as Goliad, a former mission.

Ehrenberg wrote in his book that earlier that month Fannin had decided to aid the defenders struggling in the Alamo, but had changed his mind. In Goliad he held undisputedly the first position, which rank, however, he would have to resign if he combined with the main Army. If the famished Texans had reached the nearby woods sooner, it is likely they could have had some protection and survived the battle. Starving and fighting in an open plain, they were overtaken.

Colonel James Walker Fannin, Jr.
Painting attributed to Samuel F. B. Morse.
From the Summerfield Roberts Collection of the Dallas Historical Society.

Outnumbered three to one and facing Mexico's best commander, General José Urrea, Fannin was shot in the thigh and
suffered more than fifty of his men wounded. His hope of getting help for the wounded Texans seemed to be his foremost
reason for surrender. The Texans gave up entirely to the enemy
their 500 muskets and nine cannons before marching back to

The small chapel into which approximately 300 men were concentrated.

Goliad. They were crowded under heavy guard into the church there, which became a concentration camp.[13]

"The crowded state of the prison prevented us from lying down," Ehrenberg wrote. The wounded lay groaning in the old church; several who had been struck by poisonous copper bullets were raving wildly in the delirium of a burning fever, and others tried to tear off their bandages, with the hope perhaps of bleeding to death.

Following three nightmare nights in the narrow room that had served as a small chapel, the hundreds of prisoners were released into the quadrangle of the fort, where they continued to endure misery. The violence of one of the men is described in detail by Ehrenberg:

"Suddenly a light flashed. . .[with] a terrible jarring of the air. Impenetrable suffocating smoke . . . rolled heavily over the dark green prairie. Wildly the horses of several of the enemy officers reared up and frantic with fear rushed out with their stupefied riders, in uninterrupted speed with ruffled manes and flying tails into the safe distance. . . Still half stunned, we went to the place where the explosion seemed to have broken loose. The powder magazine had disappeared. . . Around the place lay several men wounded and a black body that barely looked like one of a human being. It was still alive but not able to speak. It was burnt coal black like the color of a negro, and it was impossible to tell who the unfortunate one was. The roll was called and the missing man was Johnson.[14] Was it an accident or was it really his plan to kill himself and as many Mexicans as possible at the same time?. . . He must have ignited the magazine. But as the lid was not locked, the main blast exploded upward, and thus his terrible plan missed its purpose."

After a week in nightmare conditions, the Texan prisoners were joined by approximately 100 more men, all volunteers from New York who had been captured on the Texas Gulf coast in a surprise attack.

On the morning of the eighth day all the men were ordered to leave the fort right away. Most thought they were marching to a Texas port to embark for New Orleans. Not until they heard screams did they realize what was taking place. At the places of execution, they were ordered to kneel down, and the firing began.[15]

The shooting began at very close range. Those who were not killed immediately were pursued by gunfire, bayonet, or lance. Fannin and a few other Texans were put to death inside the presidio.

The physicians and also a number of carpenters with the Texan volunteers were saved, and from the stories of these survivors, Ehrenberg wrote the account of what happened after he escaped.[16] Of the dramatic execution of Fannin, Ehrenberg wrote in his 1844 book:

"Deeply he [Fannin] regretted that he had not hastened to the aid of the fallen garrison of the Alamo, or that he had not sooner followed Houston's orders to retreat behind the

Guadalupe. Tears of deepest sorrow ran down his cheeks during the slaughter of his true and faithful comrades."

Because Mexican General Urrea had recommended clemency for the Goliad prisoners, Santa Anna ordered Colonel José Nicolas de la Portilla to carry out the orders.

A Mexican officer who commanded one of the firing squads wrote in his diary: "What spectator could view it without horror! They were all young, the oldest not more than thirty, and of fine florid complexions. When the unfortunate youths were brought to the place of death, their lamentations and appeals which they uttered to Heaven, in their own language, with extended arms, kneeling or prostrate on the earth, were such as might have caused the very stones to have cried out in compassion."

Decades after the massacre the ground was unmarked, as noted by Jacob De Cordova, empresario, author and "Publicist of an Empire" in the first encyclopedia of Texas he published in 1858: "Although over twenty years have elapsed since these brave men were butchered, there is no other monument raised to mark the spot than a rude pile of loose rocks [six feet tall], thrown together by some patriotic individual. . ."[17] A monument was erected in April 1885, located in the town's City Park since the committee felt the actual grave was an isolated spot. In 1936 the Centennial Commission appropriated funds for the erection of a monument over the grave. The present monument at the battlefield was dedicated June 4, 1838, one hundred and two years after the massacre.

Although H. Yoakum wrote in 1855 in his *History of Texas* that 330 suffered death and twenty-seven escaped[18], the *New Handbook of Texas*[19] states, "A man-by-man study of Fannin's command indicates that 342 were executed at Goliad on March 27. Only twenty-eight escaped the firing squads, and twenty more were spared as physicians, orderlies, interpreters, or mechanics largely because of the entreaties of a 'high bred beauty' whom the Texans called the 'Angel of Goliad' (Francita

Señora Alavez, heroine of Texas.
Mural by Jessie Bubin, Goliad State Historical Park

*Bust of Señora Alavez in
the Presidio Bahía
Museum at Goliad.*

Photography by Natalie Ornish.

Alavez), and the brave and kindly intervention of Col. Francisco Garay." Francita Alavez's husband, Col. Telesforo Alavez, had been ordered by General Urrea to be in charge of the village of Victoria (only a few miles from Goliad), and she intervened with Alavez to spare the lives of the Texans there, and they afterward escaped.

One of the Goliad surgeons who was spared, Dr. Joseph Barnard of Massachusetts, later wrote, "I must not here omit the mention of Señora Alvarez [sic], whose name ought to be perpetuated to the latest times, for her virtues, and whose action contrasted so strangely with that of her countrymen and deserves to be recorded in the annals of this country and treasured in the heart of every Texian. . .When, on the morning of the massacre, she learned that the prisoners were to be shot, she so effectually pleaded with Colonel Garay (whose humane feelings so revolted at the order) that with great personal responsibility to himself and at great hazards at thus going counter to the orders of the then all-powerful Santa Anna, resolved to save all that she could; and a few of us, in consequence, were left to tell of that bloody day.

"Besides those that Colonel Garay saved, she saved others by her connivance with some of the officers who had gone into the fort at night and taken out some, whom she kept concealed until after the massacre. When she saw Dr. Shackleford, a few days after, she burst into tears and exclaimed: 'Why did I not know that you had a son here? I would have saved him at all hazards.'

"Her name deserves to be recorded in letters of gold among the angels who have from time to time been commissioned by an overruling and beneficent power to relieve the sorrows and cheer the hearts of men. . ."[20]

Actually, Mexican General Antonio Lopez de Santa Anna, according to Mexican law, had the right to execute any rebels invading from the outside. The decree of the Mexican Congress stated: "1. Foreigners landing on the coast of the [Mexi-

Antonio Lopez de Santa Anna,
General and at various times President of the Republic of Mexico.
From Pictorial History of Texas *by Homer S. Thrall*

can] Republic, or invading its territory by land, armed and with the intention of attacking our country, will be deemed pirates, and dealt with as such, being citizens of no nation, presently at war with the Republic and fighting under no recognized flag.

"2. All foreigners who shall import, either by sea or land, in the places occupied by the rebels [the Texans] either arms or ammunition of any kind, for their use will be deemed pirates, and punished as such." The decree became law on December 20, 1835.[21]

Although technically the massacre may have been legal by Mexican law and outsiders had been warned of the consequences of an invasion, citizens of both Mexico and the United States were appalled.

When they learned of the massacre, the citizens of Mexico were moved and held Santa Anna to account. The general told his people that he ordered the men killed because there was not enough food for them. The citizens of the United States were repelled and angered, especially since so many of their relatives were killed. Overnight United States neutrality changed to a fervent sympathy for the Texan cause. The battle cry of the Texas Revolution became "Remember the Alamo! Remember Goliad!"

On March 2, 1836, the delegates elected by the Texas colonists had met in Convention and officially declared Texas independent from Mexico. They formed the Texas navy, whose four schooners were important because they blocked supplies en route by sea from Mexico to Santa Anna's army. On April 20 the Texan army under Sam Houston reached the San Jacinto River near Houston. The Texans burned Vince's Bridge over Sim's bayou which cut off Santa Anna's army from supplies. On April 21 Santa Anna's legions were in retreat, and the general spoke his famous line, "You have conquered the Napoleon of the West."

Ehrenberg's story tells how he survived after escaping the Goliad massacre by cleverly impersonating a German traveler and living with the Mexican army. He stayed with the Mexicans for a month. It makes fascinating reading. When news came of Santa Anna's defeat and capture at San Jacinto on April 21, Ehrenberg and another Texan prisoner escaped and pushed on to Matagorda, occupied by Texan troops.

On June 2, 1836, two months after escaping Goliad, Ehrenberg received an honorable discharge from the army of the Republic of Texas. His documents read:

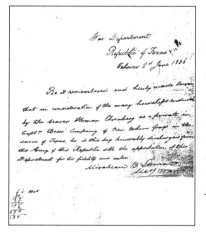

Document states: War Department, Republic of Texas, Velasco, 2d June 1836. Be it remembered and hereby made known, that in consideration of the many hardships endured by the bearer Herman Ehrenberg as a private in Captn. Brees' Company of New Orleans Grays in the service of Texas, he is this day honorably discharged from the Army of this Republic with the approbation of this Department for his fidelity and valor.

Mirabeau B. Lamar, Sec. of War.

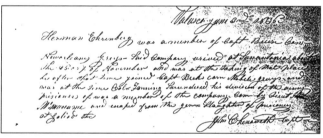

Document states:

Velasco, June 3rd, 1836. Herman Ehrenberg was a member of Capt. Breese Com., New Orleans Greys—Said company arrived at San Antonio about the 26 or 7 of November and was at the taking of that place. He after that time joined Capt. Berks com. Mobile Greys and was at the time Col. Fanning [sic] surrendered his division of the army prisoners of war a member of the company com. by Lieut. M. and escaped from the slaughter of prisoners at Goliad.

John Chenoweth, Capt.

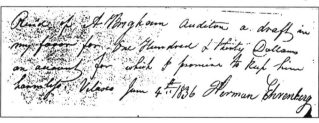

Receipt with Ehrenberg's signature.

For his service Ehrenberg was given a draft on the empty treasury for $130.

A ship's registry reveals that Ehrenberg "got on in Galveston; disembarked in New Orleans June 7, 1838."

In 1840 he returned to Germany, where he reportedly studied mining at Freiburg University. In the 1840s, in ads in Germany and in a letter to Ashbel Smith, a Texas envoy living in Europe, Ehrenberg said he was an English teacher at Halle University.

While in Germany, Ehrenberg wrote his book which was published in 1843, 1844, and 1845. In 1925 Edgar William Bartholomae translated the 1845 (third) edition into English, and in 1935 Henry Nash Smith edited and Charlotte Churchill translated a greatly condensed edition for children. The version included in this book is a full translation of the 1844 edition.

In 1843 he was seeking money with which to return to America. Adolphus Sterne likely had been contacted to help, as on June 6, 1843 Sterne entered in his diary (later published), "Wrote to Judge Terrell respecting the monay [sic] he owes me, also requesting him to look in the [Republic of Texas] War Department about the land and monay [sic] due to Herman Ehrenberg. Sat on the Board of Land Commissioners, issued two certificates. . ." This entry in Sterne's diary is contradictory to accounts that Ehrenberg abandoned his claims to land in Texas after he fought there.

Ehrenberg wrote Ashbel Smith, *Charge d'Affaires,* Republic of Texas, who was then living in Paris, France, requesting Smith loan him $40 with which to return to Texas.[22] Likely someone else sponsored his trip.

After returning to the United States in 1844, Ehrenberg traveled from St. Louis, via Independence, Missouri, overland to Oregon. "Went over the Rocky Mountains to Washington and Oregon in 1844," he wrote. He was part of that monumental movement westward over what was called The Oregon

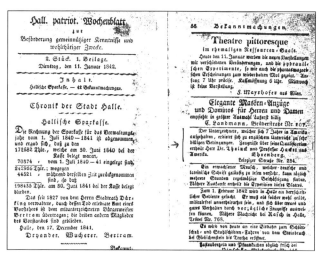

TOP: Ad in Halle Weekly Newspaper, *Tuesday 11 Jan. 1842, states Ehrenberg spent "7 years in America and taught English there. Certificates of these qualifications were sent to Herr Dr. Tholuck [?] and Professor Hacket, from America.*
Ehrenberg
Leipziger Strasse No. 284."

BELOW: "Address book [city directory] for the year 1843, City Library of Halle," lists:
"Ehrenberg, Hermann [sic], Language teacher, Markerstra. 445."

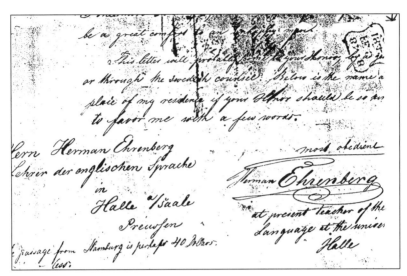

Signature of Herman Ehrenberg on his letter to Ashbel Smith,
requesting Smith loan him forty dollars to return to Texas.

Trail.[23] Travel in the 1840s from the Mississippi River to the Pacific was a severe test of endurance, and many died, but it was another challenge Ehrenberg handled. The trail crossed Nebraska; Fort Laramie, Wyoming; Fort Boise, Idaho; and ended in Oregon. Ehrenberg stayed in Oregon from late 1844 through early 1845.

In spring of 1845 he was in the Vancouver-Portland area, and boarded a vessel on the Columbia River headed for the Pacific Ocean. In company with the future governor of the Provisional Territory of Oregon and others, he sailed to Hawaii, then called the Sandwich Islands. The "Passenger List for 'Chenamus' From Columbia River, May 25, 1845. . ." in Hawaii Public Archives lists "Herman Erenberg [sic], 29, surveyor, New Orleans." The list was prepared by Avery Sylvester, Master of the brig *Chenamus*.

In Hawaii, at the request of the government, Ehrenberg surveyed streets and drew the first map of Honolulu. This is

On the Oregon Trail.

Imaginary portrait of Ehrenberg.

Art by José Cisneros, El Paso, Texas

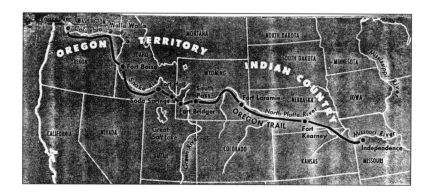

documented in the Hawaiian publication called *The Friend,* which at least twice (Oct. 1, 1845 and Jan. 15, 1847) published a copy of his map or plat. It also was pictured in a German language publication. The October 1845 article said, "The town of Honolulu. . . is the most important sea port in the north Pacific ocean. The population, native and foreign, has been estimated at from 8 to 10 thousand. Mr. H. Ehrenberg, a German Engineer, has recently been employed by the Government to survey the streets, and draw a map of the town."

Ehrenberg then visited a number of South Pacific islands. He was reported seen in the Marquesas islands, a group of eleven Polynesian volcanic islands about 740 miles south of Hawaii and north of Tahiti. He also sailed to Samoa and the Society Islands. Capital of the Society Island group is the seaport of Papeete on Tahiti in French Polynesia.

In late 1845 or early 1846 he sailed south to Tahiti, where he became an intimate friend of the then young Queen Pomare IV who governed from Papeete. He won the favor of the dusky young divorced queen of Tahiti and might have spent the rest of his life fishing and diving for pearls, but adventure called. In a biographical poem about him by one who knew him well, the writer described the relationship between Ehrenberg and the queen as, "He was her diety"[24] and "He was received with great favor by the then youthful queen."

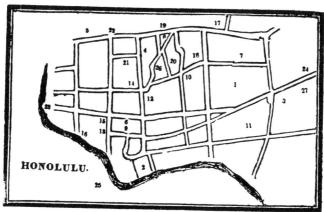

HONOLULU, OAHU, S. I. OCTOBER 1, 1845.

HONOLULU.

The town of Honolulu, (measuring five sixths of a mile long, and two thirds wide,) the most populous of all upon the Hawaiian Islands, is situated on the south side of Oahu. It is the Capital of the Islands, and most important sea port in the north Pacific ocean. The population, native and foreign has been estimated at from 8 to 10 thousand. Mr. H. Ehrenberg, a German Engineer, has recently been employed by the Government to survey the streets, and draw a map of the town. He has politely placed at our disposal a small map, designed for a wood engraving for the columns of the Friend, and by the gratuitous services of Mr. Dimond, of the Am. Mission, we are happy to present our readers with the above view of Honolulu.

The following description of localities may aid the reader, abroad, in obtaining a more correct idea of the place, than he would otherwise be able to obtain.

1 PALACE,
2 Fort, and residence of His Ex. Gov. Kekuanaoa.
3. King's Chapel, (or Rev. R. Armstrong's Church.)
4 Roman Catholic Chapel, (or Rev. Abbe Magret?)
5 Native Church, (or Rev. L. Smith's!

6 Seamen's Chapel, (or Rev. S. C. Damon's.)
7 Young Chiefs, School, (Mr. Cook, Principal.)
8 Mansion House, (Carter & Thompson.)
9 Government Offices.
10 Government Printing Office.
11 Oahu Charity School, (Mr. E. L. Stetson Teacher.)
12 C. Brewer & Co's. Store.
13 Hon. H. Bay Co's. Store.
14 Hospital, American Seamen.
15   "   English   "   "
16   "   French   "
17 Residence H. B. M. Consul General
18   "   U. S. Consul.
19   "   French   "
20   "   U. S. Commissioner.
21   "   Seamen's Chaplain.
22 Road to Nuuanu Valley.
23   "   Ewa.
24   "   Waikiki.
25 Inner Harbor, (always good anchorage.)
26 Hotel de France.
27 Premises of the American Mission.

It must not be understood that any of the above mentioned buildings occupy the whole

First map of Honolulu, drawn by Ehrenberg.

*Queen Pomare,
about 1847.*

*Autographed letter from Queen Pomare to her French doctor: "Come
quickly! Don't be lazy . . . I have pain in my chest and in my back."*
[Private Collection]

Queen Pomare was born a few years before Ehrenberg and was around age 32 at the time Ehrenberg was in French Polynesia. During her twenties, an unusual event took place. The ships of the Royal Navy of France frequently brought presents to the queen. This delivery, however, was conditional — only by first refusing to give her the gifts he had brought could one commander persuade Pomare to turn over to him a pirate she had been hiding.

The queen's entourage often included a man described as "a naval writer," and possibly this was the role Ehrenberg fulfilled. Also included were ladies-in-waiting, elder relations, servants, women who were part high-priestess and part witch-doctor, and the queen's physician. Also close by were priests who, in later years,

The Queen opens the ball.

read to her if she had insomnia. "At her feet there were three maids to massage her until daylight."[25]

Pages 34 and 35: Queen Pomare lived in the largest house in Papeete, described thus in 1830: "It has only one floor, a thatched roof, and a large veranda spanning the facade. It is situated in an enclave of greenery. For a royal residence it is rather humble. At the door there are three sentinels. Their postures indicate they are concerned only with their own comfort." The queen only entertained guests in this house in the center of Papeete, residing other times in two huts near the water.

Courtesy University of Hawaii at Manoa

Despite the prohibitions of the missionaries who seemed to have no say in the matter of dancing, she remained Tahitian in her soul and hosted constant parties that featured women who danced, often seductively, for entertainment.

During the day, the queen received most of the visiting dignitaries. In 1851 she was described as "sitting on a red velvet couch wearing a crown of flowers, simply dressed and natural in appearance; . . . Her look commands respect, and that is what no one dares refuse the Queen of the Society Islands."

After Tahiti, Ehrenberg returned to Honolulu and embarked on the schooner *Louise* on a trading expedition to Baja California and South America. At Valparaiso, Chile, he joined Col. J. D. Stevenson's regiment organized in New York for the purpose of occupying California, which was still a Mexican province.

A map shows Herman would have had a shorter trip to sail from Tahiti to Chile and not go back to Honolulu. What probably

Passenger list for the General Kearney.

Courtesy Hawaii State Archives, Honolulu.

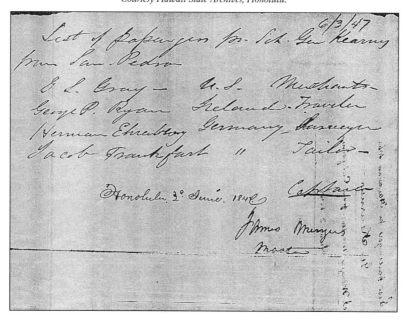

took place is that Ehrenberg made two trips across the Pacific Ocean, because the *Polynesian* for June 1847[26] mentions him in the passenger list aboard the schooner *General Kearney*: "June 5, 1847, Saturday, 'Marine Journal'. Arrived June 3, Schr. Gen. Kearney, Menzies, 21 ds. fm. San Pedro. Passengers: Messrs. G. L. Gray, George P. Ryan, Herman Ehrenberg, and Jacob Frankfurt."

There were several towns named San Pedro, but in this case the San Pedro port of departure was part of the port of Los Angeles. In the Hawaiian State Archives one can look at the ship's manifest and also learn that the ship did sail from Los Angeles to Honolulu. If Herman arrived in Honolulu in spring of 1845 after departing from the Columbia River area, how could he also have arrived in Honolulu on June 3, 1847, from America if he had not made two visits to the Pacific? No other writer to date has made this conclusion.

Writers have stated, "Early in 1847 Ehrenberg returned to Honolulu [implying from Tahiti] where in June he embarked on the schooner *Louise* on a trading expedition to Lower California."

U.S. Army in Mexican War, 1847.
Art by José Cisneros.

Actually, further research reveals that the name of the *General Kearney* was changed to the *Louise,* which has confused some historians. If Ehrenberg arrived in Honolulu on June 3, 1847, surely he would not have turned around and immediately (in June) returned on a three-week overseas voyage back to where he started from. It is not likely he subjected himself to six straight weeks on the seas.

When he did return, he visited the west coast of Mexico

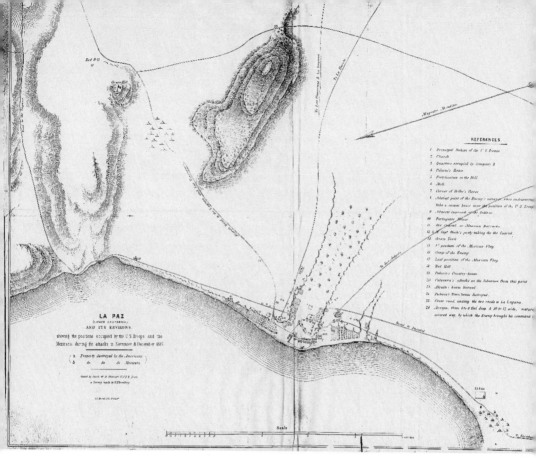

REFERENCES

1 Principal Station of the U.S. Dragos
2 Church
3 Quarters occupied by Company B
4 Palacio's House
5 Fortifications on the Hill
6 Mill
7 Corner of Belcher's House
8 Advanced point of the Enemy's attempt, when endeavoring to take a second house near the position of the U.S. Troops
9 Advanced approach of the Indians
10 Portuguese House
11 Old Quartel, or Mexican Barracks
12 Left Capt. Steele's party taking the Old Quartel
13 Grass Yard
14 1st position of the Mexican Flag
15 Camp of the Enemy
16 Last position of the Mexican Flag
17 Red Hill
18 Delacro's Country-house
19 Calaveras's attacks on the Schooner from this point
20 Mesalts's house burned
21 Pedrosa's Town house destroyed
22 Cross road, uniting the two roads to La Laguna
23 Arroyo, from 4 to 6 feet deep & 10 to 12 wide, natural covered way, by which the Enemy brought his command

LA PAZ
(LOWER CALIFORNIA)
AND ITS ENVIRONS.
showing the positions occupied by the U.S. Troops and the
Mexicans during the attacks in November & December 1847.

Property destroyed by the Americans
do   do   do   (Mexicans)

Drawn by Lieut. W.H. Warner U.S.T.E. from
a Survey made by R.E. Ehrenberg

Scale

Little known history is the fact that even after the Texans' victory at San Jacinto, Mexico continued to invade Texas for another ten years, all during its republic era (1836-1846). Mexico did not renounce claims to Texas until the Treaty of Guadalupe Hidalgo at the end of the Mexican War of 1846-48. During this war, Ehrenberg aided U.S. troops in Baja California and made maps. In November and December 1847 he saw action near Baja's tip, in La Paz, Mexico. (See Ehrenberg map above.) In March 1848 he rescued Americans in Punta San Antonio, on Baja's northern coast on the Pacific Ocean.

Cartography Collection, The University of Texas at Arlington

including Baja California. At that time, Mexico and the United States were at war (1846-1848).[27] Ehrenberg is credited with being among those who helped rescue Americans held captive during the Mexican War in Baja California. The rescue was made at Punta San Antonio in the northern half of the Baja peninsula, around 225 miles south of San Diego and Tijuana. He earned the praise of the American commanders for participating in the rescue of seven naval officers and marine privates who were imprisoned at the Mexican headquarters there. He drew a "Sketch of the Capture of [Punta (Point)] San Antonio, [in] Lower California; and rescue of American Prisoners. March 16th 1848." When American troops abandoned Mexico's Baja California, Ehrenberg also left, traveling north to Sacramento and San Francisco.

The population surge of San Francisco in one year resulting from the California Gold Rush is graphically shown in the above two views of San Francisco Bay in 1848 and 1849. From Eldorado by Bayard Taylor, 1850

Ehrenberg wrote that in 1848 he "Arrived in California." Between 1848 and 1860 California's population increased from approximately 20,000 to 379,994 as thousands of persons dramatically rushed to establish mining claims.

Ehrenberg was a Forty-Niner and participated in the California gold rush. In the spring of 1850 he discovered the mouth of the Klamath River that flows in Oregon and northern California.

Northwest corner of California, extending 70 miles inland from Port Trinidad, showing mouth of the Klamath River, discovered by Ehrenberg.

Courtesy New York Historical Society

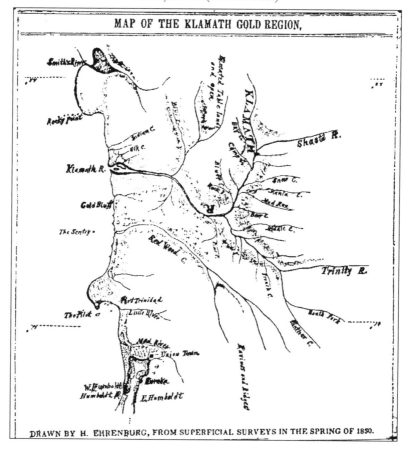

Coming down the coast he discovered the gold-bearing metallic sands since known as Gold Bluff. The San Francisco *Weekly Pacific News* of August 15, 1850 published what they labeled "Map of the Klamath Gold Region/ Drawn by H. Ehrenburg [sic], From Superficial Surveys in The Spring of 1850."[28] In August of 1850 Ehrenberg and A. Sydney Myers surveyed a town site for the town of Klamath and opened a real estate office there.

On September 28, 1850, Ehrenberg informed the census taker in Union Town (now Arcata, near Eureka) California that he was 28 years old. He continued making maps of the California gold regions. Although he was a topographer, map draftsman, and mining engineer the *San Francisco City Directory 1854* lists his address as 152 Washington and his career as "lithography." The first

Ehrenberg listing in 1854 San Francisco City Directory. Column 2, middle.

Courtesy San Francisco Public Library

Ehrenberg map of the Gadsden Purchase, however, says, "Litho by Alex Zakreski"[29] of San Francisco.

Ehrenberg was what oil explorers refer to as a wildcatter — one who pioneers new places to find minerals — and this led him down from San Francisco to the northern Mexico state of

With the Gadsden Purchase, the United States bought part of Northern Mexico, including Tucson, from Mexico's president Santa Anna for $10,000,000.

Sonora, which shares a boundary with Arizona, the beginning of Ehrenberg's widespread interest in Arizona.

With the Gadsden Purchase, the United States purchased a disputed strip of land in what is now southern Arizona and New Mexico. No sooner had the advance news come out, even prior to the purchase being official in 1854, Ehrenberg left San Francisco and his job as a lithographer and went to prospect the area being acquired by the United States. He took the brig *Zoraida* February 19, 1854 for the port of Guaymas, Mexico. Accompanying him from San Francisco to Mexico were several companions, including Charles D. Poston.

Poston, an articulate, ambitious and persuasive young Kentuckian,[30] lived from 1825 to 1902 and eventually became "Father of Arizona." When he and Herman had met, Poston was employed as a clerk in the San Francisco Custom House. For the next decade the destinies of this pair would be interwoven in connection with the silver mines of southern Arizona and Sonora, Mexico.

It was the belief of mining men that no other part of Mexico was so rich in minerals as northern Sonora. In 1853, shortly before the Gadsden Purchase, Poston became acquainted with

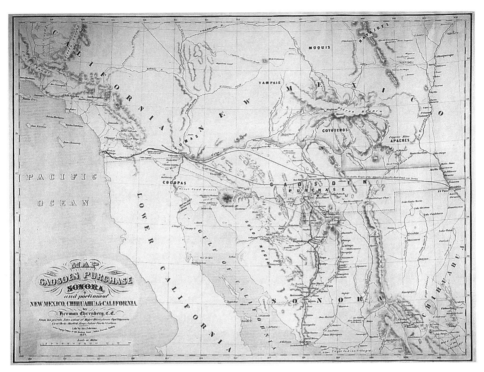

Ehrenberg 1854 map of the Gadsden Purchase.
The Huntington Library

the agent for the Iturbide family. These relatives of the late Emperor of Mexico were allowed as compensation for his services and execution to select a tract of land in Sonora, Baja California, or Sinaloa. A syndicate financed by French bankers became involved in the Iturbide Grant. Poston became involved with the French bankers and left San Francisco for Guaymas, Mexico, in search of potential land sites.[31]

The *Zoraida*, a British ship, proved unseaworthy and was blown off course and shipwrecked. Ehrenberg and Poston were among the men who stayed and finished the trip overland. En route, they were taken prisoners. Suspected of filibustering, the group persuaded the alcalde to release them as they were on their way to the Gadsden territory.[32] Finally Ehrenberg, Poston, and the group reached Guaymas, and from there went to Hermosillo. By then about fifteen men including Ehrenberg were in the party. The journey through the desert was arduous and (with their mules perishing from thirst and drinking their own urine) the adventurers finally walked the last fifteen miles, crossing the Mexican boundary into the Gadsden Purchase close to the very day, June 30, 1854, that the treaty was proclaimed official by the president of the United States.

The Gadsden Purchase became an important milestone in American geography and history. James Gadsden, United States minister to Mexico, also was a railroad promoter, and Ehrenberg's first map of the Gadsden Purchase shows "Probable route of the Atlantic & Pacific Railroad via Texas," from El Paso to San Diego.[33]

Gadsden had negotiated the land purchase with the same Santa Anna who had commanded the Mexican army in Texas during the Texas Revolution. Eighteen years later, in this real estate deal between Santa Anna and the United States, Mexico received $10,000,000.

When the Mexican War had ended in 1848, there was doubt as to the boundary between Mexico and the United States, although the most significant border was the Gila River, which runs east-west a few miles south of Phoenix. With the Gadsden Purchase, 45,535 square miles of Mexican land south of the Gila River — including the town of Tucson, then a presidio — were added to the United States.

The journeys of Ehrenberg and Poston continued. They ventured along the Gila River to its junction with the Colorado River, near where California, Arizona, and Mexico meet, a significant geographical intersection. They surveyed a town in June, 1854, which was the first real estate development in Arizona. Although they registered the name officially in San Diego as Colorado City, the name later was changed to Yuma.

(Top left):
Charles Debrille Poston
at age 28, when he and
Ehrenberg first met in
San Francisco.
Frontispiece from Apache-Land,
A. L. Bancroft, San Francisco.

(Top right):
Poston at middle-age.
The National Archives

(Left):
Poston as an elderly
man.
Research Division, Arizona
Department of Library,
Archives and Public Records,
Phoenix

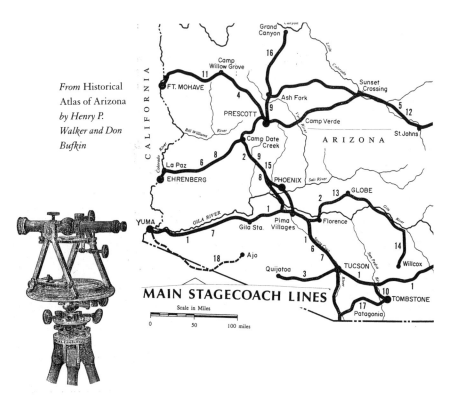

From Historical Atlas of Arizona *by Henry P. Walker and Don Bufkin*

Surveying instrument from A Manual of Instruments Used in American Engineering and Surveying *by W. & L.E. Gurley, 1856.*

While in this area Ehrenberg and Poston became acquainted with the military commanding officer of nearby Fort Yuma, Major Samuel P. Heintzelman.[34] They became friends and later business associates. The major, a West Point graduate, indicated he could introduce Poston to his friends in the East, especially Cincinnati, who had investment resources.

In the fall of 1854 Ehrenberg and Poston rode "to the cool breezes of San Diego and from there by steamer back to San Francisco." By that time steam had replaced sail in most Western water travel. These entrepreneurs/visionaries founded the Sonora Exploring and Mining Company, with Ehrenberg mining and topographical engineer and Heintzelman as president. Poston was named "commandant and managing agent."[35]

From San Francisco, Poston and some associates journeyed in 1855 across the continent to Eastern cities to raise funds. His itinerary included New York, Philadelphia, Wilmington, and Cincinnati, taking along maps and specimens of minerals. Poston later wrote [36] that Ehrenberg did not go on the New York trip because of ill health.

From San Francisco, Ehrenberg went south to locate possi-

SAMUEL PETER HEINTZELMAN

Samuel Peter Heintzelman

ble mines. While Poston was in the East, Ehrenberg spent much of 1855 and 1856 in Sonora, south of present-day Tucson, examining mines and scouting for a location for a Mexican railroad.

Poston and his group traveled from Cincinnati back to the west via San Antonio and El Paso, Texas — over a thousand miles in hostile Indian country[37] — during the summer of 1856, arriving about August 22, 1856 in Tucson, where Ehrenberg met them.

Poston brought with him cash and credit with which to launch the mining projects with Ehrenberg. Besides working as mining and topographical engineer, Ehrenberg also served as the company's metallurgist, surveyor, cartographer, and interpreter. He spoke at least three languages — German, English, and Spanish. He located a 17,000 acre ranch, which he and Poston purchased for the company, the Sonora Exploring and Mining Company of Tubac, Arizona. A month after the purchase,

Ehrenberg 1858 map of the Gadsden Purchase,
lithographed in Cincinnati, Ohio.

The Huntington Library

the celebrated Heintzelman Mine was discovered. When the men were not in the field exploring, they spent the winter in the village of Tubac, an old Spanish presidio only about fifteen miles north of the new Mexican border. Ehrenberg and Poston

(Above): The Heintzelman Mine near Tubac, Arizona. Offices and storehouse near the Cerro Colorado Mountains are seen at top. Refining furnaces are at right. Also seen are huts for laborers and a corral for mules.

Frontispiece, Brunckow Report.

(Right): Note Poston's autograph and 1859 New York address.

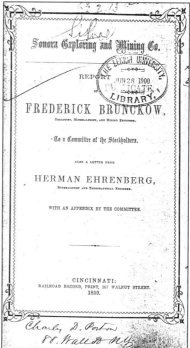

also purchased smaller tracts of land around Tubac and, joined by two mining engineers, Frederick Brunckow and Charles Schuchard, they began to discover mines.

Ehrenberg's mining reports were published and widely quoted, and his second map of the Gadsden Purchase and Sonora was lithographed in Cincinnati and widely distributed in 1858. That year Ehrenberg journeyed to New York and Cincinnati with Poston, to supervise publication of his map, as well as to promote the company. They reported, "even statesmen listened to the silver story of Sonora."

Led by the knowledge that Sonora was full of silver mines, American prospectors and settlers in the middle 1850s marched into this last Southwestern frontier.[38] However, this company started out suffering severe losses. To promote the mines and to try to sell stock in the company, Poston and Ehrenberg took another trip, riding on horseback to San Diego and then going by steamer to San Francisco. The high cost of sending ore to smelters in San Francisco for processing left little or no profit for the company, which was saved from bankruptcy by Samuel Colt, the Connecticut armsmaker and inventor of the revolver, who became the largest single stockholder and president in 1859.

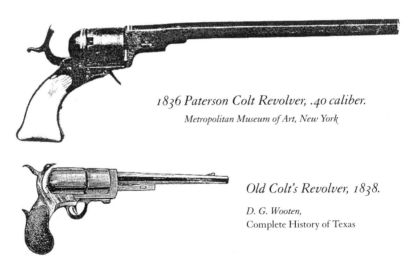

1836 Paterson Colt Revolver, .40 caliber.
Metropolitan Museum of Art, New York

Old Colt's Revolver, 1838.
D. G. Wooten,
Complete History of Texas

When a printing press came in a caravan to Tubac, Arizona, in 1859, the *Weekly Arizonian* was born. An important contributor was Ehrenberg, writing about the mines in Sonora, Mexico, and the leading cities, providing tables of distances for travelers, and describing best methods of mining silver. Ehrenberg, having resigned from the Sonora Exploring and Mining Company, traveled to New York and obtained financing for his own company which he called Cahuabi Mining Co.

When gold was discovered in the Colorado River placers in January of 1862, many miners were attracted to this area, including Ehrenberg who arrived in early autumn. Over the next few years he became part owner of many gold and copper mines.

He tried to bring civilizing influences to the mining frontiers and wrote proposals for uniform mining laws for all the Territories, which were published in a leading Eastern mining journal. In 1862 he attended a territorial meeting near Yuma, where many of his proposals became law.

Ehrenberg worked out of La Paz, a sprawling, brawling town that had sprung up rapidly on the Arizona side of the lower part of the Colorado River that flows between Arizona and California. The townsite, which he had founded, included 1,920 acres. The development association,

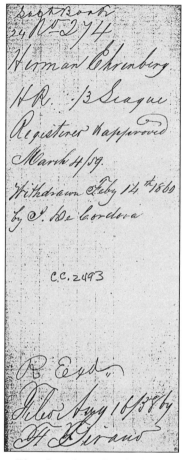

Ehrenberg focused on his Texas land about the same time he resigned from the Sonora Exploring and Mining Company and started his own company. Document for Hr /3 league Registered and approved March 4, 1859 and withdrawn Feb. 14, 1860 by Jacob De Cordova. (Originally filed Aug. 10, 1838 by H. Girano.)

Texas General Land Office,
Archives and Records Division

headed by Ehrenberg, included the Hawaiian Consul in San Francisco, a stage operator and government contractor, and Ehrenberg's friend Michel (Big Mike) Goldwater, who became grandfather of Senator Goldwater.

On January 12, 1862, Pauline Weaver found gold in the Arroyo de la Tenaja. Since January 12 is the feast of Our Lady of Peace in the Catholic faith, they named the town La Paz. A boom mining town quickly developed, having at one time over 5,000 residents and a Wells Fargo station.[39] A change in the course of the Colorado River in 1869, three years after Ehrenberg's death, brought commercial disaster to La Paz, which was left high and dry. In 1870 the county records were taken down the Colorado on the steamer *Nina Tilden* to present day Yuma, and La Paz was on its way to becoming a ghost town.

The town's beginning was as dramatic as its end. How the city was developed was told by Ehrenberg to a friend, who reported it in a book published in 1870:

". . . The next morning we reached Colorado City (opposite Fort Yuma) on the Colorado river. This place, consisting of one house, had a curious origin, which was told me by a friend, who was also the founder [Ehrenberg]. Soon after the purchase of

(Below and Right): How the mines were worked.

(Published at the WIDE WEST OFFICE, 151 Clay Street, San Francisco.)

Arizona, my friend had organized a party and explored the new region. Wishing to raise capital in California to work a valuable mine, he was returning thither with his party, when they reached the Colorado river at this point. The ferry belonged to a German [L.J.F. Jaeger], whose fare for the party would have amounted to about $25. Having no money, they encamped near the ferry to hold a council over this unexpected turn of affairs, when my friend, with the ready wit of an explorer, hit upon the expedient of paying the ferriage in city lots. Setting the engineer of the party, and under him the whole force, at work with the instruments, amid a great display of sig-nal-staffs, they soon had the city laid out in squares and streets, and represented in due form on an elaborate map, not forget-ting water lots, and a steam ferry. Attracted by the unusual pro-ceeding, the owner of the ferry crossed the river and began to interrogate the busy surveyors, by whom he was referred to my friend [Ehrenberg]. On learning from that gentleman that a city was being founded so near to his own land, the German became interested and, as the great future of the place was unfolded in glowing terms, and the necessity of a steam ferry for the increasing trade dwelt upon, he became inthusiastic [sic] and

The Huntington Library

[Published at the WIDE WEST OFFICE, 151 Clay Street, San Francisco.]

began negotiations for several lots. The result was the sale of a small part of the embryo city, and the transportation of the whole party over in part payment for one lot. I must do my friend the justice to say that he afterward did all that could be done to forward the growth of the place. . ."[40]

In mid-December of 1863 Ehrenberg and three companions blazed a new trail from La Paz eastward to the Weaver Diggings[41], which the *Arizona Miner* promptly called **The Ehrenberg Road**. From the mining district, the road went toward Prescott.

On February 4, 1864, Ehrenberg wrote to Governor Goodwin of Arizona, enclosing a tracing of the wagon route from La Paz to the Weaver Mines, imploring the governor to open more watering places along the route, to make it a first class road. (Without water, both travelers and horses could not travel the road.) Ehrenberg wrote, "I consider this route of such high importance that half a dozen failures in wells . . . . should not cause it to be abandoned; the success of the country and this wagon route are identical, one and the same thing, if one fails

(Below and Right): Scenes from actual life at the mines.

the other will haved a miserable existence. . . I take more of a scientific than pecuniary interest in the matter. I have already expended 11 years of my life in mapping Arizona and Sonora and in developing its mineral wealth, and desire Apacheria unfolded and my task completed." He described himself as a civil and mining engineer.[42]

Of his explorations, Ehrenberg also spoke at the September 5, 1864 meeting of the California Academy of Natural Sciences. He also wrote for newspapers and was a regular correspondent to the *Alta California* newspaper of San Francisco. So valued were his judgments that it was often said that his approval of a mining property at once established its reputation.

Jack Swilling, founder of Phoenix, Arizona, said,[43] "The man with us who really knew about where to look for minerals, though, was Herman Ehrenburg [sic]. One of the few to escape from the Fannin massacre, back in the Texas Revolution, he'd become a mining engineer and was with Charles Poston when the latter led the first American prospectors into the Gadsden Purchase. If precious metal was in the vicinity, it could no more

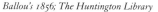

Ballou's 1856; The Huntington Library

Ballou's, 1856.

hide from him than a pheasant from a trained pointer; and up the Colorado at La Paz he made one of the best gold finds to raise cheers in Arizona. . . There's nothing quite like it."

Swilling continued:

"I became less interested in prospecting than in what Ehrenburg [sic] was doing in the matter of channeling the Colorado [River] into a sluiceway that would wash through a large number of claims and make it easier to pan at a deeper level. . . Arriving mostly from California, about twelve hundred stampeders came to La Paz, making it Arizona's metropolis. . . The still-continuing Civil War could have been on a different planet as far as these treasure seekers were concerned."

During the Civil War, at the height of the Confederacy's advance into Arizona, the head of Fort Yuma referred to: "the map of Arizona and Sonora and the adjoining territory known as German Ehrenberg's map." With it they could locate a route that Union troops could use to cut off the Confederates at Tucson, according to the U.S. War Records Office.

"During the Civil War and for a long time afterward all the patronage of the government . . . was contributed to a line far north of Arizona, and none of the pioneers ever received any reward," wrote Poston. He felt the presidents of the United States at that time "had hot work nearer home than Mexico, and Arizona and Sonora receded into barbarism for nearly twenty years."[44]

U.S. Civil War Union sergeant, circa 1864.

Art by José Cisneros

The Civil War caused eventual closing of military posts in southern Arizona, and Ehrenberg wrote to Poston, "Nearly all the managers of the mining companies have been assassinated either by Indians or by Mexicans, and the property carried off. Every mine has been baptized in blood . . .What country and business can prosper under such monstrous adversity? And what man would settle his family in these blood-drenched valleys?. . ."

On May 15, 1863,[45] Ehrenberg was appointed Special Indian Agent for the Mojave (Mohave) Indians by Poston, only a few months after Poston's appointment as Superintendent of Indian Affairs. Ehrenberg served in this post for a year and then resigned. However, Poston had neglected to notify the Indian Office in Washington, D. C., of the appointment and when Ehrenberg applied for his salary, he was told there was no record of his appointment. After proof of his service, he was offered half-salary. On September 16, 1866, while in San Francisco, he finally was compensated by a government agent.

Ehrenberg started riding south from San Francisco, heading for his home in Arizona, and while at a desert stage-coach station he was murdered during the night of October 9, 1866. The location was reported by the *Arizona Miner*, October 30 and November 10, 1866 issues, as Dos Palmos [also spelled *Palmas*], halfway between San Bernardino, California, and La Paz, Arizona, his home. Senator Barry Goldwater, in an oral history interview for the book *This Land,*

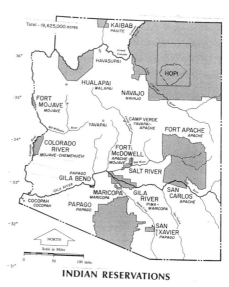

INDIAN RESERVATIONS

From Historical Atlas of Arizona *by Walker and Bufkin*

(Above):
Mohave
Agency on the
Colorado
River.

The Southwest
Museum, Los
Angeles

(Right):
Mohave
children,
Patricia and
Elizabeth
Atheqfuatha

The Southwest
Museum, Los
Angeles

These Voices, said Ehrenberg was shot to death near Indio, California. Since Herman was traveling in a southeasterly direction, he would have been about ten miles past present-day Palm Springs and Palm Desert.

Senator Goldwater said that his grandfather Michel (Big Mike) Goldwater did business in La Paz. After leaving his native Poland and living in France and England, he came to California by way of Cape Horn. After stopping briefly in San Francisco and then living in central California, the family heard of the gold strikes on the Colorado River. Since they were not doing well, "Mike, my grandfather, loaded up a wagon with merchandise and went to what was then Colorado City — the present site of Yuma.

"Mike didn't find any gold, but he found he could sell merchandise so he moved to the little town of La Paz [Arizona] as business partner of a friend from Los Angeles. . . Now La Paz was about six miles back from the normal course of the river, but sometimes the river would swing over and they could unload freight at La Paz. . .

"In the fall of 1866 my grandfather and my uncle — my Uncle Morris who was then a mature fourteen — were traveling back from San Francisco and they found Herman Ehrenberg, who was probably one of the greatest of the early Arizona pioneers, shot to death near Indio.

"About that time the river meandered away from La Paz, so they moved their warehouse downstream about six miles to a little settlement called Mineral City, which had a better river landing. Mike renamed it Ehrenberg in honor of his murdered friend."

Ehrenberg's death was reported nationally, including newspapers in San Francisco, Galveston, and New York.

The editor of the *Arizona Gazette,* Vincent Ryan, in a lengthy report shortly after the murder, wrote an article headlined "THE MURDER OF EHRENBERG."

"La Paz, October 14, 1866. EDITORS ALTA: Presuming that the sad news of the killing of Herman Ehrenberg (which occurred on the night of the 9th inst., at Dos Palmos, a station

Three generations:
(Above): Senator Barry Goldwater's grandfather, Michel (Big Mike)
Goldwater, who was a close personal friend of Herman Ehrenberg.

The senator's uncle Morris
Goldwater (with Masonic medals).

Senator Barry
Goldwater.

about half way between here and San Bernardino) has reached you, I write to correct the information which, it is feared, may be formed in San Francisco as to the manner of his death. It was not the result of any regular Indian raid, and should not lead to the idea that such is to be feared on the road from San Bernardino to La Paz.

"Mr. Ehrenberg had started from San Bernardino about two weeks ago, in company with Messrs. Cushenburg and Noyes, (who have since passed through La Paz, on their way to Prescott,) but remained behind on account of the failure of his riding animal. He fell in with the next party that came along (teamsters,) and remained with them until they reached Lone Palm, eight miles from Dos Palmos, where the teams continued, while Mr. Ehrenberg determined to ride on to the station at Dos Palmos. He arrived there about nightfall, and retired to bed on a pallet, which is kept outside the door for the convenience of the traveller, it being generally too warm to sleep inside with comfort. About midnight, W. H. Smith, proprietor of the house, was awakened by the discharge of a gun or pistol, and coming out of an inner room where he had been sleeping, found Mr. Ehrenberg lying some few feet from his bed. He was then nearly dead, and survived but a short time. Next morning the teams spoken of arrived and the body was buried.

"On examination, it was found that some goods were missing from behind the counter, and although no human eye witnessed the tragedy, it may safely be stated that it happened as follows: The proprietor of the Dos Palms [sic] House has always been surrounded by Cahuilla and Chemahueva Indians, with whom he has lived in perfect peace. All travellers, including the writer, have rested at his station, with numerous Indians around, without fear of danger. Some evil disposed one of these Indians, with the purpose of plunder, must have entered the house, not knowing that anyone but Smith was there, and upon Ehrenberg rising, shot him down. It is just such a case of murder and robbery as is ever liable to occur anywhere, in the crowded city as well as the desert. The Indians along this road have been perfectly peaceable and friendly, and the crime of one reprobate among them should not be visited upon them all.

"The villains ball selected a shining mark, which will make the atrocity of more notoriety than had an unknown person fallen; but let us stick to the stern maxim, ' Let justice be done though the heavens fall.' I believe that if the proper measures were taken by persons from San Bernardino, the Cahuillas at Martin's ranch would do all they could to discover the murderer.

"Mr. Ehrenberg was a Prussian, aged about 46: He was a man of fine scientific attainments, and, as you know, had wide fame. An outline of his life is briefly furnished in the following extract from a letter he wrote to a friend in the East some years ago: 'In Texas I belonged to the New Orleans Greys; was the third man (boy) who signed his name for Texas as a volunteer, in the Arcade building. Was at the storming of San Antonio — Fannin's — [sic] and afterwards twice prisoner with the Mexicans. Went over the Rocky Mountains to Washington and Oregon in 1844; '45 and '46 in the Sandwich Islands, and numerous groups in the southern hemisphere and South America; returned to California; '46 and '47, west coast of Mexico; '48 and '49, California; '59, discovered the mouth of Klamath river and the Gold Bluff, and the *first* gold in the sea shore — consequent great excitement in California, notwithstanding my reports against it; '54, went to Sonora and Arizona, and there ever since.'

"Mr. Ehrenberg was one of the very best of our people, and his untimely death will create the deepest gloom in every section of the Territory. A man of the greatest integrity, the purest morals, and the kindliest simplicity of character, he leaves no enemy in this Territory, where he was more generally known, perhaps, than any other person. Had he died among us, of natural causes, or even in combat with the Indian enemy, we should have been grieved far less; but for so noble a man to become the victim of a midnight robber and assassin, has left us all aghast. Yours truly,

Vincent Ryan, Editor Arizona *Gazette*."

Reporting that the murder was not the result of an Indian raid but the work of a lone individual, the editor attempted to maintain peace in the area. The obituary was reprinted in the *Daily Alta California* for October 31, 1866, page one. The manager of the stage house became a suspect later.

Another printed version stated: "Herman Ehrenberg was shot at Dos Palmas, on the road from San Bernardino to La Paz, one night last week. There is a mystery about the affair, but so nearly as we can learn he had preceded his traveling companions to that place, and was sleeping in the house. The station keeper says he found him dead in the morning, and charges it to someone on the outside. Others think the keeper may have been in liquor and shot him by mistake. He was not robbed. We presume a full investigation will be had." *Daily Arizona Miner*, October 23, 1866.

An editor for the *Arizona Miner*, October 27, 1866, wrote: "Arizona has suffered an irreparable loss in the sudden and violent death of Herman Ehrenberg. . . He was cautious in the extreme and a man of acknowledged integrity. He was both scientific and practical; a careful and accomplished student of geology, mineralogy and metallurgy, and a high authority on all matters relating to the science of mining. His reports, never in the least overdrawn and based upon an excellent judgment and thorough investigation, were everywhere received as worthy of entire confidence; indeed, to have Ehrenberg speak well of a mine was to establish its reputation at once. As a writer he was clear and precise and his contributions to the various mining journals of the country would make a valuable volume. As a pioneer he was fearless and enthusiastic. He loved the frontier and was never so happy as when rambling among the wild hills

Desert scene where Herman Ehrenberg was shot to death in
Indio, California, near Palm Springs and Palm Desert.
Photography © by Natalie Ornish

of Arizona, eagerly examining their varied, rich metallic forma-
tions. As a citizen he was unobtrusive, industrious, progressive
and patriotic. Repeatedly offered office, he persistently refused
to accept it, although in all that pertained to the welfare of society he had the liveliest concern. Not only throughout the Territory and the Union will his loss be sincerely mourned, but far
beyond our borders, in the scientific circles of Europe will his
untimely death be deplored by many who held his character
and services in hearty appreciation. Our Pioneer and Historical
Societies, of which he was a respected member, and all our people, should pay the highest honors to his memory. . ."

His friend Poston wrote that he had spent the night before
in the same stage station. "I slept on a bunk under a ramada in
front of the station the night before, but having just been
defeated for Congress and going out of the country, was not
supposed to have enough money to be worth killing. Ehrenberg

slept on the same bunk the night afterwards and was known to have about $3,500 in gold, with which he was going to buy a mine. There is no doubt in the writer's mind but that he was killed by the station-keeper.

"Thus miserably perished one of the most intelligent men. . . He rests in the eternal silence of the desert without a tombstone. . . The memory of many years faithful companionship and a thousand and one nights' pleasant conversation will excuse this extended memoriam."[46]

The following [unsigned] feature article/editorial appeared in the *Daily Alta California* for October 13, 1866:

"THE MURDER OF HERMAN EHRENBERG.

"A telegram from Los Angeles announces that the Indians murdered Herman Ehrenberg, a few days since, at Dos Palmos, on the road from San Bernardino to La Paz, about half way between the two places. The deceased leaves many warm friends, and few enemies. His career was an eventful one. He was a native of Germany, and must have come to the United States while quite young. In 1836 he was in the Texan army, and was under the command of Colonel Fannin when the latter surrendered to General Urrea, under an agreement that the party should be treated as prisoners of war, and sent to the United States on the first opportunity. In violation of the terms of capitulation, the party, three hundred and fifty-seven men, were, on the 27th of March, taken out, in four successive divisions, to be shot, and Ehrenberg among them. With his associates he knelt down to die, and the fatal volley was fired. He was astonished to find himself alive and unhurt, and immediately started to run. A thick smoke from the muskets covered the place, and he had got a considerable distance before the Mexicans discovered him; he succeeded in reaching the chaparral and finally escaping.

"Mr. Ehrenberg came to California in 1847, and has resided on the coast since. After the discovery of gold he went to the placers, and sometimes was miner and sometimes civil engineer.

He engaged in many speculations and was the leader of the party which discovered the mouth of the Klamath River and laid off a town there in 1850. He made his home for a time in San Francisco, and when Southern Arizona was purchased he went thither and engaged in mining for silver and copper, which has been his main occupation for the last few years. The Arizonians consider him one of the leading pioneers and most prominent citizens of the Territory. Mr. Ehrenberg was a very modest, taciturn, brave, kind, honest, and in every way worthy man."

A Phoenix historian, James M. Barney, (whose uncle had a store at Ehrenberg and was its first postmaster) wrote about Ehrenberg the pioneer and Ehrenberg the town in a column published May 27, 1961, almost one hundred years later: "Of old Ehrenberg — once a beehive of business and social activities — there is now nothing left but a few moldering adobe ruins. The rich merchants who once held sway there and the men and women who sang and danced and played in the gaudy saloons and dance-halls have long since passed on."

What will never pass on is a natural monument to Ehrenberg, designated by those who admired and respected him. The

December 12, 1952

Mr. Allen Belden
Acting Executive Secretary
United States Board on Geographic
Names
Department of the Interior
Washington 25, D. C.

Dear Mr. Belden:

I wish to express my thanks for your courteous letter of the 8th instant respecting the name Ehrenberg applied to a certain point in Grand Canyon National Park in accordance with a decision by the United States Board on Geographic Names.

As the works kindly mentioned by you are available in the library of this Museum, it will not be necessary for you to pursue the question further, although your desire to do so is greatly appreciated.

It interests me to know that the name was proposed by Mr. Frank Bond, who was Executive Secretary at the time I was a member of the Board as representing the Smithsonian Institution.

Cordially yours,

F. W. Hodge
Director

FWH:P

DEPARTMENT OF THE INTERIOR

NATIONAL PARK SERVICE

GRAND CANYON NATIONAL PARK
GRAND CANYON, ARIZONA

July 5, 1953

Dr. F. W. Hodge
Southwest Museum
Highland Park
Los Angeles 42, California

Dear Teluli:

Delightfully surprised to have your air letter of July 1. It was good to have word from you.

Now, regarding your inquiry on the location of "Ehrenberg Point" in Grand Canyon National Park.

You will find the point named on the U. S. Geological Survey topographic map of Grand Canyon National Park., Arizona (East Half) 36° 15' north and 111° 55' Range 4 East. It is located off the North Rim overlooking Nankoweap basin, down which the Powell Party under Thompson cut a trail. There is a ridge that fingers out into the basin from the rim. This ridge has three buttes in line, named from the rim successively, Brady Peak, Alsap Butte and Novinger Butte. Ehrenberg Point juts out almost directly north from the central butte named Alsap.

I am sending, under separate cover, the above map with Ehrenberg Point indicated by a black arrow for quick and ready locating. This will be better than a wordy description.

Our very best wishes go forward to you and here's hoping we can get to see each other soon. Regards to M. R. also.

Most cordially,

Don Louis

Louis Schellbach
Park Naturalist

United States Board on Geographic Names has honored him with "Ehrenberg Point" in the Grand Canyon National Park.

For historians, Ehrenberg's greatest legacy is his account of the Goliad massacre, considered the best account ever written about any facet of the war for Texas independence.

NOTES

[1] See appendix section for parentage.

[2] See appendix, "About the Translator."

[3] Records of the Bureau of Customs, Record Group 36, National Archives, Washington, D.C.

[4] Charles Poston, "Herman Ehrenberg: In Memoriam," *Arizona Daily Star*, Feb. 19, 1880.

[5] Archie P. McDonald, ed., *Hurrah for Texas! The Diary of Adolphus Sterne*, p. ix.

[6] Marquis James, *The Raven*, p. 199.

[7] Sterne diary: McDonald, p. 19. Llerena Friend, *Sam Houston*, p. 100. Harriet Smither (ed.), "Diary of Adolphus Sterne," *Southwestern Historical Quarterly*, 31: 78, 80.

[8] Additional Sterne biography in Bertram W. Korn, *The Early Jews of New Orleans*, pp. 206, 329-330.

[9] The author of this book has used the spelling Greys with an *e* because that is the style used by the *Handbook of Texas* editors. However, the following spelled Greys with an *a:* (1) Mirabeau B. Lamar, discharge papers of Ehrenberg, Velasco, 1836. (2) Herman Ehrenberg, letter in his handwriting to Ashbel Smith, 1842. (3) Yoakum, *History of Texas*, Vol II, 1855, pp. 22, 23. (4) Thrall, *History of Texas*, 1879, p. 237. (5) Wooten, *A Complete History of Texas*, 1899, p. 190.

[10] T. C. Richardson, *East Texas*, Volume 3, page 1406.

[11] In December, 1841, Sterne wrote in his diary: "Got a petition introduced into the House of Representatives to Audit my Claim of $950.00 for transporting Troops in 1835, passed all round and has become a Law — but have no money, nor no chance to get any —" Sterne, *Diary*, p. 75. One claim, for $820, was approved in 1837 but not paid until 1842.

[12] Crockett was one of the few mature fighters, most of the volunteers being teen-agers. He arrived in Texas just in time to die two months later.

[13] When this author experienced a memorial service in this very chapel in the Presidio on Palm Sunday, April 1997, attendance was approximately 150 persons, all seated, with standing room only in the rear. For this chapel to hold twice that many persons, they would have to exist elbow to

elbow, all vertical. See appendix on Re-enactments of the Massacre.

14 For Edward Isaac Johnson's biography see Natalie Ornish, *Pioneer Jewish Texans*, pp. 38-39, based on interviews with his descendant, Lawrence P. Johnson of Cincinnati, 1981. Edward Johnson left Cincinnati in 1835 to come to Texas, where he fought in the center of the hottest action in the Revolution. He served under General Burleson in the storming of San Antonio, and fought in Captain King's company in the Battle of Refugio, where King and 150 Texans were killed. He then marched with Dr. James Grant's forces to Goliad, where he joined a company under Captain Burr H. Duval, who also died at Goliad (and whose brother survived and wrote of the massacre.) At Refugio, as many Texans were killed as died at the Alamo; however this battle has fallen through the cracks of history as the events there were too painful for the citizens to remember.

15 The Texan troops were divided into three groups of approximately 100 men each and were marched to three separate areas: one northeast on the road to Victoria, one northwest on the road to San Antonio, and one south on the road to San Patricio. The men were massacred in these three locations. See map in Part II. Ehrenberg was sent on the northeast route. They were marched out under different pretexts. Some were told they were to be taken to Copano and sent home; others that they were going out to slaughter beef, and others were told they were being removed to make room in the fort for Santa Anna.

16 The doctors were saved because their services were needed to take care of the Mexican wounded. Dr. Joseph H. Barnard of Massachusetts and Dr. Jack Shackleford of Alabama, who were hidden, later wrote of their survival. Carpenters were spared who had done work that pleased Mexican colonel Garay, who hid them. John Henry Brown, *History of Texas*, Vol. I, pp. 598, 613. Others who wrote of their survival include John Crittenden Duval, who escaped along the San Antonio road and wrote *Early Times in Texas* published in 1867 and 1892.

17 Jacob De Cordova, *Texas: Her Resources and Her Public Men*, p. 223.

18 H. Yoakum, *History of Texas*, Vol. II, p. 100.

19 1996 edition.

20 Brown, *History of Texas*, Vol. I, pp. 613-615, quoting Dr. Barnard.

21 Ibid., Vol. II, p. 44.

22 Archives, Center for American History, University of Texas at Austin.

23 The journey lasted six months and settlers had to contend with flooded rivers, Indian attacks, little food, and disease.

24 Charles Poston, *Apache-Land*, pp. 51-52. See Appendix this volume for poem.

25 Patrick O'Reilly and Raoul Teissier, *Tahitiens. . .* Paris: 1975.

26 In Public Archives of the Territory of Hawaii.

27 At the close of the Mexican War, by the Treaty of Guadalupe Hidalgo, the U. S. acquired from Mexico the regions of California, Nevada, and Utah, most of Arizona and New Mexico, and parts of Colorado and Wyoming. H. H. Bancroft, *History of Mexico*, IV (1886). See also John Edward Weems, *To Conquer a Peace: The War Between the United States and Mexico.*

28 A brief resume of Ehrenberg's account of his northern California explorations accompanies this map that appears in the *Weekly Pacific News*, per steamers *Columbus* and *Carolina* (San Francisco, Cal.) Thursday, Aug. 15, 1850, p. 1, cols. 3-5. The National Archives, Bancroft Library and the New York Historical Society. An illustration of this map is included in: John E. Parsons, ed., "Nine Cousins in the California Gold Rush," *The New York Historical Society Quarterly* XLVII (Oct., 1963): 387. Described in Carl I. Wheat, *Mapping the Transmississippi West*, Vol. III *From the Mexican War to the Boundary Surveys, 1846-1854* (San Francisco: 1959), pp. 131, 295. See also Diane M. T. Rose, "The Maps of Herman Ehrenberg," *Prologue: The Journal of the National Archives* 9 (Fall 1977), for detailed listing and locations of other Ehrenberg maps.

29 The name may have been at one time Zakrzewski, formerly a Polish officer in the Revolution of 1830-31, according to Edmund L. Lowalczyk of Worcester, Mass., as stated in Carl I. Wheat's *"Maps of the California Gold Region 1848-1857.* Director F. W. Hodge of the Southwest Museum in Los Angeles wrote to Lowalczyk in 1953 hoping he could furnish information regarding Ehrenberg. Hodge described Herman as a topographer, mining engineer, and map draftsman.

30 Poston was born near Elizabethtown, Hardin County, Kentucky, April 20, 1825, son of a printer. His parents were Temple and Judith Debrille Poston. Charles was orphaned at age twelve, and became an apprentice to the county clerk for seven years. In 1848 he married the county clerk's daughter, Sarah Lee Haycraft and they had one surviving child, Sarah Lee. When Mrs. Poston became paralyzed in 1851, she was cared for by her daughter but supported by her husband. Poston left Kentucky 1851, taking a ship in New Orleans and arriving in San Francisco Bay January 28, 1851. Soon he was chief clerk in the customs house at a salary of $300 per month. John S. Goff, *Arizona Territorial Officials*, III, p.17.

31 Dates vary slightly as to this journey. Author Goff stated the men left San Francisco in late 1853 and arrived in Guaymas January 14, 1854. John S. Goff, *Arizona Territorial Officials*, III, p. 18.

32 Ibid., p. 18.

33 The Gadsden maps by Ehrenberg show the following: The area between California and Texas was all called New Mexico. Names on first map: "By Herman Ehrenberg C.E., from his private notes and those of Major Heintzelman, Capt. Silgreaves, Lieut. Darby, Bartlett, Gray, Julius Froebel, & others." The "Ehrenberg Poston Party" appears on both maps to be in a part of Sonora not included in the Purchase. The 1858 map says, "from his private notes and those of Colonel Gray, Maj. Heintzelman, Lieut. Parks and others."

34 William H. Goetzmann, *Army Exploration in the American West.* Yale, 1959, pp. 259-260. See also *Weekly Arizonian*, March 3, 1859; *Arizona Weekly Star*, May 13, 1880.

35 Poston was described as "the alcalde who dispensed justice, performed marriages and generally watched over matters."

36 "In Memoriam."

37 Vivid descriptions of similar trips are reported in Bayard Taylor's *Eldorado,* 1850. Gary F. Kurutz, author of *Western Americana in the California State Library*, cited Taylor's book. Ornish int. with Kurutz, April 1997.

38 H. H. Bancroft, *History of Arizona and New Mexico 1530-1888* (San Francisco 1889), p. 497. See also Howard R. Lamar, *The Far Southwest 1846-1912*, Yale University Press, p. 417, who wrote, "So vigorous was this grand reconnaisance [of topographical engineers] that in a short fifteen years the United States had been able to compile as much information about the region as the Spanish padres and explorers had accumulated in over two centuries."

39 See also A. C. Greene, *900 Miles on the Butterfield Trail*, 1994.

40 Raphael Pumpelly, *Across America and Asia*, 1870, p. 60.

41 This refers to Pauline Weaver (1800-1867), a man who became a legend in Arizona mining and served as a peacemaker between Indians and white men.

42 Ehrenberg 1864 letter to Governor Goodwin was published in the *Arizona Historical Review* (July 1936), pp. 88-89. A copy of the letter is on file in the office of the Secretary of State. The letter is in longhand and written in ink on double-size foolscap paper.

43 Author John Myers Myers quoted Swilling in his book *I, Jack Swilling: Founder of Phoenix, Arizona.*

44 C. Poston, "In Memoriam." See also R. W. Paul, *Mining Frontiers of the Far West 1848-1880*, p. 157.

45 Date of appointment is from "Herman Ehrenberg" document written by Hon. Carl Hayden, U. S. Senate, 1940.

46 Poston, "In Memoriam."

Book II

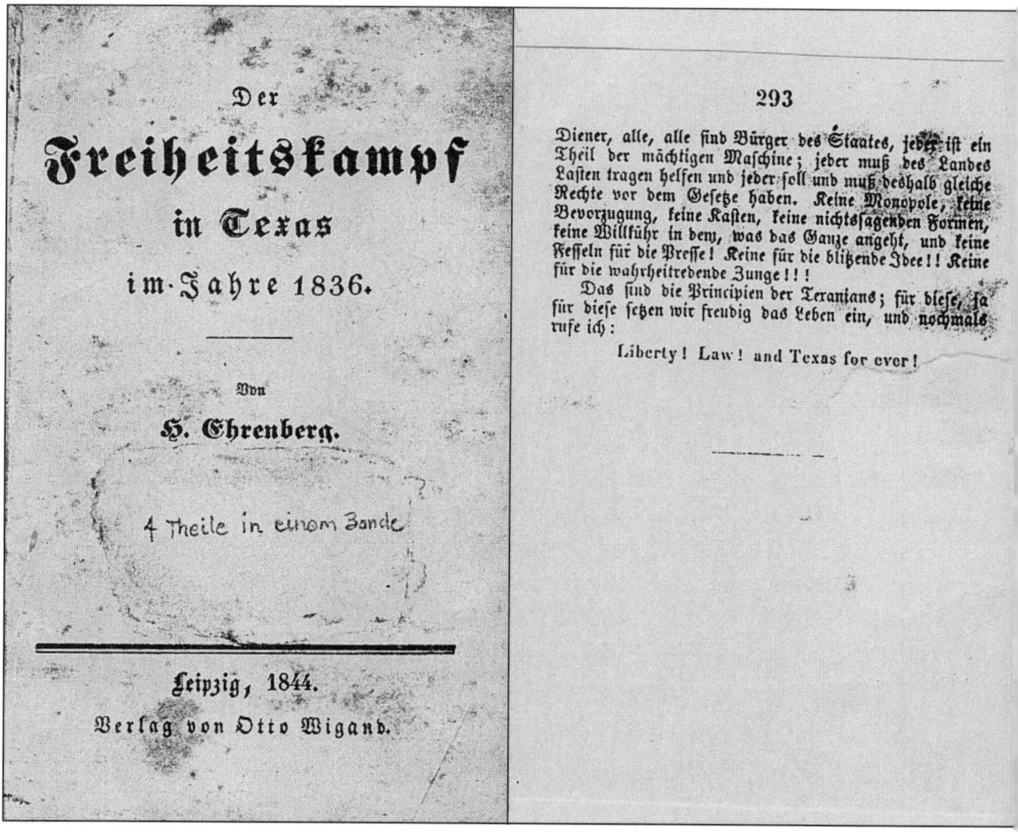

Der

Freiheitskampf

in Texas

im Jahre 1836.

Von

H. Ehrenberg.

4 Theile in einem Bande

Leipzig, 1844.

Verlag von Otto Wigand.

Diener, alle, alle sind Bürger des Staates, jetzt ist ein Theil der mächtigen Maschine; jeder muß des Landes Lasten tragen helfen und jeder soll und muß deßhalb gleiche Rechte vor dem Gesetze haben. Keine Monopole, keine Bevorzugung, keine Kasten, keine nichtssagenden Formen, keine Willführ in dem, was das Ganze angeht, und keine Fesseln für die Presse! Keine für die blitzende Idee!! Keine für die wahrheitredende Zunge!!!

Das sind die Principien der Texanians; für diese, ja für diese setzen wir freudig das Leben ein, und nochmals rufe ich:

Liberty! Law! and Texas for ever!

Second edition of Ehrenberg's book on his capture at Goliad in 1836, published in 1844. First and last pages are shown above.

Natalie Ornish Collection.

Der Freiheitskampf in Texas im Jahre 1836

(The Fight for Freedom in Texas in the Year 1836)

by Herman Ehrenberg

Translated by
Peter Mollenhauer

with annotations by Natalie Ornish

Although the Spanish Inquisition reached its epitome of evil in Spain,
it included North America, where "heretics" were burned at the stake
in Mexico City. Lasting for centuries, it did not cease in the New
World until 1821. Ehrenberg came to Texas-Mexico in 1835,
only fourteen years thereafter.

Art from Fray Bartolomae de Las Casas' *Regionum Indicarum per Hispaños,* 1598.

The editor has inserted phrases in brackets into the text
to make for smooth reading. This information is relevant
to understanding Ehrenberg's writing.
The footnotes are Ehrenberg's.
The illustrations have been added to Ehrenberg's memoirs.

CHAPTER ONE

Mexico Before 1835

BEFORE THE WAR FOR INDEPENDENCE, the permanently established Spanish officials and the aristocracy had done everything
in their power to hamper the respect and independence of the
Mexicans through fraud and bloody executions: Slaves—worse
than slaves, dogs—were the people of the especially beautiful,
lofty plains of Anahuac [scene of the first real collision between
the colonists of Texas and the military power of Mexico in
spring of 1832, when William B. Travis, a leading citizen, was
jailed by Col. Juan Bradburn, an Anglo in service of Mexico].
Yet those bloodsuckers were not the worst enemies with which
the Texans had to battle: Another far greater enemy, working
hand-in-hand with the Spanish military and aristocracy, also
had brought out terrible weapons against the inhabitants.

With the aid of the torture rack and the pyre [People were
burned at the stake in Mexico City for not converting to
Catholicism by the Spanish Inquisition, which crossed the
Atlantic and came to the New World.], the disciples of Loyola
had forced upon these peaceful people an established religion
that was deadly to the spirit. These servants of God began with

demoralization to proselytize the Indians to Christianity; and indeed they were most successful in this endeavor. Here they showed their masterpiece, and it was evident that their cruelty here was not one step behind that of their brothers in South America. One gazes in horror from the borders of North American free states down to the south; magnificent, incomparable lands sprawled out here; but all these fertile lands are covered and soiled with murder and lust.

Mexico's indescribable misery finally had reached a point that to stay there would have required superhuman effort. Furiously, frantically arose the people clad in rags, and poorly armed or armed not at all, they went to battle. To war! To war! was the cry to the hills of Teotihuacán [a town north of Mexico City], and it resounded with a thousand voices thunderously from the south and east, north and west. Down with the *Gachupines* [derogatory word used by Mexicans to refer to Spaniards]! Down with the dogs! Let Mexico be free! Free! *Viva Mexico*! [Long live Mexico!]

For eleven long years the opposing parties fought and murdered; and groups clad in rags, even naked, not unlike robbers if such they were, wandered about the land. "Blood, blood" were the rallying words from all sides. One of the groups, the Spaniards, carried the murderer's sword because of greed to promote slavery; the other group, namely the Mexicans, acted out of revenge toward suppressors who for several centuries had wielded the whip over their heads.

The year 1821 approached and with it the last hour of Spanish despotism. The viceroy's government was forced to recognize Mexico's independence. After long arguments among the chieftains of the leaders, [Augustín de] Iturbide now took over the helm of the state machine. Iturbide became emperor of Mexico.

Notwithstanding its structure, the new government might have been able to work benevolently for the country; but by worrying only about treason, Iturbide only thought about making the newly liberated people slaves again. Numerous envious

DON AGUSTIN DE ITURBIDE,

ARAMBURU, AREGUI, CARRILLO, Y VILLASEÑOR,

Generalísimo de los Ejércitos del Imperio Mexicano, Gran Almirante de su Armada, y Presidente del Supremo Consejo de Regencia.

Por cuanto atendiendo la Regencia del Imperio *á los méritos y servicios de D. Ignacio Paz y Tagle, Alferez de Esquadron Provincial de esta Corte.*

ha venido en concederle *el grado de Capitan de Milicias Provinciales*

y estando autorizado por el expresado superior Gobierno para expedir estos Despachos provisionales.

Por tanto, el Capitan General, ó Comandante general á quien tocare, dejará usar de este permiso al expresado *D. Ignacio Paz y Tagle* previniendo lo conveniente para ello á continuacion de este Despacho provisional, bajo de su firma, á cuyo efecto se le ha de presentar dentro de un mes contado desde la fecha de el, como tambien al Intendente á quien tocare, para que lo haga anotar en la Contaduría principal del mismo Ejército donde sirviere dentro del expresado término; en inteligencia de que será nulo faltándole cualquiera de estos requisitos.

Dado en México á 27. de *Diziembre* de 1821, *primer* año de la Independencia del Imperio.

Agustin de Iturbide

Fran.co de Paula Alvarez

La Regencia del Imperio concede á l. Alferez d. Ignacio Paz y Tagle el grado de Capitan de Milicias Provinciales.

Decree of Augustín de Iturbide.
Signed with his rubric and engraved coat of arms. Iturbide is the person who signed the first permit for the settlement of Anglo-Americans in Texas for Stephen F. Austin's colony.

people who observed the emperor's actions with distrust took the opportunity to joyously depose him, and after one year of ruling, the imperial government was destroyed. Iturbide was banned and now, in 1824, came an extremely free constitution. With the exception of a few articles, it coincided almost entirely with that of the constitution of the state federation of North America [United States of America].

If at that time the people only had an approximate sense of political freedom, now the people could play practically just as significant a role in the world theatre as their neighboring republic. But the indolent slaves of the priests yielded the political field and the reins of the government to a few ambitious, excellent soldiers, without making use of their rights to participate in the struggle and victory.

The Spaniards had been chased away; Mexico's glowing hatred subsided. And again the people sank into a state not far removed from that of animals. Sensuous pleasure and a life without work was all that was desired. Various parties emerged but all of them strove to acquire for themselves the ruling power and control of the government. Their various paths crossed each other, and they approached each other as enemies. Through misrepresentations and appeals of the priests, the ignorant people were incited bulldog-like one against the other, without knowing for what cause they should shoulder the musket.

So up to the year of 1832, this literally garden of the New World was the arena of dark deeds. In this year, however, [Antonio López de] Santa Anna proclaims the restoration of the constitution of 1824. He makes himself leader of the liberal party in order to overthrow the despotic rule of [former General Anastacio] Bustamante. He succeeded in this [becoming president of Mexico in 1833] and again Mexico's incomparable phlegmatic nature began to reveal itself and come to the fore: Again the people gave way to their preferred inactivity and, with the exception of the inhabitants of Zacatecas, they had con-

Santa Anna.

fidence in the two-faced nature of the victor and trusted Santa Anna. [In 1834 Santa Anna stated that Mexico was not ready for democracy, crushed the liberal Zacatecans in 1835, and advanced on Texas in 1836.]

It was a favorable moment for him and he used it. The just restoration of the legal constitution previously promised was again negated and the laws of the dictator were enforced with the bayonets of the coarse, brutish soldiers—Indians. And all states that revolted against this violent overthrow and had revolted against their own annihilation were suppressed by his [Santa Anna's] troops. A centralized government was to be established, the free sovereign states were to be converted into mere provinces and the whole nation was to be placed under martial law and governed by the military.

Now, the most northeastern province, Texas, appears in the foreground, and a few words are necessary in order to understand the following.

Until the war for Mexican independence, Texas had only a small Mexican population which concentrated in the towns of San Antonio, La Bahía (Goliad), Nacogdoches, and a few missions where they were by virtue of their numbers protected against the violence of the wild Comanches and other prairie Indians.

The reason that such a land as Texas should contain not more than six thousand inhabitants lay on the one hand in the jealousy of the Spaniards toward the neighboring states, from whose liberal institutions they had everything to fear, and on the other in that the Indians mentioned made all cultivation and farming of the land unusually difficult. Their hordes swarmed about in the border provinces and penetrated even deeper into the remaining states. In Texas the Mexican authorities recognized the Comanche authorities; and when one of the red chieftains honored San Antonio with a visit, the commander of the troops was obliged to obediently hold horse and stirrup for the chief.

In order to stop these Indian raids, the Spanish government, shortly before its fall, accepted the plan of an American, Moses Austin, who proposed to found a colony of his countrymen in Texas as a protection of the frontier lands. Moses Austin died soon after he had laid the foundation of the colony; his son, Stephen F. Austin, continued the work. Hundreds and hundreds of families came over from the states. The Mexican war broke out; freedom was victorious, and another policy friendlier to the colonies was adopted by the new government. They received their former rights, as well as some new ones and also a special constitution especially suitable for the American population. From year to year the settlements grew larger, and new ones were laid out with the approval of the general government.

Comanche warrior.

Excerpt from document signed by Moses Austin, 1811.
Natalie Ornish Collection, Dallas Historical Society

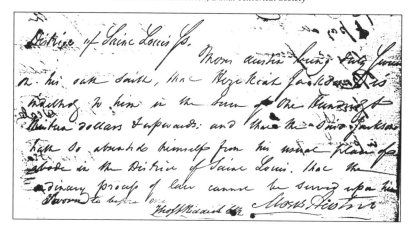

The settlers were able to live with increasing security on the plantations, and soon the Indians didn't dare to trifle with the determined, vigorous North Americans as they had been in the custom of doing with the Mexicans. The attention of the Texans was also fixed on Mexico. And only too clearly did they recognize the weaknesses of the various governments that so quickly succeeded one another. Texas was too remote from the center of the struggle to participate in a vigorous way effectively, but on their own soil the Texans always contended for

Stephen F. Austin.

the Constitution of 1824, whereas it was distressingly distorted by the parties in Mexico.

Up to the year 1832 several undesirable laws had seriously affected the very essence of the welfare of the colonists. The settlers felt highly insulted and they obtained justice on a few points only after determined protests to the weak authorities.

The bold people of North America looked down with contempt upon the sensuous nation [preoccupied with daily concerns and not intellectual idealism] with which they were to become brothers—with a people who did not cast a single glance beyond the present time and who remained the tools of deceitful priests.

The more enlightened settlers could not possibly co-mingle with this race of Negro, Indian, and Spanish blood, which could not comprehend its freedom and which was not conscious of its own rights. And yet the colonists still hoped for the best from the future.

Already several disquieting movements had taken place in Texas, and just now a part of the citizens were under arms against several garrisons because of their unjust actions, when suddenly the news came to the colonies that Santa Anna had placed himself at the head of the liberal party. At once the same flag was raised, to which the occupying forces had to swear allegiance.

However, Santa Anna, as previously mentioned, became untrue to his political pretensions, and his government came to be viewed with greater suspicion than any previous one had been by the colonies in Texas. The petition of the Texans to the general government to found their own state, which they were ready for and to which they were constitutionally entitled, remained without results. Their representative, Stephen F. Austin, was imprisoned in the city of Mexico and was held a long time without trial. Peaceful citizens were arrested without cause on barest suspicion and other excesses were committed.

In the summer of 1835 Austin returned from Mexico after a two-year stay, and the insulted colonists received him with rejoicing. [Lorenzo] de Zavala, a Mexican hero of the revolution who had opposed Santa Anna's violent and illegal measures, was compelled to leave Mexico, and he placed himself under the protection of the Texans.

[Domingo de] Ugartechea, the military commander of the Texans at the time—[In 1835 Ugartechea, respected by the Anglo-Texans, was made military commandant of Coahuila and Texas and put in command of the forces at San Antonio de Bexar Presidio.]—received an order from Santa Anna to march into the colonies to forcibly put de Zavala into chains. General Cos appeared from Matamoras soon after with reinforcements and orders to take supreme command of the Texans. With him came a number of senseless laws for the Texans, of which I will mention only the following two:

All of the arms of the Texans were to be handed over. As evidence of special consideration the inhabitants of five plantations each were to be allowed one rifle.

The colonies further were forbidden to build churches.

How senseless and wicked the first of these laws is in a land like Texas at that time surrounded on all sides by marauding Indians! How unjust the other!

And how illegal all the rest! All other mandates of the Mexicans also were beyond the possibility of execution. I guess I do not have to explain all of them here and have said enough of the rights of the colonists to apply force against force.

And now, to the revolution!

CHAPTER TWO

New Orleans

THE WORDS "PUBLIC MEETING" were projected in two-feet-high letters on corners of the uncommonly straight streets of New Orleans. "Great public meeting tonight at eight o'clock in the Arcade. Liberty is at stake, the sovereignty of a people in whose veins flows the blood of the Anglo-Saxons—Texas, the prairie land, has arisen in order to oppose with arms the tyrant Santa Anna and the greedy, arrogant, and domineering priests of Mexico. The liberal citizens of the Union are being asked for aid. We have therefore called for a general meeting of the inhabitants of our city and we hope to see our citizens in large numbers in the plaza."

THE COMMITTEE FOR TEXAS

The numerous periodicals of the city hastened to advise the public of the new happenings in Texas. The sympathy was widespread, and the publications of the Whigs as well as those of the Democrats and the smaller neutral newspapers combined in their support of brethren beyond the Sabine:[1] United, they thundered their weighty voices among people of the united free states of North America.

Independent journals privileged to convey the truth to the people are the main support of the state; they help the progress of civilization and inspire citizens to noble deeds. They exchange views and protect against intrigues of the Jesuits of all confessions whose aim has always been the tyrannization of the world. Here, too, the journals inflamed the minds of people; Americans as well as Europeans and Protestants as well as Catholics armed themselves in order to make sacrifices on the holy altar of freedom.

Slowly the Catholic cathedral's clock struck eight o'clock, and a Mississippi-like stream of people flowed toward the gigantic coffee-house called the Arcade. Already thousands stood under the roofed promenades with tall colonnades and shoulder-to-shoulder formed lines in the crowded galleries. Speaker after speaker ascended the podium. The unrestricted noise of the people subsided and a desert-like stillness settled over the audience. Vigorous speeches were made that proposed to convey to the public the causes of the national uprising of the Texans; other speeches contained the pleadings of the settlers to the inhabitants of the free states for support against the usurper, Santa Anna, who in conjunction with the priests had destroyed the Constitution of 1824. But even the short speeches of several citizens touched the hearts of the masses that crowded close around the speaker's podium, and happy was he who could speak to the people that day. Even though his speaking ability might not have been the best, the cause for which he raised his voice was much in his favor: and at every pause the public thundered its applause for the fight for the fertile prairie. [Texas]

The enthusiastic citizens crowded round the subscription list lying on the stage, and even before the assembled people had left the colonnades, ten thousand dollars had been subscribed. Another list was opened for volunteers who wanted to support their former countrymen in the struggle. A six-foot Kentuckian now ascended the speaker's platform and signed up at the top,

with the thundering applause of the enthusiastic crowd that surrounded him; because "Old Kentucky" had always been the first
to take up the rifle when it came to fighting for what is right. The
meeting was closed and the lists were left there in the same building to allow further participation and sign-up in the morning.

Squire [Adolphus] Sterne, the representative of the Texans, a
native German, was highly elated over the result. On the next
afternoon, October 12, 1835, the [ship] *Washita* led with the first
Texas volunteers, the first company of Greys, who wanted to sail
up the Mississippi and the Red River and then make the journey
to Texas overland. All of us had speedily acquired for ourselves
clothes suitable for life on the prairie, clothes which we found
ready-made in the numerous storehouses. From the grey color of
these garments originated the name of our company. Our
weapons were rifles, pistols and the Bowie knife, famous in

Adolphus Sterne.

Indian wars.[2] We also received from the Texan committee several cannon that were to make the journey on board the ship with us. A day after our departure a second company of Greys left New Orleans going, however, through the Gulf of Mexico to Texas. The next expedition to be fitted out was the Tampico Blues whose destination, however, was not Texas but, as the name indicates, the Mexican city of Tampico. It was composed of Americans, Englishmen, Frenchmen, and several Germans. Our two companies, the Greys, numbered six Germans.

The *Washita* soon left the mighty waters of the Mississippi and turned into the narrow but deep Red River. Here it was that we first tried our rifles, and it was on the countless strongly-armored alligators that were lying on the numerous old tree-trunks with which all streams in the jungles are bordered. They sunned themselves and were in the habit of paying no attention to the passing Greys until a few bullets from us threw them down into the mud. Very seldom did the home of a planter appear on the damp, impenetrably forested banks: and only in the vicinity of Alexandria, a small town on the right side of the Red River, did a few settlements peek over the jungle.

The arrival of the Greys was already expected here, and soon the whole militia was on its feet in order to be hosts to the champions of freedom. However, our impatience to enter the war zone did not permit us a very long stay; but after we had emptied a glass of real Holland or a few more tasty champagnes toasted to the welfare of the colonies, we marched in pompous parade back to the panting *Washita*. And as the last sound of the signal bell had resounded in the forest, the boat was roaring upstream through the thick turbid waters. Before we had reached Natchitoches we were through with the election of officers. [Thomas H.] Breese was elected captain without opposition.

In Natchitoches we were received in the same manner as in Alexandria; and as we had to wait here for a few articles, our camp was pitched for the first time under the primitive trees of the stately forest. The openhearted citizens immediately sent us out a wagon-load of provisions of all kinds; and when we walked through the streets, we were invited to friendly meals from all sides. Notwithstanding this pleasant life, on the second day after our arrival, due to inactivity, some dissatisfaction broke out in the company. None too soon, Captain Breese appeared in camp around two o'clock and issued orders for immediate breaking of camp. The important news had just arrived that the colonists aimed to make an early attack on San Antonio. We, therefore, had little time to spare if we would have a share in this glorious undertaking.

Hardly had a half-hour passed before we were already hastily marching through the meanderings of the forest that abounded in game, and by nine o'clock in the evening we had already covered a distance of forty-two miles. On the next day we had to encircle a fort occupied by Uncle Sam's[3] troops which stood here on the boundary to protect the American settlers from attacks of the wild Indian tribes. Nor was the commanding officer to allow us to march through to the Mexican, now Texan, boundary if the friendly relations between the Union and Mexico were to remain undisturbed: consequently we proceeded cautiously.

A few miles beyond the line of observation we made camp for the night with a gentleman named Thomas, and from there we reached on the following day the mirror-bright Sabine, a part of which borders the United States. The silvery waters that offered a more friendly view than the thick, loamy waters of the Red River, rolled softly toward the Gulf; and on the opposite bank — Texas — we were received by the men of the region who had remained behind to protect their homeland and families.

The tender hand of a Texas woman gave us in the name of all beauties of the land a splendid blue silk flag on which the following inscription appeared: "To the first company of Texan Volunteers from New Orleans."

We kissed the soil of the new homeland, received the holy ordinance of citizenship, and Captain Breese expressed in so many ways to the ladies our abundant gratitude. Then we marched on enthusiastically and on the second day following we reached the new little town of San Augustine.

Barely had we left the forest that surrounds the town when the splendid militia marched out to meet us with the deep roll of the drum, out of which the drummer in harmony with his own steps put forth the most direful sounds. His strokes fell on the flabby hide in a regular beat and the echo rumbled back out of the dark forest like the voice of a ghost. This kind of music is well adapted to stimulate sentimental thoughts, but these didn't at all agree with those of the enthusiastic Greys. Consequently our drummer began to beat the lively "Beer in the Mug" march which caused quite a stir in the surroundings, but had the effect of making our ears suffer somewhat less from the death march of the militia that was about to meet with us.

On command of the citizen captain his drummer was made to cease his activity, and also the tones of our drum died away just in time for us to hear the hurrahs of the worthy back-woodsmen. The tri-colored flag flew past us in a rustle, and again the deep toned drum accompanied the serious march of the militia that paraded by us two men deep and then joined our column to march, the old citizens and the new ones, widely spaced to avoid stepping on somebody's heels, into the market place of San Augustine. Three small cannon roared us a welcome, but what truly pleased us the most were the really gigantic beefsteaks and roast beefs which were awaiting our arrival in the huge chimneys, in order to soon embellish the glistening china plates and white linens on the tables. Large glasses of milk and sparkling water stood at each splendid setting, so that full provision had been made for all the adherents of temperance societies in our group. But for those of us for whom an affiliation of this kind is a terrible thing, nicely ground bottles with cognac and Holland gin in the center of the table were available and the simple laconic "Help yourselves" of our hosts constituted the only ceremony at this meal.

After nightfall four companions and I, together with our host and his sons, sat by a brightly flickering chimney fire, and the first northwest storm of the season was sweeping down from the far distant mountains through the woods of northeast Texas. Inwardly happy, we sat comfortably in the cozy home of the old colonist who delighted us with fiery anecdotes from the freedom fight of the states [the War of 1812]. We sat motionless in a wide circle about the singeing amber from the fire with the serious inhabitants of the West; only the old gray-headed planter who sat on the right side of the corner, whose sharp features were overcast with a glowing hue that gave him a scary appearance, was constantly in motion. With the poker in his right hand, he constantly stirred the fire from one side to the other: No sooner did his firewood lay in one position to allow the flames to break forth brightly through the intervening spaces, when his expert hand in several minutes brought everything into a new position again with the iron; and notwithstanding the disturbance, the flames soon crackled forth anew. Meanwhile we newcomers in the wilderness listened with delight to the spirited accounts of the farmer and marveled at his tireless industry and skill, while his eighteen and twenty year-old sons amused themselves, as it seemed, by whittling neat little figures out of wood. But barely were these created when these artists made countless alterations with their sharp little pocket knives, and the stick became shorter and shorter, until finally the last figure flew into the fire and another piece was fetched to make the time fly by that evening. From these appearances we would have recognized immediately the farmer as an immigrant from hospitable Kentucky. Moreover, his accounts of the triumph of the Americans over the British at New Orleans had indicated that he was one of those excellent marksmen who fought under "Old Hickory", as General Jackson was called because of his unyielding disposition, who had commanded not to fire on the charging enemy until they could see the whites of the eyes of the British. The order was strictly obeyed, the first line of the British fell, and after a short but terrible contest the remainder fled in great confusion over the marshy ground of the region back to their fleet. But the city of New Orleans, which was six miles from the battle, as well as the freedom of the Union were saved, and all hopes of the British crown to subjugate the Atlantic colonies again had disappeared forever.

From time to time good advice for us and his sons flowed in laconic form from his lips. He could not strongly enough recommend economy with the gunpowder, because every misfire from our side would inspire the enemy with new courage, whereas a sparing but effective shot would evoke horror among the enemy.

It was about eleven o'clock when we threw ourselves on a pile of bear and buffalo skins in order to break camp by sunrise the next morning for Nacogdoches, which was two days' journey away. From there we wanted to embark on our 490 mile ride on horseback to San Antonio.

The signal for the departure to get going sounded, and after an invigorating breakfast prepared by our kind and beautiful hostesses, we marched away; a salute from a little cannon wished us good luck on our journey, and the echo of the forest conveyed to the friendly people of San Augustine our hearty thanks.

A few weeks later we saw the men again; the gallant men of San Augustine did not want to be found missing in the struggle for freedom, and once more, the old planter seized his bright rifle, which since 1815 had been used only on forest animals. With youthful spirit he stepped once more into the role of fighter and, united with his slender sons, he was always to be found in the most persistent gunfire.

---

[1] The river that serves as the border between Louisiana and Texas.

[2] A huge knife bearing the name of the inventor, Bowie.

[3] The United States was given this name by the British during the Revolutionary War since their foot soldiers had the letters "U.S. United States" on their backpacks, which was interpreted to mean Uncle Sam.

CHAPTER THREE

Nacogdoches

THE SECOND DAY AFTER OUR DEPARTURE from San Augustine, we intended to arrive at Nacogdoches, but the approaching frosty night found us still scattered in different parts of the forests and most of us spent the night on the scattered plantations that lay from five to six miles apart along the road. But the nearer at that time that a person approached the town, the less seldom did he find the homes of the white man, notwithstanding the fact that this was the most thickly settled part of the land.

Already quite a while had passed since the last rays of the sun had disappeared, when several of us together anxiously began to look around for the house of a planter. We looked about in vain in the dense forest enveloped with darkness and were thinking of camping in the open. Suddenly we saw an open treeless region that we at first mistook for the fields of several planters; we soon decided, however, that it was a prairie, the first of importance that we had encountered on our journey.

Not far away several dogs began to bark, and soon we saw a low log cabin and from its little windows a bright light glistened.

The inhabitants, a small family, sat around the fire and, busy, they took little notice of the disturbance from the loud barking of the dogs.

A slender, strong man of the Virginian type stood with his rifle on the dark side of the door and looked keenly at us as we came nearer. However, as he noticed our color he lowered the rifle and in a friendly manner invited us into the house, to the beckoning fire, and an invigorating cup of coffee. After we had informed the host that we were volunteers from New Orleans, he again shook our hands, whereupon he explained to us his cautious position in front of the house. He had only recently moved across the Sabine and intended to settle here with his family; but as the Cherokees and the Coushattas occasionally frequented these parts, and as one could not really trust them, on our approach he had gone out to determine what kind of wanderers were making their way so late through the lonesome prairie. "Of course," he added, pointing to the glowing hostess, "I always have the satisfaction of being laughed at by my old woman on my return, but I think a little precaution is better than a little thoughtlessness." We laughed also, but agreed with him, especially as he was a newcomer in the land.

Since we were informed that Nacogdoches was only six miles away, we made a quick decision to still make that two hours' march, and disregarding the persuasions of the host and his handsome family, we stormed out once again into the darkness; not, however, before we helped eat supper consisting of ham and beefsteak, which is seldom absent from the American table.

Strengthened by this meal we soon reached the end of the prairie, and again entered the forest which stretched from there to the town without interruption.

At last after a march that seemed forever, the dark figures of the homes of Nacogdoches arose about us. Unnoticed we found ourselves in the southeast area of the little town.

Thoroughly tired we knocked at a two-story house, the outside of which, like the others, did not betray any signs of being inhabited. Still, it was not necessary for us to go further, as an old Negro opened the door and with a friendly light in his hand welcomed the first Greys of New Orleans in the name of his master.

We found ourselves in the house of Squire Sterne, who already had made all preparations for our reception, and in a few minutes an inviting supper steamed on the table. After the march of two hours we were again in a position to attack the mighty roast beefs, excellent roast venison, and game.

During the meal, nobody spoke except the old Negro who from time to time gave us the benefit of a few flourishes of his gumbo-English. And we were just laughing heartily as our kind host, highly pleased with our arrival, entered. He too had just returned from the Queen of the Mississippi and had been expecting us for a few days: besides, he was rejoiced to find a few native Germans among us.[4]

"Bob," he called to the old Negro, "Bob, four of the long, slender ones out of the corner on the stand, do you understand?"

Adolphus Sterne home.
Courtesy Sterne-Hoya House Library and Museum

"Bob understands, Massa," replied the old Guinea Negro, as he departed to obey.

"Now," the squire asked us, sitting down, "how do you like our Texas?"

"Heavenly, Squire," replied Peter Mattern, "and the people are all so hospitable and truly decent, so I would not like to be back in Frankfurt for the present, especially as I hope that Santa Anna will have his hordes attacking us soon."

"There will be work enough for all of us," said the squire, "every honest white-skin will have to shoulder the musket to protect his family and property from the greed of the enemy; but we will compel no one—no one, gentlemen. Everyone must go voluntarily and courageously into battle, because it is a sublime and just cause calling our nation to the struggle. It is for our religion, our God, that we are fighting, and are sharpening our Bowie knives[5] for the freedom of our children.

"And for that," interrupted George Curtman, "do we also want to attempt to see if our bullets will hit the mark, and as a citizen of the new state, I swear to you all to give the last drop of my Germanic blood for the new republic—"

"Stop, my countryman, shh! shh! Do we wish to stir up the whole of Mexico against us? Even the liberal party? No! Another time. Shush! We are still too weak to stand alone, and only by combining with this liberal party can we overthrow Santa Anna. Perhaps in later times when many more of our brethren are clearing out the forests on this side of the Sabine and are defending the land with guns and strong arms, can we unfold the banner of independence, and only there first, only then, can we proclaim the freedom of the prairies."

"Does the honorable squire mean to say," I interrupted him, "that we came to Texas to bow anew under absolute rule after we had barely become acquainted with the life of a free people? Does the worthy gentleman mean that the Greys entered the prairies to clear out the primeval forests under Santa Anna or any other copper-faced slave driver, in order to break the land for their priests, or to raise large herds so that when that clique should once have a desire to do so, they might do to us even as the archenemy is now doing, swinging the dagger of despotism over the head of Mexico? No—we beg to be excused, Squire. We will not stop half-way on the journey. We are going the 'whole hog' as our friends in the states say. My countrymen need not be afraid even now; the long anticipated time has arrived. Old Kentucky, true to his character, will not now stand idly by, and I wager ten to one that even now the cry to arms is resounding through the hills of this hospitable state: 'for your brothers in Texas!—for the liberty of America!' And shortly all the Southern states will send their aid, if independence is at stake. If however, you wish that the tri-colored flag of Mexico shall continue to fly over Texas—these colors that are now, because of their falseness, merged into a sombre grey—and that from day to day take on an increasing appearance of the kind with which the whole group of Jesuits and their adherents and followers would so gladly darken the whole world—then the nation through whose lands the mighty Mississippi winds, and whose coasts are bounded by the waves of the Gulf, the still waters of the Atlantic, and the great seas of the north, will not sympathize with the inhabitants of the Mexican province of Texas. If she will at once energetically shake off the yoke, immediately raise up a flag whose colors will glow in the glitter of the southern sun, only then the South and the West will send its youths across the Sabine to aid the new republic that is just now springing into life. Therefore, once again, Squire—To the Republic!!!"

"Stop, young man, here comes Bob. May we strengthen the word with the grape juice of the Fatherland." Bob, who entered with four bottles, placed them on the table, and the squire filled the glasses to the brim, and as a true German took his glass and explained, "May the venerable old Rhine wine in this sparkling glass be like the waves that stream through the land of a single, great, free nation."

"The old German Rhine wine!" repeated the chorus composed of many nationalities, and the flowing gold of the first glass rolled over our tongues.

"And now, Squire," said Peter Mattern, refilling his glass, "The Republic of Texas! May the Rio del Norte [Rio Grande] become the border that separates us from Mexico; and once that has happened, we won't have any trouble dealing with Uncle Sam."

"Gentlemen, I drink this toast with pleasure: if you want your arms to be successful, conceal this toast deep within yourselves. Spies are among us. Santa Anna and the gold of the priests work in the dark in order to make us hated by the whole nation, and it is still not, as I remarked a while ago, the time to lift the mask, that would incite the nine million Mexicans against the prairies and forests; but the day will soon come when we can act as free men, and then will all the people declare the republic, and then will I shout: the free and independent State of Texas! and for this let us empty our glasses."

"For this era!" we chimed in, emptying our glasses, and one more time we emptied our tumblers for the Father of Texas, Stephen F. Austin.

Although it was past eleven o'clock and the beds were awaiting us, we liked Stern's suggestion to go to the Mexican coffee-house. There we found the Mexican people of Nacogdoches, who comprised nearly one-half of the total population, a colorful crowd. A group of men, women, and girls made their way through the smoke-filled room that we entered.

4 He was a German.
5 A long, heavy knife of fifteen to twenty inches.

CHAPTER FOUR

The Coffee-House

DISGRACEFUL, AMBIGUOUS DIRTY JOKES in broken English issued from a group of people resembling a band of Gypsies. With every fourth word one could hear either a damn or a Spanish *carajo* [a Spanish slang, curse word generally meaning male genitals or feces or s_ _ _] emanating from a person in the center of the room, accompanied by loud applause from those standing around. The squire, who had for many years seen scenes of this kind, pushed his way through the spectators, who were curious about our appearance and made room for us as we approached.

"Now," said the squire, "the Greys shall see with what kind of an enemy we have to deal. As you here see the Mexicans, so is the whole nation with the possible exception of a few of Spanish descent, which represent the Mexican nobility. But in a moral sense they are all alike. A murder on the conscience of one of them does not weigh much. While the rich, the so-called cultured classes, absolve themselves of their own sins, the *padre* in San Antonio forgives the poorer, uncultured classes their minor transgressions for a few *pesos*; and a good well-trained mustang for his reverence, the apostle of Rome in the West, will overbalance all

100

criminal cases and soothe the conscience completely as well as release the souls from purgatory, where we heretics must languish and suffer without mercy."

By this time we had penetrated the inner side of a circle of people, where we discovered a little man no taller than four and three-quarter feet tall, jumping about in graceful movements, if one can call the movements graceful, around a much taller Mexican doña. We were astonished at the vulgar words and very suggestive positions of the two who danced the fandango nobly, in a so-called decent society. And we seemed rather to be among those people who several years ago in "Natchez under the hill" lived in the most lascivious way. However, traces of those times vanished in the latter place and large storehouses and trading companies cover the spots from which the decent citizens had chased away those creatures.

The brown lady understood the dance completely and with her castanets kept the beat to a miserable English translation of a Mexican song that her hardly visible companion screeched out to us in the cawing voice of a raven. He was in fact most charming to look at. His long coal-black hair flounced in wild twirls about his comparatively large head, so that we could get only an occasional glimpse of his copper-colored, wild features and his wide open mouth.

An old fiddler, also a descendent of Montezuma, stood in awesome delight at the edge of the circle, and as his brown bow screeched across the three strings of his musical instrument, his little time-stamping foot moved with amazing rapidity, following the not very slow movements of the *señora*.

The *señor* was smoking a real Havana cigar and the *señora* a lovely small cigar, which was very becoming to her cute mouth, pretty enough to kiss, and to her whole person. The Mexican, Ole Bull with his magic fiddle, stood enveloped in terrible fumes, and encircling over the heads of the very respectable dons and doñas hovered grey clouds of smoke.

"Squire," said I, "this is sufficient, abundantly sufficient, for one evening's entertainment; let us seek fresh air. This coffee-house is a highly interesting place, but what a tremendous difference there is between the fandango here and the fandango on the floor of the St. Charles[6] in New Orleans!"

The squire replied laughing, that he always enjoyed himself very much whenever he came to this place. "However," he added, "we have not seen everything yet. Step through this door

Spanish fandango.

A Mexican Fandango

Art by Hogan in Beyond the Mississippi *by Albert D. Richardson, 1867.* Ornish Collection.

and you will find the black room here not any less interesting." The black room was really a black apartment. The smoke of one hundred thousand cigars had settled on the one-time white walls and formed a complete covering for it.

Black, as if covered with velvet, were the floors, the walls, the ceilings, the window frames, the chairs, the cabinets, and the shriveled-up inhabitants; even a few rather small, pretty Mexican Amazons appeared to have been darkened by this casino atmosphere. Most noteworthy was the furrowed face of an old matron. The rising vapors encircled her drooping Roman nose in mottled, encircling cloudlets, and one cup of coffee after another rolled down her thin, long throat. Her grey head was constantly in motion when she was not busy with her coffee or concerned with the sale of coffee, grog, or other things; and as the master fiddler with his three strings lured forth the most melting sounds, her mossy head waved back and forth now fast, now slow, over her ever-constantly empty yet ever filled cup.

Only the table was clean because of its constant use. The endless rubbing of arms had wiped the smoke away. Every place on the benches was occupied, and piles of silver were stacked up on the table. On one side sat a colorful, crafty, one-eyed, gaunt creole from Louisiana guarded by two professional gamblers,[7] former, but now banished, inhabitants of the undesirable section of Natchez. They had barely escaped the Manila ropes of the citizens of that place. Their early departure from the country had saved them from the fate of their black feet companions, who were suspended in the air of Vicksburg to dance to the howling of the winds and to the cawing of the crows. These three gentlemen, this noble trio, migrated with great speed over the Sabine to flee from that terrible country where they attach "perfectly honest" people of their type to limbs of oak trees for decorative purposes as a matter-of-fact, routine procedure.

Now they were here to give a few demonstrations of their black art in return for the Mexican *pesos*, and the stack of silver dollars behind the Pharoah's table grew from minute to minute. With every hand that the Creole drew, the "knights of the white metal" collected without any feeling or consideration of the agony with which the loss of the last *peso* tightened the chest of the loser. Without saying a word, the greedy eyes of the players rested on the disappearing money.

The brown, really pretty, features of a girl dressed in black contracted convulsively. An unnatural column of smoke, coming as from a crater, rose from her cigar into the super-charged atmosphere; her dark eyes fixed on the card that concealed the fate of her last dollar; the devilish one-eyed man began dealing, and with mechanical precision the three noble companions of Natchez took the last dollar from the unfortunate girl. She got up in anger, struck the table with her doubled fist and burning torch [cigar] with such force, causing sparks to fly, and stormed out of the door, only to return again after the air had somewhat refreshed her, to win back her lost money tomorrow night, the Lord permitting. The little Black Forest clock that hung in this hell struck twelve as these revelers of the night decided to lock the bank and close for the day, not because they had already won enough but because they had won all there was. The Mexicans with grater-rough faces floated slowly through the black apartment.

"*Señora*," yelled the creole to the napping Sybil, "—damn it *señora*, grog, grog! Doesn't the old lady see that we are thirsty? Damn your eyes! Come here with your brew! The *señoritas* are warm and the cold norther is blowing on the outside. The pretty ones will take a deathly cold if they do not immediately take an invigorating glass of your rum cocktail. So make it quick, old lady, hurry up!"

"How many glasses," crowed the old lady, "did the *señor* order?" "Damn you," the creole broke loose again, "two, three, four glasses for everyone, as much as my worthy friends wish to drink; Do you think, old cab-horse, when Sam Johnson treats that he will act niggardly over ten, fifteen, or twenty dollars? No, never, damn his soul! If he were such a skinflint, he would not deserve to be called the son of his noble father. Damn it, how often have hundreds of dollars flowed forth from me, but Sam Johnson is still Sam Johnson."

"It is easy for you to speak that way," mumbled the old lady. "You rake the *pesos* together with such ease that one is almost persuaded to believe that you were in league with"—She made three crosses—"Mother Mary, keep us in the fold."

"Shut up, you old wrinkle, and hurry and get your hellish drinks ready instead of making inappropriate and wicked insinuations, unless you want my friends and me to give old Patrick our business."

The magic strains in the other room had ceased and the dancers had disappeared. A few of the victims of the gambling table still sat in half despair in the black room to drown their sorrow with the fiery stupefying drink that the old witch of Nacogdoches had brewed in her smoky corner. We too went home and told the squire of our surprise to find here in Texas the cunning thieves who had been driven out of Natchez some time ago. They had come to Texas to begin a new era among the Mexicans with their low-down business. "That will continue only for a short time," replied the squire. "Soon the last dollar will have disappeared from the pockets of the Mexicans; and Sam Johnson and Company with nothing more to do will follow our army to San Antonio; I see no difference between the effect of a bullet from a respectable planter and that from a respectable pickpocket—both respectable gentlemen in the presence of the enemy, provided that each does his duty."

"What, Squire?" I responded surprised, "do you believe these fellows who devour everything and brag about it will ever have the courage to step out in front of the enemy? There the honorable squire is most assuredly mistaken. At the sound of the first gun, sir, you will see such a hasty departure of this thieving gentry that you will be amused to see them march off in all their glory to the Rio Grande to gamble for Mexican silver in Matamoras or other places."

"That may be true," replied the squire indifferently, "It will all be the same how we get them across the border. If they do not wish to fight—well—then they may run. If they do not want to run—well—then they will have to dance."

"What—dance, squire? How do you now get on the subject of dancing? Please, how do you mean that?"

"Well," continued the squire. "I mean that the noble lads whom we are discussing will be permitted to dance. Sam Johnson knows the Highland fling completely, and someday he can dance it to the tune we whistle."

"Squire, you are an unsolvable riddle. I have to ask you, if it is permitted and you hold the Greys worthy of confidence, to lift the veil from those obscure dark words."

"Why shouldn't I?" mumbled the thoughtful Texan. "Well," he continued; paused a while and began anew. "I mean, if they do not wish to fight, they will, like a superfluous garment on the nail, be hung on the first convenient sycamore."

We were startled with surprise. "The squire is not speaking seriously," said Curtman. "To hang people, sir, is no small matter."

"Just because, sir, it isn't a small matter we must use it. What do these gentry care for small matters?" continued the squire.

"But," responded I, "have the Texans a right to put their countrymen out of the world this way if they have committed no crime within the border of Texas?"

"Why—I don't know—concerns me little—we do it just the same," answered the squire.

"Why," interjected Peter Mattern, instinctively imitating the squire. "Why—we do it—that is said easily enough, but what right do you have to do so?"

"What right?" continued the squire, "What right have the States to chase a bunch of pilfering thieves over here to us? Who allows this thieving rabble to disgrace our prairies by their presence—especially since Mexico has seen to it till now that the hated province, Texas, always had a good assortment of this kind of article on hand. But things will have to change. Soon, soon shall they march, pack and bundle, to their soul-comforter over the Rio Grande, or to him in hell. They have to go, and the province must be free of these vagabonds in a few years. Run, fight, or hang—these are the choices they have—we want a free land, unstained by such thieving birds; and with our independence a strict rule of justice must enter. The laws must be respected. But pardon will come for those who will forsake the old paths. It will be the last time that a hand will be extended them to draw a curtain over their black past, the last time, gentlemen."

"Squire, you are terrible but just," I added, "yet it would be agreeable to me if we could win our freedom without the aid of these losers; it is such a sacred matter for them to take part in."

"Wild imaginings; when the victory is won, it will make little difference to us who did it. It is better for the deer to fall than the faithful cow—better for the last cock than for the brooding hen. If one of the gamblers fall, a good act is done the world. On the contrary, if a colonist falls, we lose a good citizen and have a distressed family in the land. A fourth of a load of lead in the gun of the former might have saved his life. No, gentlemen, no one is so contemptible that he could not be employed somewhere in helping us to roll back the central-colossus from our El Dorado. Everywhere leading personalities will offer themselves to support our cause, and the resulting force will roll back the colossus over the Rio Grande that borders our land. And then will be the time for us to set our internal affairs in order."

We now found ourselves at our stopping place and, really tired, we wished each other a good night's rest. Soon our wishes for sleep were fulfilled, but notwithstanding all that, my mind generally did an encore of the whole coffee-house scene.

6 Theatre.

7 Literally, *black feet*, a term used to describe professional gamblers and confidence men.

CHAPTER FIVE

The Banquet

"THE VOLUNTEERS FROM THE STATES!" cried a large strong man who sat at the head of the 150-foot-long board table. "The Greys!" he cried and poured down the foaming champagne as he gave the toast. The two rows on the sides of the heavily loaded table raised their glasses at the same time and eighty dollars worth of the precious beverage disappeared to the benefit of the Greys.

In the center of the table stood, in festive decorations, Mr. Petz, a large black bear, hide and bones, meat and claws, and between his grim teeth he held the flag of the Constitution of 1824. The remainder of the table was occupied by raccoons, squirrels, and turkeys.[8] But two large nicely roasted hindquarters and the backbone of an ox decorated the table also. As the satellites surround their planets, so stood the foaming champagne and the sparkling Rhine around the fried, although still wild appearing animals in a colorful array.

Hopping Johnson arose to make a few remarks. I must here observe that he was not the notorious Sam Johnson. But he was a famous gentleman-squatter who had conquered the world up to now in a triple-hopping, and at that on his left leg. He also carried the nickname: the Better or the Great Hopper. But in general he was known as Hopping Johnson. The Cornbreakers'[9] nature radiated from all of his features; the blood that flowed in his veins was completely Virginian. From the day that the old Johnson, the great-grandfather of our Hopper, had set foot on the new continent in order to become a Virginian squatter (at that time the Alleghenies were still called the backbone of the colonies and Old Virginia was a wild, disorderly land frequented by Indians) none of the Johnsons had ever gone beyond the boundaries of the state, which seldom happens among the people of Uncle Sam's territory. But our young Hopper had left the good old land against the will of his father and traveled for many years through the states with several exceedingly fine thoroughbred race horses that his father, who was a breeder of thoroughbred stock, had raised. He became widely known for his excellent fast horses. Later on he settled in Texas.

"Gentlemen," sounded his clear voice from the center of the table. "Gentlemen, the men of Nacogdoches have prepared a banquet for the Greys of New Orleans, and the ladies have taken charge of the work of the kitchen. Vain patriotism, gentlemen; the red Cherokee has tracked the o'possum and laid low with his gun the raccoon; the young warriors have furnished our table with guineas and squirrels. But Sam Johnson has searched the jungle for three days, living on the game of the forest, that he might sacrifice this gentlemen here"—pointing to the bear before him—"for this festival of freedom. Long did he quietly track him and only on the third day did he discover him growling in a dense thicket. The rifle bullet dropped him. Sam returned victorious to the village to get more help to bring Petz home. Petz, gentlemen, was brought in and now stands in our midst. Nicely roasted, he wishes us *bon appetit*." He drew a deep breath, wiped his brow and continued, "Your glistening plates, gentlemen, are surrounded by the noble juice of the Rhine and of champagne. With these are polished crystal glasses. You will miss the knives and forks—which actually are missing. And that is why Sam Johnson has been appointed by the patriotic ladies' committee to explain their absence. Hear—hear—gentlemen, Sam Johnson has never concerned himself about the kitchen department. If he had his steaks and cornbread, together with a little glass of Kentucky wine[10] at mealtimes, he did not ask for anything else. For the simple reason that the ladies in their haste could not secure sufficient of these instruments of destruction, or at least without an additional amount of trouble, gentlemen, there will be nothing left for us to do"—drawing his Bowie-knife—"but to imitate the red warrior, who fells his enemy with his tomahawk and shortens his existence with his scalping knife, or who similarly kills the roe and prepares the meat for his nourishment. So, my hopeful soldiers of the prairie, out with your Bowie knives and away with the well-roasted slices of Mr. Petz. O'possum, Coon & Company's fat hind-quarters. Dig in! Dig in!"

"Long live Sam Johnson, the Hopper, the tireless bear-hunter!" cried the occupants of the table and drank a glass to his health.

The Hopper took a deep breath, expressed his thanks and drew the skin of Mr. Petz to the side, and the otherwise black "gentleman bear" in death made a more tempting appearance than he ever was able to do in life. The two-foot long knives were drawn from their sheaths and wrought destruction on Mr. Petz and the rest of the meats. One toast after another was made. Then political speeches were made; the causes of the war were discussed; inflammatory appeals resounded; thought was also taken of the women as they sat at their hearths, and it was already very late when the feast was over. One person after another, with revolution on his mind and boundless courage in his heart, had quietly left his seat to look up his sleeping place, and each dreamed enthusiastically of prophetic figures in infinite variations. The next morning our horses were gathered, and in the afternoon we galloped down the streets and out of the little town. The cheers of the inhabitants followed the delighted cavalry troop of Greys until it disappeared in the dark forest.

8 Coons, squirrels, and Welsh chicken [guinea hens].
9 The nickname of the Virginians.
10 Clear brandy or corn whiskey.

CHAPTER SIX

The March to San Antonio

THE JOURNEY DID NOT PROGRESS as rapidly as we had expected, but we came a little nearer to our destination every day. The colonists along the road received us with great joy, and they offered the best in their homes to us. In several places they wanted to give us a banquet, as had been done at Nacogdoches, but the Greys had no more time to spare. Forward! was our motto, in order that we might arrive in San Antonio before the militia made a major strike. We hastily crossed the rushing Angelina [River]. The majestic Trinity with its incomparably rich lands and broadly forested banks soon lay a few days' journey behind us. Before us in a long black line lay the forests of the Brazos River. The innumerable varied changing colors of the many kinds of trees, the vines and parasitic plants added to the already heavenly scenery and indescribable magic. Autumn, the most beautiful season of the year on the new continent, revealed its festive colors in these magnificent landscapes.

We stayed a few days in then new Washington [on the Brazos]. Several hundred new dwellings were going up in the forest, which resounded with the industry of the immigrants. Hour after hour, the splendid oaks and the majestic pecans and hickories fell; many a noble persimmon had its almost ripe, pretty, reddish-yellow fruit scattered about on the ground. Large piles of brush, crooked limbs and tree trunks were burning in every direction to clear the ground, and only recently did the sun send its warmth down to the damp, fruitful, dark brown earth below. The place contained several coffee-houses, one lodging house, supply stores, stores connected with warehouses containing ready-made clothes, cloth, and all other needs of the settlers. We also found a good billiard room, and as everywhere in America, a courthouse;[11] and, finally, the never-failing gunsmith shop.

A few miles from this place, the prairie regions begin and extend clear down to the coast. For days now we trotted through a constantly changing park; and disregarding the cold northwest wind, nature here displayed an indescribable fullness and splendor.

The prairies here are not like those immense stretches between the Guadalupe [River] and San Antonio that reach clear up to the mountains, or that enormous grass ocean of Tamaulipas that extends in varying widths of a hundred miles or more from the Gulf to and over the mountains made of rock, to those practically unknown treeless regions further north. But rather an open country, everywhere decorated with the most exotic groups of trees, appears before the traveler. To the right and left one always sees at great distance the horizon bordered with dark forest; and near the traveler, small forest areas alternate with open meadows. Occasionally a little brook, whose course is marked with a string of trees, winds its way down from the mountains. Again the scenes change. Now the post oaks stand in regular rows around large meadows, which in their square shape resemble the meadow regions of the Old

World. They differ only from these in that the meadows of Europe are encircled with willows and poplars, while the little prairies are surrounded with oaks. Everything appears so orderly that one is almost persuaded to believe that human hands had part in the planting of the trees.

In the vicinity of Bastrop, approximately one hundred miles from San Antonio, the country becomes somewhat hilly; and, agreeably surprised, we found ourselves again in dark resin-wood forests, the first that we had encountered since our departure from Nacogdoches. We rode through the gigantic needle-wood forest and momentarily expected to enter a little prairie, or to see the long-sought town of Bastrop. The sun passed behind the pinnacles of the gigantic pine trees and evening was beginning to get dark. However, we still saw for a long time the golden hue that spread itself out over the majestic tree tops, but it finally disappeared also. We rode on slowly, step by step, through the night that enveloped us in its darkness. The only road sign was the open strip of light over our heads that permitted us to gaze on the starless, deep blue heavens.

The horses stepped cautiously forward and searched for the way that was invisible to the human eye, while we peered ahead to keep from being torn from our horses by the pine limbs that at times reached far out over the road. It must have been near midnight, and we would have pitched camp long ago, but no forest brooklet or spring flowed across our path where we could water our faithful, exhausted horses, nor could we find a suitable place to graze them. We had to move on.

Suddenly the leading horses neighed lustily into the thus far uninterrupted night, a sign that something agreeable was near. We looked around and discovered several lights of a little town in a tremendously low area to our right. The road shortly led us down the steep hill, and soon we were passing through the streets to the waters of the Guadalupe to water our horses. The citizens of the town, however, took charge of this job, and, since they had been expecting us for some time, we were able to at once eat an invigorating supper with several of the colonists.

After we had finished, we stepped out into the broad streets, where the inhabitants started a number of large fires. From eight to ten tree trunks had been laid in layers on each pile, and their sparks flew up into the dark night above us.

It was late when we rolled ourselves up in blankets and laid down around the fires, disregarding the wishes of the people that we sleep in their houses for the night. We had so accustomed ourselves to camping in the open that we declined the invitations with thanks. As we wished all a last good-night, we drew the covers over our heads and slept for the last time in the colonies. Tomorrow we were to continue our journey over the one hundred-mile prairie to San Antonio. Since we had nothing to fear of the redskins in the center of the town, we slept without sentries.

This was the fourth day after our leaving Bastrop. Up to this time we had not come upon the home of a single colonist in this lonely wilderness, and from time to time the bent-over bleached grass, in other places tall as a man, indicated traces of a Comanche troop that had probably just come down from the mountains.

We now kept ourselves closer together than formerly, while we rode through the colonies. Our muskets were always loaded, partly to kill the necessary game for our support, partly because we were now passing through a level stretch of country that the unfriendly Indians often frequented in large numbers during this season of the year. Woe to the erring hunter if he should fall into the barbaric hands of his red colleagues; a terrible death would be his fate. The character of these hunting tribes is cruel, but similar to the brown inhabitants of Mexico, they are characterized by their cowardice.

The Comanches have sworn eternal enmity to the world. Their five thousand to six thousand red warriors chase about in troops of from one- to four-hundred men, together with women and children, over the regions of the Guadalupe and San Saba mountains. Formerly they even came down into the lower regions of Texas. At times they swoop down like a thunder cloud on the Mexican side of the Rio Grande and return again to their valleys with large herds of stolen stock.

All male Mexicans are scalped, and the women and children usually are led away as slaves and given their freedom only on payment of a heavy ransom.

Their cowardly nature, however, does not permit them to come down anymore among the settlements of the Texans except under the guise of friendship. At such times, especially in the spring, they exchange furs and silver bars for lead and woolen blankets. Alcoholic beverages are repulsive to them, contrary to all other brown hunters of the West. They are characterized by wearing little scrubby beards which their red brethren prevent growing by tearing out the roots during early youth. They are constantly on horseback, hunt on horseback, and attack the enemy only on the prairie where they can make use of their skilled horsemanship. They sit in council on horseback; and armed with lance and buffalo shields, they invade the lands of other Indians. The weaker side is destroyed without mercy, but not very often do these terrible hunters of the prairies suffer appreciable losses in these massacres because those nations, who are at home on the prairies

Trading with the Indians.

as well as in the jungle, are stronger and more courageous than the others.

On the western horizon black clouds were arising, without our knowing the reason for their appearance. Our aim for today was a little shady island ahead of us. Splendid live oaks spread out their enormous branches and formed the most attractive incomparable arcades. From the evergreen pyramids hung silver grey garland, the so-called Spanish moss, almost down to the ground, giving the grove a melancholy appearance. On our arrival the horses were unsaddled, a nice place for the campfire selected, the food brought forth, and preparations for supper made, and soon we could enjoy the heavenly evening in comfort.

[11] *Gerichtshaus.*

Indian horsemen.

CHAPTER SEVEN

The Prairie Fire

WITH PURPLE, MORE BEAUTIFUL than on the dark waves of the roaring sea, did the sun disappear as it sank behind the unknown mountains of clouds in the west, and terrible black masses rolled up like gigantic dragons against the clear starless horizon. Anxiously we gazed at them, hoping to discover an explanation. Our thoughts floated to San Antonio; we saw a sea of fire destroying the town; heard the battle-cry of the combatants, whose freedom banners were victorious; and here we were without any prospect of getting any further ahead during the night, without being able to take part in this fateful event. We listened with keenest attention toward the lightly blowing wind to catch a possible distant sound of the deep thunder of the cannon, but all was in vain.

Brightly flickered the fires around which we were lying. Silently we roasted huge pieces of beef and quarters of venison on the frying spits—they alone looked good to us—and watched the grease trickle down. The company first cut piece by piece from the surface of the roasted or done side, while the other side was being roasted. After we were through with the one side we turned the roast over and ate quietly from the other. We reflected deeply upon the peculiar lot of mankind and of these hind-quarters that an hour ago were the parts of living beings and now were the best tasting fry that had ever gladdened our tastes and stomachs.

Depressed, we looked into the flickering fire, where a mighty iron kettle was boiling the brown brew that was to serve as refreshment and aid to digestion after our delicious meal; I shall never forget how excellent the coffee tasted. I had never drunk any better. I must give our cook *pro tem* credit for knowing how to cook this invigorating beverage, regardless of whether it is for old ladies or for hunters in the wilderness. Every one sat still and watched the cook, when suddenly he called out,

"Bill, where is the coffee? Is it already ground? And come here. Put it into this boiling water so that it will mix quickly. The water is boiling up." A sudden stillness set in, a quietness such as precedes an earthquake. The cover began to rise, a cover of ground coffee that had formed a crust over the water. As the earth cracks apart, so this cover split in twain. Seething, the precious fluid boiled forth. In an instant the coffee was ready.

An oppressive stillness lay over the immense region. A faint glow had somewhat reddened the clouds; our guards were lying at their posts as it is more expedient to lie on guard duty in the prairie than either to stand or walk. Every visible object is noticed by the marksmen of the forests at amazing distances, and the uncautious and careless guard soon becomes a victim to their adversaries' skill and cunningness. Even the mustangs were crowding around the dying campfires. Moved by secret misgivings of the mysterious stillness, they pressed in friendly manner near their masters as if anticipating danger.

All of a sudden the shrill barking of a dog sounded sharp and cutting through the stillness of the night, now tapering off as a death howl, soon again so penetrating that the ears rang and the body shuddered. Without moving, we stared into the dark night as a second and slightly deeper voice chimed in, and a few moments more a third, then a fourth, a deep base. A few moments more and thousands upon thousands entered the great chorus. This music of hell of the prairie dogs [coyotes] was intermixed with the frightful howling of the great black wolves that live in company with them. That deep sound that issued from the depth of the throat as from a cavern and that can be compared only to the howls uttered by a number of dogs on hearing the sounds of musical instruments that are unpleasant to them, it is in itself terrible; then think of the howling of a thousand voices.

We were still standing in amazement; there, quick as lightning, everything quieted. As still as the grave was the night. Only the monotone calls of the whippoorwill and his mate penetrated the darkness. Melancholically he calls her name, and the mate answers in the same manner. One is agreeably surprised. We listened with pleasure to the duet, the tender calls, as if they were exiled spirits in the splendid expanses of the West. There again we heard the terrible yelling sound as before, the second, the third, the fourth, and then the whole chorus.

Rudely awakened, my comrades sprang up, seized their guns and peered into the darkness for the hellish spirits that had interrupted the quietness of the night, pregnant with commotion. Barely had we recovered from our amazement, when another pack of these spirits of hell in the opposite direction raised their horrible voices. At first we could distinguish the howling of the two parties, but soon it melted into one immense deafening din. Thousands upon thousands of shrill tones like the awful war-whoop of the redskins pierced the air. Then again one could perceive the difference between the two parties for a few moments. Now the noise became weaker from moment to moment, and after a few minutes more only a few long drawn-out sounds like weeping and moaning cries came across to us. The wolves and the packs of dogs [coyotes] had made short shrift with the sad duet of the whippoorwills. But immensely more frightful was that of the former. The echoes now resounded, faint across the lonesome prairie, like the groans on a battlefield at night after the bloody work of the day before. But the inhabitants of the country, accustomed to such nightly confusion, did not let the turmoil disturb them in their quiet sweet slumber. And now only the winged ruler of the night, the owl, cried his terrible farewell song to his nightly companions in his hollow tones as from the grave.

With the exception of the guards, we again stretched ourselves out around the fires to seek slumber under the covers. The horses also began to move out on the prolific mesquite grass to graze. Today was the fourth day that we were in the region of the mesquite prairies. This beautiful nourishing growth, which resembled a ripe field and was from three- to four-feet-high, concealed the tender young blades from the gaze of the casual human observer, but not from the horses. Greedily they plucked the delicacy, to them until now unknown, which yearly draws down millions of buffaloes from the mountainy rock to graze here during the winter when the cold northwest wind takes their food in the higher altitudes.

"Who's there?" "Relief!" "The Password!" sounded in monotones through the now softened nature as the corporal relieved the several sentries. "Corporal, you let me wait a long time," mumbled Bill. "I have been here at least three hours, because the pale star there stood high as I came on duty and in three or four minutes now it will disappear behind those big hills."

"Exactly two by the watch," was the answer, "but is there nothing to report?"

"Hm, I don't know: Many a shy wolf led me into temptation to use my gun, and the rabble of Who Who Whoing [of an owl], how the devil it cried! Comes by me unannounced, moves no limb, flies around me and yells her 'Who Who Who' into my ears. At first I thought it was the ghost of old Mother Fiskins, my honored grandmother, who was surprised to see her grandson, Bill shoulder the musket. Thought that she was laughing at me. I had a notion with her—"

"Forward, march!"

"Stop!" cried the interrupted one. "Stop, corporal, a moment—Comrade, look out—I believe the light[12] is coming back because that black cloud in the west looks like the rosy hue of morning."

Truly the black cloud, which had gradually taken in half of the horizon was illuminated with a purple glow similar to the northern aurora. Ever bloodier did the heavens become. Awakened for the second time, we newcomers in the prairie marveled at the bright illumination.

"The prairie is on fire—the redskins are near—" at last said Bill, "they were hunting today; many a poor deer, to escape the fire, no doubt, ran into the deadly musket of the brown hunters. We must—"

Suddenly like an army in a storm the wildly lashing flames charged over a slight elevation about a mile away and raced with the wind down upon us. As our horses began to panic, we jumped up and rushed them over to a small island of greenness which, like an oasis in the desert, marked the fresh water in the prairie. Here the burning rays of the sun could not penetrate through the densely growing moss-covered oaks to dry up the grass. Consequently we were secure from the flames in this retreat. However, there was really no danger, because one could jump through the flames. Like wild animals, the horses, if left to themselves, would have taken to flight in the opposite direction and would have run as long as the flames followed them. The prairie Indians used this technique of *drive hunts* in hunting game by utilizing the fire as a driving force and then posting themselves in a place a few miles ahead of the wind, where

Indians.

the wind blows against the flaming torch. Once they were
flushed out, the easily sighted game would fall in spite of the
mediocre rifles.

The Comanche, like all sons of the wilderness, never shoot
more game than their needs require. He regards the deer and
buffalo of his territory as his property. The largest part of the
prairie Comanches are divided into tribes of several hundred
each, and migrate northward during the spring from year to
year with the immense herds of buffalo; but the winter drives
them back to these barren but still productive regions. In company with the buffalo and other game, they prefer the southern
climate to the northern winters. This is the time for the squatters
and the rangers[13] of the far west to be on the lookout for their
horses and stock. As long as the red man can live on tame cattle,
he will never kill one of his friends, the deer or the buffalo.

We expected the sea of fire without shores to move forward, and it did; nearer and nearer crackled the flames. Black clouds rose up and rolled slowly along over the fire, when suddenly as far as the eye could reach, the whole line was extinguished. Only for a moment single flames here and there flickered up, then everything was over. Nothing remained but the smell and the still rising black smoke.

The dew was now falling as thick as fine rain, and it alone is what preserves the vegetation, as it often does not rain for months. The singeing rays of the sun would burn up everything if it were not for the refreshing dew. The lonely wanderer who pitches his camp in the open will draw up the cover after nightfall, and at times over his head, because it gets fresh, really cold, and as just mentioned, the dew falls in such quantities that it gradually smothers the fire unless it is a very strong one.

Nothing interrupted the latter part of the night. During these few remaining hours we slept undisturbed, but by five o'clock everybody was awake with the first glimmer of the rising sun.

Our watch fires flickered cheerfully, but became more pale to the degree that the sun rose higher. Finally she stood there in her full splendor, and the blue mists that were lying low on the prairies fled like clouds from the fiery god and soon disappeared completely. But how different was the view today from that of yesterday! Yesterday waving fields, similar to ripe grain; today, what awful appearance as far as we could see. From our feet down to the remote edge of the horizon was an uninterrupted black shroud. No tree, no twig, nothing but a black sea.

The bugle sounded lively for the break-up. The quartermaster and a few others trotted out over the black ground. I soon followed on my little Cherokee,[14] well pleased with the continuous good weather and full of hope of arriving in San Antonio in time to fulfill my wish to participate in the first battle for the freedom of the prairie.

In my mind I already saw the city with its solid, proud walls, stately domes and churches, and the formidable fortress, the Alamo, and over it the tri-colored standard of Mexico, rather, the standard of the flag of Santa Anna, as he represented the nation, and his will had to be done when he gave an order.

The wind blew black clouds of ashes toward us. This was highly unpleasant as it filled our noses, mouths and eyes to such an extent that we could barely see. Toward noon we, the first four, arrived at the high rock bluffs of the Cibola, one of those remarkable rivers of Texas, which when the water is low, disappears in places for ten miles or more in the riverbed and flows along underground in the same channel, and then again appears on the surface at various points in significant strength. The riverbed of the Cibola is about a half mile [old German mile] and covered in some places with oaks and in others with mesquite wood.[15] However, the larger part is covered with immense pieces of chalk rock which reflect the sun rays, thereby increasing the heat and brightness. No breeze blew in this section. The high, white bluffs obstructed the easy northwest wind. When the Gulf breeze did not cool us off, the northwest wind constantly streamed down out of the rocky hills through the endless open prairies.

For a long time we searched in vain for water for ourselves and our thirsty horses. Finally, behind a large chalk rock, we discovered a considerable pool of clear fresh water that was kept in constant motion by many fish.

Today, it was not to be that we reach the longed-for San Antonio. However, the scenery had changed. More timber, many herds of deer, wild turkeys, and flocks of other birds that were frequently seen put us in a good mood. We camped for the night on the Salado [River], six miles from San Antonio. Strong guards stood all around the camp but nothing disturbed us, and nothing interrupted the stillness of the night except the calling, far and near, of the many whippoorwills. The whole forest seemed to be alive; but as the pale moon disappeared around twelve o'clock, the sad notes of these inhabitants of the forests died away also.

Only the relieving of the guards was heard from time to time. The fires flickered, and hour after hour hastened by drearily.

It was the last watch before the break of day, and I could barely wait as I sat dreaming before the fire and gazing into the flames, when—listen! The winged morning wind wafted the muffled thunder of the cannons of the Alamo[16] toward us. The first fiery light in the east announced the coming of day. In a moment everybody was on his feet, breakfast was prepared, coffee was cooked, horses were saddled and everything was ready. But a guide was lacking, as no one knew the way, much less the location of the camp of our friends. We were told to wait at the Salado, and that's what we did. The sun had disappeared again when at last two persons, a Mexican and an American, came in sight, and they led us to the main army. It was late at night when we arrived at the camp.

Our drummer and an Englishman had separated themselves carelessly from the troops and missed the right way. Nelson, the Briton, marched cursing along the road in the opinion that he had already gone too far, and his tired horse fully agreed with him; and only against its will did it follow the freedom fighter, who was pulling it with all his strength. Soon he cursed the long road, then his mount, and then again the Texas horsemiles when one had to go on foot. A salvo of not very tender expressions rolled from his lips to wail his protesting saddle pony when a repeated bold "*¿Quién vives?*" [Who goes there?] was called out to him.

"O ho, what kind of gibberish is that, all Turkish [We would say 'Greek to me'.] to me, but farewell my faithful nag, and farewell, gentlemen, *Quién vives*. I'll answer tomorrow; I first have to learn Spanish."

But the gentlemen who asked *Quién vives*, for whom the answer was not sufficient, sent something Mexican in the form of musket bullets after him, one of which put an end to his innocent horse while another deposited itself in his side, which he however, since he was in a considerable hurry, did not notice until he fell head over heels into a pond several hundred yards away from the sentinels. He did not notice the pond in the darkness. Here he lay unpursued until the next morning, when some of our people found him and brought him into camp nearby.

Our drummer also had his troubles. A cutting hunger and burning thirst plagued him considerably. With his drum hanging limply in front of him, and leading his faithful horse (which did not exceed Nelson's mare much in slenderness) by the leather [reins] which he had put over his shoulder, he went slowly forward. By the way, I must mention that the five hundred-mile trip had cost our horses a good piece of flesh. Several times hunger drew the stomach of our drummer together so angrily that he was about to beat the alarm. Now he stood still to reflect what should be done in such a despairing situation. In expression of his wishes for the people who were not exactly his friends, the Mexicans, and also regarding his highly stubborn mare, he didn't do any worse than the Briton, Nelson, but had the advantage over Nelson in that he was master of three languages. And a flood of French, Spanish, and English words gushed forth, and would have continued to do so—because the Creole was inexhaustible—if a strange voice had not addressed him with a "*Buenos noches.*"

The cunning drummer, a Creole from Louisiana, thought quickly when he found himself among the Mexicans and told them in Spanish that he was a negotiating officer. A parley officer with such a horse and out here at night appeared a little suspicious or phoney for the Mexicans; but when he added that four thousand volunteers from the States were on the way to destroy all the descendants of Montezuma in Texas, the matter became a little more serious for them. He was taken as a highly dangerous and embarrassing fellow to the Alamo, where, after a hearing, he was informed in correct order of the day that he would be shot in a few days. What a good consolation! But the Louisianian did not lose courage; didn't Uncle Sam's boys stand before the Alamo, and had the old man [Uncle Sam] ever been beaten!

[12] Sun.
[13] Rangers, companies of strong men who roam around the outer borders of the white population, in order to keep a vigilant eye on the Indians.
[14] A small Indian horse.
[15] A thorny, small type of tree which has beautiful blossoms.
[16] A fortified mission that dominated the city of San Antonio.

CHAPTER EIGHT

The Camp of the Militia

THE AUTUMN SUN, which had just risen above the constantly clear southern horizon and flooded the already stirring camp of the backwoodsmen with its fiery rays, showed the Greys, after the greeting from the Alamo and the reveille had died away, a camp that differed radically from what anyone had seen before. In spite of our active imagination and the descriptions and accounts of the war of independence in the States that we had read and heard, we had not pictured that an army composed of volunteers and militia fighting for freedom would look that way. Practically all of us had seen the roaming trappers along the western border of the States, and several of us had partici- pated in their excursions through the prairies. We also had wandered through camps of the Indians in the forests of the States and on their invitation not only had smoked the peace pipe with them but also had helped to eat captured game with them. Yes, even a few of us equipped with gun and beaver traps had traveled through the regions of the rocky mountains. Thousands of miles from civilization they once marched through the domains of the Black-feet,[17] the Flat-heads and the

130

Crows;[18] but never did they see anything similar to the camps surrounding the Texans.

To our left flowed the warm San Antonio [River] which had its source only a few miles from here. It already had a depth of from six to eight feet and a width of from eighteen to twenty yards. It formed a respectable stream and flowed down toward the enemy, forming a peninsula on the way. On the upper outside edge of the bend lay our camp. On the opposite lower bank, however, also on the right bank of the stream, lay the old, honored San Antonio, which was concealed from our view at the camp by the forest that borders all the Texas streams. Between us and the town lay a corn field, which extended for about an English mile along the river. But it was now barren. On the opposite treeless bank, and only separated from the town by the river, stood the main fortress of the former province of Texas, the previously mentioned Alamo, about three-quarters of an English mile from our camp. Immediately around us a flat area at least a half mile wide lay the camp of the citizens of Texas. On the other sides it was surrounded partly by large corn fields and partly by prairies, which were overgrown in places by mesquite brush and by enormous groups of gigantic cactus. Among these the horses and the cattle of the troops grazed peacefully in the tall grass. When one walked across adjacent fields, millions of blackbirds[19] would darken the sky. Stirred up, they would rise like a black cloud, swarm around in circles a few times and settle down again a short distance away to look for food on the ground. But the field where usually much cattle were shot and butchered had its inhabitants also. Great flocks of vultures of various kinds looked for their food on this slaughter place, which was to be had, too, in abundance, or they sat with outspread wings and open beaks on the dry limbs of the nearby pecan trees and warmed themselves (a true picture of the Mexicans) in the pleasant rays of the sun. A few large wolves and coyotes also wandered, as if they belonged to the army, among the heads, skins, and other refuse of the slaughtered cattle and had their breakfast undisturbed as well.

The roll of the drum now sounded through the camp. The muster rolls of the companies that had pitched their tents and built their huts deliberately as they pleased here and there without any regard to order, were read one by one. In order to give a true picture of the organization of the army it is necessary only to select any one company of those patriots against whom guns and valor, all discipline, and even the overpowering numbers of the enemy could not avail.

This was similar to the protection of the human rights in the colonies of the States under the great Washington. The result of their arms is known to the world; that proud Britannia was compelled by land and sea to strike her colors before the Yankees; and so were the Mexicans before the colonists of Texas, even when it was without any auxiliary force or help and with a population of twenty-seven thousand, which had to battle against eight million.

The company that lay opposite was, like the others, called out of its pleasant occupation of roasting its meat on the spits furnished by nature. But soon a small number of not fully-clad warriors stood in front of their sergeant, who was waiting with the list in his hand waiting for the arrival of the others. They were without firearms, and most of them had in the one hand a friendly wooden frying spit ornamented with good smelling roast and in the other the famous Bowie knife. Several did not fall into line, as their partially roasted meat did not permit them to leave it to its own fate, or possibly the threatening condition of the coffee did not allow them to leave the campfire. These certainly were important reasons, and the sergeant decided to begin even if all the men of the company were not together. Alternatingly, now from the ranks and then from the fires, sounded the sonorous voice of a backwoodsman. Once a muffled "Here!" broke forth from under a bundle of woolen blankets in a tent, followed by a general laughing of the company. The sergeant, although a little provoked, passed it up as nothing unusual. After he had finished reading the names, it was not necessary for him to give the dismissal order, as every one, as soon as he had answered to his name, returned again to his former place at the fire. The last one to stand in line carried a steaming coffee can in his hand.

We looked at each other alternatingly, especially we Europeans, and didn't know whether we should laugh at what had just happened or at the seriousness with which it was executed. It is true that the European soldiers possessed more discipline than prevailed here—with them at least some form existed. If there were no necessary detentions, the troops appeared *en masse*. But with us here, we were more laid back. The roll was never called in the morning. After the signal to rise had been given and after the fire was made, we prepared breakfast. We then broke into small groups if there was nothing to fear from the Indians or large groups of the enemy and galloped away as we pleased.

Only in one respect were we very strict, that is, on the journey the quartermaster with two or three men always rode several hours ahead to let the people know of the approach of the Greys; citizens then prepared everything for our reception. Everyone had to do his part of the work; there was bread to be baked, corn to be ground, coffee and tea to be boiled, steers to be butchered and other similar necessary things. If things were not as we wished them to be and the quartermaster was to blame, he was immediately removed from office; similarly other officers shared the same fate and had to take their places in the ranks as common soldiers. But I must say that we were never obliged to depose our captains, as Captain [Thomas H.] Breese of our company and Captain [William G.] Cook[20] of the other company of Greys knew how to command respect, and the latter particularly was well liked.

Toward nine o'clock we went out into the corn field that lay between our camp and the town to enter a small entrenchment that had been thrown up mainly by Captain Cook's men. It was fortified with only two small cannon, which my comrades used to bombard the old Alamo. We could in fact see pieces of the old walls roll down from time to time. The whole thing was being done for amusement and every effective shot was accompanied with loud applause from the Greys. The enemy wasn't lazy either, and his grapeshot from the openings of eight or nine cannons swept over against the encampment and beyond it, dried up the ground in every direction, and threw up clouds of dust toward our camp. It was no easy matter to get into the entrenchment from the camp as one had first to cross from six hundred to eight hundred yards of the open field, and as the artillery of the enemy was being used far more than ours. But this latter circumstance was a lot of fun for us, as the shots got some of our men into close quarters as they ran across the field

In December of 1835, the Texans were outside the Alamo and the Mexican forces were within.

to the entrenchment. It was pure curiosity that drove us across, because we had no orders and no other purpose than to see the Alamo, which, from here, offered an imposing view and to join in the applause with the others when part of the masonry of the old building or of the deserted old church collapsed.

Eight men, including myself, set out together to cross the desolate field, while the enemy, as if he had directed all the cannon of the fort (the Alamo) against us, enveloped us with his grapeshot like heavy rain. We were obliged for a moment to seek shelter under a large pecan tree. After we had taken our place here, we looked at each other and laughed at the fact that we, eight men, stood behind a single tree while the malicious laughter of our comrades, those in the trench as well as those in the camp, accompanied every full load that struck our faithful pecan tree and the rattling down of the dry limbs.

"This is, then, what they call waging war," said one of our future heroes, Thomas Camp; "and this," replied another as a swarm of iron mosquitoes flew past us, "we Americans call the variation of Yankee Doodle."[21] "Yes, and we call it," interjected another, "the last groaning of Santa Anna with his, till now, central constitution that is destroying everything." "And we," it rattled down from the dry tree limbs, "wish that you disappear at once." But we didn't hear the end of this speech, because the next second saw us on the way to the trench. The branches of the pecan tree covered the ground where we had stood.

Everything was lively in the trench. All stood around the cannon, and alternatingly first one and then another had the pleasure of giving a blow by taking a shot at the old walls. Before firing every man was first required to indicate in advance which part of the Alamo specifically he intended to demolish, and thereby bets were placed accordingly for or against him.

"A hundred ready-made bullets against twenty!" one was heard to call out, "that I will hit between the third and the fourth window of the barracks."

"Accepted!" cried three or four voices simultaneously; the gunner fired. He had to pour bullets all of the following day.

"My pistols, the best on the ground," cried a new candidate, who was about to fire, "against the poorest ones in the trench!"

"Well! Sir—I reckon—I can risk it," said a backwoodsman in a greenish pea jacket, whose pistols, although not quite as good as the others, were at least the next best. Away flew the cannonball, and the lost pistols of the gunner ended up in the belt of the man with the pea jacket, who magnanimously drew his and handed them over to the poor artilleryman.

"Well, in order to give you revenge, comrade, I will take a shot also. If this guy doesn't hit either—well, comrade, you may have your pistols back again." After he had, with the aid of a few of the Greys, loaded the cannon and gotten it into position, he looked down over the barrel for a long time. With one eye shut, as if he had a rifle before him, his face presented a mathematical problem while his right hand drew a number of geometrical figures in the air.

The noise about him, which he could not hear by nature, did not disturb him. The cannon only could speak clearly to him, but not all human voices were audible to him.

At last he was ready; another time he cast a hasty glance at the cannon and reached for the torch. Driven by the mighty load of powder, the destroying ball flew towards its mark. The rattling of the stones indicated to us, before the smoke had cleared away, that he had hit his mark. But after the smoke had disappeared we searched in vain for the third and fourth windows. As one voice a hurrah went up for old [Erastus] Deaf Smith, as they called him, for the most gallant Texan that ever chased across the Prairie and who later rendered such fine service with his scout-corps on the Mexican border between the Nueces [River] and the Rio Grande. The figure of a backwoodsman in the real sense of the word stood before us.

It was dangerous for any enemy soldier that got within the range of this man's musket, as he never missed his mark; while hunting, he never shot his game other than in the head. For that reason he looked down with such disdain on the Mexicans, with whom it was pure accident if the bullets of their muskets reached their aim.

While we were thus engaged with the demolishing of the Alamo, several shots were fired from the tall grass and bushes on the opposite bank, which made it inadvisable for us to look out over our trench.

Indignant at the impudence of the enemy, we decided to drive them away and proceeded to do it immediately. Thirty to thirty-five men of the Greys with their rifles took position in the woods on this side of the river's bank, where we were protected from the artillery fire of the Alamo, and through effective shooting soon silenced both the guns of the enemy and also probably some of the enemies themselves.

Becoming excited by the continuous firing and being some distance away from the camp, we as one man, without consulting anyone before, attacked the men posted in front of the city, who, although they were stronger than we, immediately cleared way for us, whereupon we followed in triumph. The enemy seemed not to have expected this at this time, and all inhabitants and soldiers fled toward the center of the town, which was very strongly fortified, and from which all the streets could be reached by cannon fire. Triumphantly we entered the captured houses and brought forth much-needed cooking utensils. While some loaded themselves down, the rest of us fought with the appreciably increased guard. From the center of the city, the bugles sounded the alarm, and the roll of the drums called the carefree enemy to arms. The Mexican cannonade toward our trench slowed down, but the trench still continued from time to time to send its smashing balls to the Alamo. We pressed forward energetically from house to house and from street to street while the enemy in proportion to his superior strength defended himself comparatively weakly, and fled out of the active range of our excellent rifles. After we had penetrated a small part of the town in this manner and, drunk with victory, were loaded down with booty for the kitchen, we thought of retreating, because we would soon have the whole Mexican army on our necks if we didn't. But it was too late. Before we could begin, the Mexican grapeshot fire from the right, where they had almost surrounded us, pierced the air over our heads. At the same time two four-pounders on the roof of the church in the center slung their balls right in among us: however, they usually bounced off and whistled away over our heads. Instinctively our men made real submissive bows to the disappearing balls. They were obliged to yield to necessity even if the deep bowing is in bad taste with a free republican. A full volley down the street from the center also accelerated our retreat. We directed a few shots to the artillery that was to the rear, but which now, since we had retreated, was to the left of us. We compelled the men to leave the cannon, but we could neither spike it nor take it with us, as the Mexican blue coats were swarming out of the streets like bees. It was high time for us to return to our comrades at camp, from where the rolling of the general march sounded over to us.

Barely had we left the captured cannon, before the Mexicans returned and followed us with its balls. However, since we could feel the vibration of the air and hear the report of the fire a little earlier, we did as before, bowed, and the swarm of copper pills that General Cos, the commander of San Antonio, had intended for our benefit rattled away over us: But when we came within the range of shots of the cannon from the church and also from the Alamo, from which we had been protected by the woods and banks of the river, we were hard put how to dodge them.

Soon the whole corn field, (from the town to within a short distance from where we were), was covered with the infantry of the enemy, and we were saved only because the soldiers did not take definite aim at the objects at which they were shooting. They held their heads far away because their muskets were more dangerous for the men behind them than for the men before them. A single shot will change the color of a white man's face in a moment and make it look like the color of the southern sky. And the bullet, instead of hitting its aim, whistles away twenty to thirty feet over it. And that's the way it was here. Bullets that were intended for us flew a quarter of a mile further and fell to the ground near our companions. Hard pressed and in danger of being accidentally hit and wounded, we hurried to a group of trees which reached out about one hundred and fifty steps from the river and lay across our path. Here we took a definite stand and sent our bullets effectively among the enemies. Conscious of their enormously overwhelming numbers, they would not let themselves be held back, and with a wild mixture of blowing of bugles they pressed forward to surround us. There was nothing left for us to do except to flee under most dangerous circumstances; but suddenly, imagine our pleasure! the old strains of Yankee Doodle chimed merrily, and around a projection of the forest came the backwoodsmen and the remaining companies, in order, as they said, to help the Greys out of a pinch.

In marked contrast with the cool bearing of the soldiers, the fearless scout of our army, Deaf Smith, rode with wild gesticulations in front of the army from the left wing to the right. In his left hand he carried the staff from which the tri-color fluttered briskly; in his right the never-failing gun. The bullets that tore his flag did not bother him nor did the deafening noise of the bugles and drums of the enemy. The Texans now awoke from their lethargy, and now went into battle against Santa Anna's soldiers under Cos. Smith had for the longest urged an attack, but he could never induce the officers to undertake one. They consoled him by waiting for reinforcements. He replied that he could take the fort and city with half of the troops already present.

But again he was to be disappointed. Barely had the Mexican soldiers seen the army of the Texans, barely had they heard Yankee Doodle, so familiar to the British, before they fled behind the protecting walls of the town; and the backwoodsmen didn't even have an opportunity to fire their guns.

We were led back in triumph to our camp together with our welcome kitchen utensils, which no one had thrown away. After that the Greys rose powerfully in the esteem of the brave Deaf Smith, and he was accustomed to call us by no other name than his boys.

Several days passed again without anything of interest happening, aside from a few brushes between the enemy outposts and our restless volunteers; also a fight was offered the Mexicans with Smith's participation. It was the well-known Grass Fight, where the Texas militia took a number of prisoners—about 160 men, whom, however, we liberated again during the night because they made us extra trouble and had to be fed from our provisions. A few would not leave because they liked it better with us than with their countrymen.

From day to day we pleaded to storm the fort and town, but couldn't induce the commander of the militia, of which the larger part of the army was composed, to do so. Finally Colonel [James] Grant, who formerly was an officer in the Scottish Highlanders but now for a number of years a citizen of Mexico, succeeded in arranging for a general assembly of the troops, where General [he was elected brigadier general of the militia in 1837] E. [Edward] Burleson, the commander of the army [colonel of the infantry], would disclose his plans. If they should be approved, it was agreed to put them into action the next morning.

With new life the drums sounded through the whole camp, and the joyous expectations of a decisive battle smiled on every face. Cheerfully, each threw his gun over his shoulder and hurried to the place of meeting, where we awaited in formation for Burleson's arrival. Not a man was absent except for a few wounded.

At last the commander appeared in company with several other officers. He immediately stepped to the front and, looking ill, he addressed the army as follows:

Edward Burleson succeeded Austin in command of his regiment when Austin was sent to the United States for aid, and he continued as commander of the militia when it encamped outside San Antonio. He also led a group at San Jacinto. He served in the U.S. congress and senate and as vice president of the Republic of Texas.

"Citizens!

"In response to the general demand to bring about a decisive turn in our war for independence, in response to demands from all sides to know whether we will in the future be permitted to stand on the soil of Texas which we have just made arable by our perspiration, while in the first epochs of the colonization the muskets could not leave our sides to keep the Comanches from our new hearths, to do justice to these demands, I have given the matter ripe consideration and have sought the advice of Major [Robert C.] Morris and Colonel [Francis W.] Johnson. It is my opinion as well as that of the colonel that, in view of the unfavorable season [December], we should withdraw behind the Guadalupe until spring, have some comfort in camp, await reinforcements from the States and undertake a sudden attack with renewed strength on San Antonio in February or March without setting up camp again as we are doing now."

Cries of disapproval ran through the lines; and even Grant, the gallant Scot, shared our opinion.

"If we withdraw," said a captain of the Greys, "the boundaries of Texas will be our destination, and barely will the Greys lie quiet and idle for five or six months. The spring would not find them in the army. No, now is the time, now to San Antonio—or never."

From all sides applause was accorded the captain, and Burleson continued:

"As I notice, gentlemen, you are not of the same opinion as I am—a matter that I had anticipated; and I have designed another plan in case this happened. If the troops find this one good and workable, I am of the opinion that it should be implemented tomorrow morning before daybreak."

A hurrah emanated from our midst, and he continued:

"We will divide the troops into three divisions of which the first, under Colonel [Benjamin] Milam, will attack the center of the city from the river on the northwest; the second, under Major Morris, will simultaneously storm the center from the west, and Mr. Smith, who has lived a long time in the town, will serve the second as guide; the third division, I will command in person and with it remain back to protect the camp and in case of accident cover the retreat."

The anger that had possessed the army soon changed itself into contemptuous laughter, and, one by one, the militia left the ranks.

Burleson, who had nothing better to submit, advised those who still remained that the present attitude of the army made a retreat imperatively necessary, and that we would have to take advantage of a more opportune time to drive the central army under Cos out of Texas.

But the Greys protested vigorously against this, especially Captain Cook. He asserted that should he leave the present camp and postpone the attack until the spring, he and his companions would not withdraw behind the distant Guadalupe but would camp during the winter a few miles from here in one of the fortified missions half in ruins on the San Antonio river.

Burleson permitted us to do as we thought best and, full of anger, we returned to our huts that we had left so joyfully.

The fires flickered forsaken in the camp; and in front of the huts and tents everybody was busy saddling the horses and packing up. Some of the militia were already riding off to the colonies, as there was no hope for a successful attack under such leadership.

A short time had passed and possibly half of the militia was already on the road to the Guadalupe. The Greys were downcast and still undecided what to do. What could one hundred and thirty men do against nearly fifteen times that many? Nothing but sacrifice themselves; on the other hand, should they lie in the colonies for three or four months? That was not the purpose for which they had come to Texas. Why did they renounce the brilliant positions and prospects that were offered them in New Orleans? Why did many leave the parental hearth? For honor, and not to become a soldier, because the regular soldier is an object of contempt to the industrious citizens of the States; only seldom does one find the sons of Uncle Sam among them; they are mainly whiskey-loving foreigners.

No, it was for the rights of their kinsmen, for the rights of every man that they entered the field without any prospect of remuneration, that they left the safe haven to plunge out into the raging sea.

But they were not to grieve long. Suddenly five horsemen came riding down the river on the side on which the camp was located. The leader, a little lean man, wore the uniform of a Mexican lieutenant, which he in reality was. A white flag fluttered in his left hand.

He asked hastily for the commander and, after we had led him there, he pledged himself to lead our troops unobserved to near the center of the town. Yes, he even said that if a part of the troops would follow him, he would lead them to under the window of General Cos.

However, his offer was not accepted, as we were afraid to trust him. Too many circumstances spoke against him. In the first place he was a traitor, secondly he was a Mexican, and thirdly some Comanche blood flowed in his veins. All of these made Smith's warning to be careful unnecessary; but his advice to attack the city, as he had suggested, was accepted after some encouragement from the side of Smith.

With new life the Greys shouted through the half-deserted camp. The militia did not agree with this plan and considered an attack now as foolhardy. Half of our troops had left us and we could not muster more than four hundred men. Nevertheless we frankly declared it our intention to try the attack, even if the volunteers would have to make it alone. I said volunteers because the slender volunteers from Mississippi had just as large part in this work as the companies from New Orleans.

A call was issued for volunteers to storm the town the next morning, "because only volunteers will fight for and win freedom." A list was passed from man to man, which everyone in favor signed. When the last had signed, the names of two hundred and thirty men could be seen on the paper. The names of only a few of our company were missing—the wounded.

The plan for the attack was this. A part of the troops, that were to remain behind to guard the camp, went up a short distance soon after midnight. They crossed the river and under cover of the night planted several pieces of artillery quite remote from the Alamo. They then waited until nearly four o'clock and made a feigned attack on the fort to draw the attention of the enemy and most of the troops in that direction. Meanwhile we marched, double quick, in two columns down two streets paralleling the river toward the center of the city. In the vicinity of the latter we purposed to take position in a group of stone buildings whose walls were three feet thick. There we were to wait for day, survey the surroundings, and make further arrangements.

In spite of the approach of the fateful day, we slept excellently. Wrapped in our blankets from head to foot, we lay around the fires with our guns near us and our saddles for pillows. In this position the northwest wind that blows down so coldly from the rocky mountains through the southern plains during the winter could not disturb us. In the early spring it often causes the death of sugar cane, and even at times cotton and corn. Often the thermometer drops to 40° F. during the night and by noon of the next day, it reaches the same high reading as the day before. Although a Northerner, whose blood has not been thinned by a Southern summer, may not find this climate disagreeable, it is just as severe on the regular inhabitants of these broad plains and more unpleasant than the cold January is to the inhabitants of the north.

[17] Black-feet Indians.

[18] Indian tribes in the Missouri Territory who are especially feared by the fur dealers.

[19] A marlin, a kind of blackbird.

[20] Now major general, quartermaster general of the Republic of Texas.

[21] The national melody of the Americans.

CHAPTER NINE

The Surprise Attack [Victory at the Alamo]

~

A NORTHER LIKE THE ONE MENTIONED in the previous chapter was piercing the prairie the night of December 4 to 5, 1835. Tents and huts were blown down and all sparks of the fire had been blown away, but we lay quietly under our covers and dreamt of the adventures of the coming day. It was just two o'clock when the guards were relieved, and now they went quietly from tent to tent to awaken the sleepers. They started up out of their dreams, but dropped back just as quickly when the icy breath of the storm whistled around their warm bodies.

But soon we stood in line with our faithful guns on our shoulders. We were wrapped in our blankets and awaited the signal to march.

It was, however, a little too early to work simultaneously with the troops that were to make the fake attack. Therefore, we had to wait a while longer. During this time, since we had started no fires, we froze terribly and anxiously waited for the time to march. At last Major Morris stepped among us and read our names out again. Only two hundred and ten men were at the meeting place to answer to their names. The night had removed many heroic thoughts, and the cold storm had blown away many weak spirits that last night glowed in our hearts like the last sparks of the fire. But this had no influence on the others whose motto was: "The fewer the number the greater the glory." We believed that those who could not face the enemy with courage and love for the cause would do more harm by their example than good.

At last it was past three o'clock and we hurried quietly across the cornfield toward the city. Not worried, the numerous enemy soldiers at the Alamo cried their "sentinels to the alert" through the night. Except for these long drawn-out words and the howling of the norther storm, we could not perceive the slightest sound. Soon we paid no further attention to the unfriendly breath of the rocky mountains, but warm from our running and the expectancy of soon seeing the enemy, our woolen blankets flew to the right and the left on the road. Without reducing our speed, the watchword "Bexar[22]" [pronounced Bear] ran from man to man.

We were about half-way across the field when a thunder different from that of the norther indicated to us that our friends had fulfilled their duty and had attacked the Alamo.

Instantly the enemy drums began to roll and the bugles pealed in motley confusion. From the fort came continuous booming toward the place from where our people with their small guns courageously challenged the entire Mexican army. The glances of our leader, the Mexican lieutenant, were focused constantly on the Alamo, which we could see to our left as a black colossus. Uneasily he peered through the darkness as if he feared that our purposes had been betrayed. At last he broke his long silence and said, pointing to the Alamo where several rockets were just rising:

"The way is clear; we are safe. Those sparkling, artificial stars are calling a part of the troops out of the town to help the

Alamo. Now, let's go briskly ahead so that we may enter the town within ten minutes. Do you see those outposts at the fire? Let them run away unnoticed. Our shooting would kill a few but would bring the whole garrison down on us. However, quickly after them, so that we will get to the center at the same time with them. The further ahead we get this morning, the more stone buildings will fall into our hands."

We were within twenty steps of the fire before the sentinels noticed us, and without uttering a sound, they fled, some even without their muskets.

Unobstructed we rushed, as stated before, in two columns into the city. The first column, with Breese's Greys in the lead, was supposed to surge down the street by the river. But for reasons of safety we hurried along on the left side of the river through the little gardens of the Mexicans, and over, in places, treeless river banks of the San Antonio toward the center. As already stated, all the streets were commanded by Mexican artillery. This, indeed, was good, because when we were within almost two hundred steps of our destination, the first load of grapeshot of the enemy swept along the street. Soon, just as the day began to dawn in the east, we were obliged to take a definite position in an enemy guard house, a substantial stone structure.

We viewed with interest the dark outlines of the quadrangle that surrounded us. We had never seen buildings of this kind before. They were all only one-story high and were built in the form of a long box. Toward the yard this structure, which served as our refuge, had two doors but no windows, whereas there were four of medium size on the opposite side next to the street. The roof was flat and surrounded with a stone wall two feet high. At the lower end of the house and parallel with the center ran a wall three feet thick and six feet high, in a right angle toward a small secondary building. From there another one of the same kind ran parallel with the river, exposing itself and the front of the dwelling to the fire of the Alamo, which was about two thousand yards away. The other side of our little fort was shut off with a few small buildings. All the dwellings of the well-to-do Mexicans are in the form of little fortresses. The walls, on an average as thick as those described, are very practical for this climate; they are cool in the summer and warm during the winter storms. Consequently one seldom sees any fire in the chimneys. Elegant furniture is nowhere to be found. In the yard an enormous steer tied to a stake by his horns was lowing discontentedly. He came in handy when we ran short of food. In the house we found a few opened barrels of Missouri cornmeal and a few remnants of sugar, coffee and cocoa.

Although it was still night when we arrived, the enemy soon revealed his location to us by his murderous fire. The whole center became a flashing line. The firing was uninterrupted infantry fire, intermixed with the groaning of all of the Mexican cannon, of which twelve to sixteen six-pounders were directed against the little fort of the first division. One of them stood within eighty steps of us and was working against the lower wall, behind which we were busy setting up a nice, long six-pounder.

The cannonballs sang us a morning song of a singular kind. In countless tones from soprano down to bass, like those of the harp of Aeolus, they vibrated over our heads. Several of our men, who had taken position on the flat roof behind the wall, were compelled to keep themselves very quiet; they had never experienced a shooting of this kind before; even behind the walls they were not safe as the guns of the church, which reached high up above all other buildings of the town, commanded our roof also. Consequently, shortly after daybreak they were obliged to jump down in the greatest haste, and had the questionable pleasure of being laughed at for their dexterity.

By eight o'clock we still did not know where our second division was. It was said that they were near by; but where, no one could say. And we finally discovered it by an unfortunate accident. From stone buildings to our right and a little to the rear, little smoke clouds issued from time to time. From the light of the fire we concluded that not very many enemies could be in the buildings. Consequently as a quickly conceived plan to take the buildings and put them in communication with us was about to be executed, several shots from there indicated to us that they were our own people, who were mistaking us for their enemies. One of the bullets struck a Mississippian by the name of Moore, which, fortunately enough, glanced off from two dollars that he had in his vest pocket. A second laid low another, the tall Mississippian. The bullet tore the brain out of its cavity and spattered it on the walls and over us who stood near him. His colossal body twitched convulsively for hours in the thick clotted blood that flowed out of the wound. It showed us novices the battle of the body with its departing life.

The clear crack of the shot and the small bullet that glanced off from the money supported the belief of a few that they were our own people who were firing out of the buildings. And several offered themselves as volunteers to Colonel Milam, who now commanded us, to jump over and inform them of their error. The offer was accepted and immediately carried out, but not until another one became a victim. It was this time a German, William Thomas, who had just taken aim to fire on the center of town. A gun cracked, smoke issued from the building of our friends, and momentarily the gun of the heavily wounded German dropped to the ground. The wounded man, driven by a mighty force, made an involuntary movement, a puff of wind blew past him and a stream of blood issued from his sleeve. Pale as marble he looked about, clapped his hand on this left shoulder and remarked that he must be wounded, although he felt no pain. The terrible pain came later. Later the shattered shoulder bones caused the surgeon more trouble than the wounds of all the other soldiers put together.

After the second group was advised of our presence, leaving nothing to be feared from it any more, a door was broken

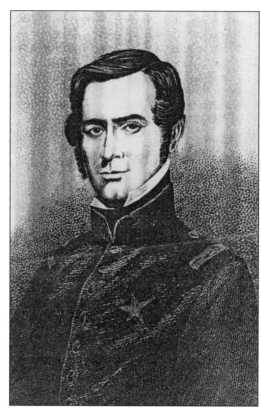

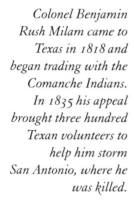

*Colonel Benjamin
Rush Milam came to
Texas in 1818 and
began trading with the
Comanche Indians.
In 1835 his appeal
brought three hundred
Texan volunteers to
help him storm
San Antonio, where he
was killed.*

Archives Division,
Texas State Library.

through the thick rock walls and a trench to our people was dug as the safest and most convenient means of communicating with each other. Running across the street was highly unsafe. As soon as the enemy got a glimpse of us, which was only after a few seconds, they would send past us a large quantity of lead and copper paradise apples, but would seldom hit.

The cannon that was firing eighty yards from us, constantly raging against our walls, and in conjunction with those of the Alamo did considerable damage, was now the main object of our attention. It was silenced in a short time as the backwoodsmen and the Greys, through little holes dug through the walls, shot down every blue coat who approached it. It, therefore, could not be loaded, much less be directed at us. On the other hand our long, bright six-pounder now played effectively on the row of buildings opposite us. We were, however, obliged to use our cannonballs sparingly, as we did not have an over supply of them.

In the afternoon we began to feel thirsty. As there was no well in the house, we alternately jumped down to the one hundred and fifty yard distant San Antonio River, dipped our vessels into the water and rushed back to our companions under a rain of enemy bullets. This finally became too dangerous, as constantly increasing numbers of blue coats posted themselves opposite this position. Soon the price of water rose from $3.00 to $4.00 per bucket. Finally no one was willing to risk dipping out of the crystal waters at even higher prices.

A Mexican woman who was in the house when we arrived and who at once cooked and baked bread for us in a friendly manner, offered to go to the stream and get water for all of us since she, as a woman, would have nothing to fear. This we, and especially Colonel Grant, roundly forbade her to do as we were apprehensive that the blue coats would fire on her just as soon as on us. She insisted, nevertheless, and said laughingly that we knew only very little of the Mexican attitude about women. And before we were aware of it, she was on her way to the stream. Hastily she filled her buckets and was on the point of returning when a swarm of bullets swept by, and pierced with four bullets, she fell lifeless on the green turf. Our men gazed with horror over the wall. Only a few seconds passed before several men rushed out to bring in the unfortunate, good-hearted woman. All the enemies had discharged their muskets, and the dead body was brought in without a single shot being fired. Others of the Greys taking advantage of this inability of the Mexicans to shoot, jumped down to the shore of the river, filled their vessels and returned safely, much to the chagrin of the blue coats.

Toward evening a call was issued in our division for volunteers to take a stone house, which stood to the right of us and a little nearer to the center of town. There was rather brisk firing through the cracks of the boarded windows, which, on account of the nearness, did not give us any great pleasure. Partly on that account did we wish to take the building and partly because its possession would put us appreciably nearer the enemy storehouse. The first company of the Greys under Breese was determined to take the building without other help, as another one had already been handed over by the enemy to the other unit. But we came too late. As we jumped through the windows and rushed forward with our wrecking bars, there stood the six foot high namesakes of the mighty Father of Waters [men from Mississippi], whose tremendous crow bars moved by their muscular arms, smashed the thick walls into pieces. Barely had ten minutes passed before the first stone fell inward. Instantly we sent the contents of our guns through the little opening into the darkness within.

A terrible crying of women and children from within indicated to us that the building was full of people who were now plaintively pleading for mercy.

At once our serious guns that meant business were silenced. But the walls collapsed anew and soon the Mississippians broke through a gate-like entrance, and a long group of women, children and men staggered out. The latter surrendered their guns and expected us to imprison them. But the tall victors, who had nothing to eat, explained to them that it was far from us to wage war against the citizens of Mexico, and that they need not be concerned about their property. With that they gave them permission to escape, which the prisoners did not have to be told the second time. They went under full wind and sail to the empty houses that lay between us and our camp.

Cook's Greys also had taken possession of another long building, and with the capture of a third one the next morning they intended to supply all of us with fresh water, as near them a canal had been built through the city.

The next dawning day was still stormy, and revealed to us on the pinnacle of the church steeple a blood red flag, truly a mirror reflecting all the sinister places and wrinkles of Santa Anna's heart. We laughed at Cos's intention to frighten us with that color. In fact it was gratifying to us in one respect, as we alone were now fighting under the tri-color and the enemy under the standard that carried despotism in all its folds and promised death to all rebels who opposed the ambitious plans of Santa Anna and who, in the uninhabited savannas of Texas, dared to take up arms when the mighty states of the Confederation had bowed humbly under his sword.

During the previous night our long twelve-pounder had arrived, the largest caliber that thundered in the valley of the San Antonio, and we proceeded at once to throw loopholes or firing slits. A number of buildings fell into our hands that day, and several mesquite fences that lay between us and the enemy were set on fire. By four o'clock they were in full flames, and by eight o'clock the cover under which the enemy might have approached us unnoticed, lay like a glowing field of amber before us. The groups of houses that we occupied were completely connected up with trenches during the second day. During the night the enemy kept up an incessant fire, and in the darkness he also used the cannon standing opposite us. In spite of the constant firing we slept as well as if we were lying in the peaceful, closely settled regions of the States.

On the third day, the battle was opened by us in grand style. We gazed with real satisfaction on our twelve-pounder as she slung her thunderbolts out of her new firing slot and defiantly bellowed forth her war whoop to the old church tower, from which the enemy molested us quite a bit with their muskets. The third shot that the German from Brunswick[23] named Langenheim sent off caused part of the dome to cave in, which was a warning to the enemy to leave this position for the events to come. In order to spare the venerable old ruin, we ceased firing

General Martin Perfecto Cos, brother-in-law of General Santa Anna, was in charge of the Mexican army during the storming of Bexar in 1835, a major Texas victory, when the Mexican troops were inside the Alamo and the Texans were bombarding and shelling it from the outside.

at it. We directed all of our artillery on a few buildings that we shortly intended to take. Our artillery, however, suffered severely. Soon all the men with the exception of the tall "Brunswicker," as we called him, lay heavily wounded. He, an attractive man six feet tall, miraculously remained uninjured, although he constantly exposed his full height to the blue coats while adjusting and firing the cannon.

We enjoyed ourselves that day at the expense of our enemies. Our people found great sport in putting their caps on poles (ramrods, used for loading firearms) and holding them above the wall. I had just returned from a round when I saw several of these punctured caps and hats on perfectly sound heads. This seemed strange to me, but the riddle soon explained itself. Just then a Grey held his cap slightly above the wall, and barely had it projected above the rim of the wall when twenty to thirty bullets swarmed around the place. With loud cries of applause from the enemies, who believed that they had laid flat another heretic, the cap sank slowly back behind the wall. A pause set in, at least from our side. But the blue coats continued to fire incessantly and it must have been much the same to them whether they fired into the sky or at us, as their bullets sang away over the buildings even when no one thought of shooting over or through the punctured walls. However, after a while another cap appeared boldly over the wall, and as expected the blue coats cried out a good morning to it. But the hail of bullets could not scare the wounded. Fearlessly, they maintained their position, while the enemy troops fired their bullets lengthwise and crosswise, over and under, the position. Soon their anger was converted into consternation. They stared over to our walls and they as well as their muskets were silent. Then sounded the loud laughter of our men, who were showing the enemy the cap in all its terrible condition.

With this, however, our fun came to an end. Following this event the enemy would not fire on our caps, nor on the broad-brimmed hats of the backwoodsmen, nor even at our real heads unless we revealed a part of the body also. After a while, however, they fired as briskly again as ever, but not at our caps and hats but at the pumpkin heads our men had decorated with their own headpieces and stuck up over the wall. This had the result that the enemy wasted away his powder and occasionally exposed himself to the eyes of the backwoodsmen or the Greys. Even if the enemy did not fall, at least his shattered arm caused him to drop his musket.

We, also, had a serious loss today; a good artillery man, an Englishman named Cook, was killed. Formerly he had been gunner in the English fleet, and in Texas he had immediately taken his place with the artillery. He was the first one to be killed in operating the twelve-pounder.

Another incomparably greater loss we suffered in the death of our gallant Colonel Milam, who fell lifeless to the ground with a musket ball in his forehead in the center of the yard where the first division lay. During the evening they were both quietly buried by us, while the enemy artillery sounded taps for them. But when they were lowered into the graves, all of our artillery in the town as well as that in the camp gave evidence of our grief and our esteem.

For the remainder of the siege we were without a clear-cut leader, and all expeditions against the enemy were carried out by calling for volunteer troops. The only authorities that were present were Major Morris and the two captains of the Greys. But I must observe in fact that I never heard a single order during the whole siege. Our own consciousness of being able to do something against despotism under the flag of the Union kept order and discipline in our ranks.

On the fourth day five hundred reinforcements under Colonel Guardechi, who had moved from the other side of the Rio Grande and had not been noticed by our rangers in the course of their march through the wild prairies to Tamaulipas, moved into the Alamo. But we had little to fear from these men as most of them were required to serve because of murder or robbery or because they had taken part in uprisings against the usurper, as had occurred in all of the states of Mexico. They were chained together in pairs, and disregarding the fact that many of them wished us infamous heretics death, it is easy for one to imagine how little there was to be feared from such rabble. They, therefore, did not frighten us in the least, and we continued our plans vigorously to conquer one part of the city after another. In fact we planned to undertake very soon a *coup de main*.

At five o'clock in the evening volunteers were called to take several buildings filled with blue coats. More than were necessary pressed forward to have a share in this major strike, and even before the sun sank into the horizon we stood about in irregular groups equipped with arms and tools near the buildings to be stormed. The militia was armed with wrecking bars to tear down the walls. Although the soft stones rolled out quickly, it seemed to take a long time because the enemy was firing unpleasantly at us from a little trench that had been thrown up across the river opposite the first division.

Meanwhile it wasn't very long before walls fell inward into the building, and soon thereafter the contents of our guns followed. The openings were enlarged, as soon as we had reloaded, and we fired another salvo. But the bullets of the enemy also whistled, although without effect, through the ever enlarging holes. Our militia prudently did not expose anything but the wrecking bars. Finally the openings were large enough to admit a man at a time, and another volley from our guns cleaned the room of the blue coats who, as we pressed in, had withdrawn to a more distant and safer atmosphere.

The door to the next room was strongly barricaded, and we were obliged to proceed with our axes, which, however had to be done with the greatest caution as the enemies were shooting wildly, and two men already were slightly wounded.

As soon as the sun had disappeared behind the western horizon, the night, as in all southern regions, settled down over the prairie and town with amazing rapidity; and already black, impenetrable darkness prevailed in the conquered room, when the door to the next room crashed down. This room had also been evacuated, and we felt about on the walls in the dark without being able to see anything, let alone find an exit. In the adjoining room shot thundered upon shot, but, as it seemed, also without aim. Only from an opening near the ceiling flashed the fire of the burning powder, and the bullets that were fired against the ceiling fell at our feet accompanied by the limestone that they knocked loose.

At last we found a barricaded door, but it also soon lay in splinters. The room was, like the other one, vacated by the enemy.

This gave us possession of the building, and we were now only about thirty to forty yards from the center of town. Nothing now remained but to remove a link from the chain of buildings that surrounded the large quadrant, the center of the city, in order to put us in possession of the stores of munitions in the church which stood in the center of the quadrant: and, I might say, to put us in possession of the whole city. But we had done enough for today and another day was designated for that purpose.

"Glory enough for one day!" cried the backwoodsmen as they rolled themselves up in their blankets to sleep.

The fifth morning, the sun broke forth in full bloody autumn splendor and sent down her warming rays from the deep blue vaulted skies. The whole divine nature lay soft and quietly around the scene of battle. The howlings of the norther had ceased and that indescribable charm that pervades the wilderness on such a day lay on the western prairie that stretches westward from San Antonio as an enormous carpet to the rocky mountains. The waving mesquite fields were not fresh and green, but appeared bleached, like the ripe meadows of Europe. The sea of grass in the unlimited distance blended with the dark clouds above us.

But in terrible contrast the deserted streets lay about us, and the desolate field, the burnt-off mesquite fences and a few buildings before us, while the buildings around us looked more like broken rock heaps than human habitations. Again, more active than ever before, the artillery of the enemy without inter-ruption jarred the trembling, partly collapsed walls of the Free Corps [Volunteers]; and without aim as before the shower of copper bullets rolled uninterruptedly from the outranked tower-muskets of the enemies.[24]

General Cos, like the chameleon, had again changed his color, and unpardonable hatred waved from the steeple of the town instead of the blood red flag; the black standard of death hung down limply from its high staff. Powerless, its folded form threatened the winning force of besiegers from whose headquar-ters the splendid tri-color was displayed with enthusiasm.

Devastation raged from our artillery as well as from that of the enemy, and the heavy fire of our old faithful twelve-pounder put in ruins the walls of the building that we expected to take during the evening. But the cannonballs for our six-pounders had been used up. And they would have remained silent for the remainder of the siege if the enemy had not occasionally supplied us with the needed article. Whenever a ball would hit our walls, our people would hastily jump over after it, quickly load it into our cannon, and fire it back at the enemy with our compliments, for which he usually thanked us with eight or ten others. But at the most, only two or three of them hit our building.

Toward three o'clock in the afternoon we saw and heard for the first time the pomp of Mexican attack. A strong unit of from five hundred to six hundred blue coats streamed forth from the walls of the Alamo. As if they intended to attack our practically deserted camp, they marched in that direction toward the river, sounding their bugles, but were driven back by a few volleys from our companions. This, however, was only a sham attack and was executed for the purpose of drawing the larger part of our men out of the town, whereupon Cos would have attacked the few remaining with his superior forces. We, however, saw through that gentleman's plans, and neither he nor his many confusedly blowing buglers could draw a sign of fear from us. But we sat quiet and expectantly, like the fox in the kettle, in our stone houses. If he really attacked our camp, the guards might be able to defend it; if they could not, they were told to turn it over to the enemy and come to us into town, inasmuch as we would need all the men and guns the following night that we could gather together in order to deliver our final attack and ultimately free the prairies of the legions of the central government.

After they had, however, at a very respectful distance, paraded around in all their splendor for a time and toward the end had received a few loads from our artillery, they very quietly and without ostentation marched back to the Alamo, seeing that their ruse was in vain.

We of our first unit determined to take an important position in the center of town this evening in which the second company of Greys, although located in another building, intended to support us; but at about nine o'clock, just as we were making our preparations, the enemy made a ferocious general attack on the first unit. All the cracking and thundering that we had heard up to now was only child's play in comparison with this attack. Any moment we expected to see the hordes of blue coats appear on the walls that had almost been leveled, and whose ruins were serving our people behind it as an entrenchment. We lay, man along side of man, with our hammers cocked, ready to drill through the first one who would be foolhardy enough to set his foot on the remnant of the wall. At the little holes they had broken through the walls stood the backwoodsmen; every bullet that left their guns laid one of the enemy on the ground. The Mexicans, as usual, considered it expedient, however, not to come too near our guns, and remained at a respectful distance. This finally became too boring for us and about twenty men of our Greys determined to attack the enemy in the flank.

Fearlessly, although we were being attacked by six hundred to eight hundred men, we rushed through a little detour and attacked the four walls of a former log cabin. The darkness was in our favor, and before the enemy was aware of it, we were situated among the crowds of the enemy that had been dishing out this murderous fire. The discharge of our guns and all of our pistols instantly caused a wild confused retreat of the blue coats behind the walls and buildings of the center of town where they, however, continued their incessant firing, especially at the roofless building conquered by us. Firing also thundered wildly from the second unit, and it seemed that they had to stand a harder fight than we did. The bugles whirred wildly out of the center of town and the drums rolled for battle. The profanity of the enemy and the incessant musket fire was completely drowned out by the cannon of the Alamo which now in short intervals thundered through the darkness. But there was something inspiring in this powerful roaring through the night. A similar feeling took possession of me as in those days when I saw the powerful tow-boat for the first time that panted up the Mississippi with a fleet of ships, frigates and schooners. With a muffled, hollow thunder the white smoke issued at regular intervals from within the lighted up monster. Long after it had passed out of sight we could still hear the puffing of the boat.

After eleven o'clock the tumult died away in every direction and we left the four walls to see how it stood after our attack on the center of town. But imagine our surprise when we found all of the buildings of the second unit empty. We were still standing about unable to explain the cause of the enemy's absence when a wounded man lying in the corner gave us the information. Immediately after the enemy's attack on the first unit, everybody hurried away to storm altogether unexpectedly the designated position from a different direction. And the plan succeeded completely. In a short time they had driven the Mexicans out of two of the largest buildings and spiked [made unusable] the cannon, so dangerous for us, eighty yards away.

It may appear to many that we proceeded very carelessly with our job, such a conclusion could especially be justified by the fact that the second unit not only left us without any assistance but also even left its position to undertake a charge while we were being attacked violently. Neither can I justify this with anything except that we considered ourselves invincible, a conclusion that later caused us deep wounds and almost caused the destruction of the new republic.

The fifth day was thus closed gloriously, and we were looking eagerly for the sixth, the tenth of December. The fire of the enemy had died down, and only occasionally a shot was fired (from the little trench on the other side of the river) whose cannonball, like a lost wanderer, carelessly hurried through the darkness and crossed that space where, for five days and practically four nights, thousands of praying soldiers had crossed themselves. The thundering roar of the artillery had died away and the quivering earth had quieted down. Only the groaning of the wounded reminded us of the bloody sacrifice that was made for freedom. Nor did we know how much more blood it would require. But the goddess demands no blood when justice is done in a peaceful manner; immeasurably more pleasant to her is the victory won through the noble feelings of the heart. If these are destroyed, if reason becomes blind, then the suppressed must take up their bloody weapons for what is right.

Lighter and brighter did the east become, and the dark shadows of the night were disappearing before the fiery December sun that was to reveal the fall of the enemy. The humble white flag of submission was waving from the ruins of the Alamo. The black flag of death had disappeared from the high dome whose pinnacle was now ornamented only with its own dignity.

The capitulation was agreed upon by nine o'clock. The Mexicans were to be allowed to march away unmolested. As a protection against the Comanches they were allowed one hundred and fifty guns, a little powder and lead, and a four-pounder. The officers were obliged to give their word of honor never again to fight against Texas. The officers and troops were to leave the town at once, the Alamo on the 12th of December and to evacuate the whole country on this side of the Rio Grande as speedily as possible.

On the designated day Cos marched away with his troops, and by virtue of conquest, we took possession of the conquered stores and the Alamo. Forty-eight cannon, approximately four thousand muskets, a considerable amount of gunpowder, ready-made cartouches, and a large supply of cannon and musket bullets came into our hands. We also found a large number of enemy uniforms in the stores in the rear of the church. But they were not of the slightest use to us as, although new, every Texan would rather have made himself, like the brown inhabitants of the prairie, a hunting shirt and a pair of moccasins out of the skin of the slain deer, than to have worn the suits of the contemptible soldiers.

The loss of the Mexicans ran up to seven hundred and twenty-odd killed, and a small number of slightly wounded who left with General Cos, while a large number of the seriously wounded were taken under the treatment of our physicians with the same carefulness that was accorded our own wounded.

Our loss was six killed and twenty-nine wounded, who were lying in the military hospital, together with a few slightly wounded who took up quarters in the town. This proportion of the enemy's loss is so infinitely large that it appears almost unbelievable. But practically all battles between these two powers show that the number of Texans killed multiplied by four hundred will generally equal that of the Mexicans.

Our treatment of the enemy was good as also was our treatment of the inhabitants of San Antonio, although they had united with Cos and opposed us. We still regarded Texas and Mexico as one large whole state. Consequently, now, as formerly, the tri-color of Mexico waved over the church. And we hoped that fame on its mighty wings would soon spread the result of our contest against the usurper's troops over the sister states of the republic, and that it would call forth a renewed uprising of the whole people to throw off the yoke of the central constitution.

---

[22] The name of San Antonio, which the Mexicans pronounced quite differently from the Texans.

[23] A town near Hanover, Germany.

[24] The Mexicans all had this kind of musket, but only the ones that could not be used by the British.

CHAPTER TEN

San Antonio

SOON AFTER THE DEPARTURE of the Mexican troops, most of us moved into the ruins of the Alamo. Each one, according to his own pleasure, searched out a favorite retreat for protection against the cold and storm of winter. A little detachment of nine men, including the Virginian Paw who had become a lieutenant, selected the rather well preserved church, which had been robbed of all ornaments, as their quarters. There were several large arches at the front entrance, under which it appeared dangerous to tarry long. The outer side was provided with several figures of the saints chiseled out of sandstone, in front of which the Mexican women regularly every morning knelt down without being disturbed in the least by the passing in and out of the volunteers. It was being said that the sandstone saints were being visited more now than ever before, and I have often wondered whether the black eyed *señoras* became so pious because they were now in such close contact with us heretics, or whether it was the presence of the heretics themselves that drew them into these desolate ruins.

After everything had gotten quiet again in the town and the country around, only occasionally resounded the discharge of our guns when a deer or a turkey was being killed for eating, and the inhabitants of the town at last returned in large numbers. Most of them had left during the siege and quietly awaited the result of the battles on their ranches[25] that lay from six to eight miles down the river.

The homes of the rich and the blockhouses of the poor soon filled up again, and the streets were alive with Mexicans and Texans moving back and forth. Through the broad streets glided many a cute *señora*, even if not as elegant and as graceful and resilient as the pretty New York ladies as they flutter by the hundreds along the magnificent Broadway, yet endowed with that charm and courtesy for which their nation is known and which so drastically is distinguished from the rougher manners and mores of the inhabitants of the north.

The Mexicans are great lovers of pleasure; they dance, ride, eat, drink and sleep their lives away. We frequently visited different families. If we came between ten o'clock in the morning and five o'clock in the afternoon, we would usually find all the members of the household sitting on a carpet that was spread out on the floor of the room. Apparently everything was happy. The dons very pleasantly chatted their time away with the brown beauties, or talked about horses, and cracked pecans, while the whole party smoked their cigarettes.[26] After five o'clock, when the rays of the sun are not burning so hot on the prairie and the evening wind is blowing refreshingly cool from the mountains, the young men drive the horses home. The brown Amazons of the west mount their favorite steeds and away they race with the men in a flying gallop through the streets and then toward the prairie, where they chase about until seven or eight o'clock. Then, however, they return to spend the rest of the night in the dance halls with the music of the fandango. The first days passed in intoxicating pleasures, as it appeared that we were welcome everywhere. Aside from the conversations composed of sign-language and a combination of

English and Spanish words, everything went briskly forward. And frequently did the peculiar combinations occasion loud laughter. But after a week, as this pastime regularly repeated itself from day to day, the charm of the newness began to disappear. Our restlessness rose again and demanded other nourishment than the endless and at last boring fandangos and the increasingly boring conversations of the inhabitants of San Antonio.

The hunting in the vicinity also wasn't good any more, as first the siege and then the constant hunting had frightened practically all the game away. 'Tis true that the prairies were covered with herds of deer; but to hunt them was tiresome and a worthless pleasure, especially, as we preferred the flesh of the cattle, that we had in abundance, to that of the deer.

We had to undertake something else. Consequently Joseph Spohn, a Creole from Louisiana, Thomas Camp, an Englishman, and I rode several miles down the stream on a pretty day, the ninth since our entrance into the Alamo, to view the old partly decayed missions that the Spaniards had erected here in beautiful style during the eighteenth century. All the buildings together with the church stood at one end of a square area of about eight to twelve hundred feet across, protected on all sides by high walls. Along these walls the Mexicans of San Antonio had lined up their corn bins.

We aimed to go to the mission of San José. Well armed, heavily loaded, and with a lunch of several fried ox-ribs buckled behind our saddle, we proceeded on our journey.

About a mile from the Alamo we saw the first comparatively well preserved church, called Concepción, in whose vicinity Colonel [James] Bowie and Captain [James W.] Fannin with eighty men had a battle with four hundred of the enemy a few days before the arrival of the Greys. Here the militia captured that pretty six-pounder that the first unit put into such good service against its former owners.

Fandango.

Painting by Theodore Gentilz, a resident of Castro's colony.
Daughters of the Republic of Texas Library at the Alamo.

On the other side of the old church we had to cross the strong current of the San Antonio, which was no small matter for our horses, as they had to go into the water up to their bodies. Two miles further on the right bank, however, lay the second mission to which we directed our horses. For quite a while we saw the steeple of its high dome projecting above the dense and dark magnolia and pecan forest; and after we passed a large corn field we saw the weather-beaten old buildings. It was an interesting sight to see in the middle of a jungle a ruin that reminded me of the Thuringian ruins of my fatherland. The grey stonework was endowed with the dignity of more age than it really had. The rough northwest storms had accomplished in a short time what would require hundreds of years from the German climate; in the hot South, also, everything ripens and dies sooner than in the cold sedate North.

The high arched door through which we just entered was the only entrance for horsemen; various cactus species covered every horizontal part of the walls. Several horses and fat calves grazed in the center of the square, but not a human being was to be seen in the whole plaza. We unsaddled in the middle of a ranch, and left it to our horses to choose whether they would take their noon meal with the other horses there or rest in the shade of the buildings.

As we entered one of the wretched Mexican huts, we found the whole company. There were probably fifteen persons seated on the ground busy with a mighty pile of pecans, opening them with great dexterity. In a dark corner sat several very old grey-headed men whiling the time away playing cards; they consisted of wrinkled skin and human skeleton. The drying atmosphere of the highland of Texas, it seemed, had not failed to affect them; and they seemed to justify the old saying of the Texans that the inhabitants of San Antonio never die, but gradually shrivel up and, feather light, are finally blown away by the wind. There are, in fact, some very old people here on whose faces one can barely discover the features of a human being for the wrinkles. But I am not quite willing to vouch for the blowing away part.

As we were very thirsty, we asked for a little milk, which was handed us, albeit apparently unwillingly. After we had bought a quantity of pecans, we set out for the church and the old cloister in the expectation of finding supplies of arms and food there. We planned to make a close examination.

The top of the steeple could be reached by steps hewn from several tree trunks. From here we had a lovely view. About us lay the forest out from which two other steeples at a little distance projected; before us lay the already described square; to the left rolled the San Antonio; behind us was that large corn field; and to the right the green savannah rolled away to the southwest. Everything except the prairie was encircled with the forests of the San Antonio. The prairie reached out over the distant rolling hills, and only occasional low mesquite trees stood on the plain among which grazed the herds of the inhabitants of the mission. No watch against the Comanches was kept, although these unwelcome visitors from time to time drove off some of their stock.

A few bats and even a screech owl flew away as we approached their retreats, and they fluttered about in the cool, dark high room of the church hall. In the desolate cloister building, which was immediately connected with it, only lived the aforementioned denizens of the night. Everywhere the floor was dug up and eaten through by destructive mice. In one of the rooms stood a large, black oak table at which the good monks must have emptied many a chalice toasting the health of the Indians, whom they were supposed to convert. A small dark room that we now entered showed the traces of devastation to a higher degree than the other parts of the ruin.

The floor was covered with lime and stones that had dropped down from the walls and ceiling. This appeared suspicious to us, and after a little scraping we discovered a loosened stone plate, which, on taking it away, permitted us to look through a narrow opening into a dark room, but we could not see the least thing. The sound of the stones that we threw in indicated to us that it was not very deep; and I decided to jump down while Tom got from our horses a rope with which he could draw me out again. After I had let myself down through the small opening as far as my arms permitted, I jumped down the rest of the way into the unfamiliar room, for better or for worse. Splendidly, our hopes were fulfilled. After about a ten foot drop I landed on from twelve to fifteen wagon loads of corn that the Mexicans had concealed here. And although it by far exceeded their needs, they would have let it rot here rather than to help support our army with it, notwithstanding the fact that we usually paid enormous prices.

After I had very carefully searched through every nook and had discovered nothing beside the corn, except a little exit that was barricaded with stones and through which a few rays of light penetrated, my companions drew me back up with ropes to the light of day. The stone plate was put back in its former position and we covered it over again like the remainder of the floor with lime and rubbish. And over it all we threw a layer of dust. Then we left the buildings, saddled our horses and hurried with the parting sun toward the town. The fire god had long disappeared when we rode through the long, dark entrance into the Alamo.

We immediately reported our discovery to the general-quartermaster, who paid much attention to such a welcome treasure as this one, considering the scarcity of food. Early next morning six wagons under the guidance of myself and assistants to the quartermaster journeyed to San José to get part of the corn. Soon we were in sight of the old ruin; and as our wagons drove through the high doorway to the small entrance that had been so artfully concealed from the outside by a pile of stones, the Mexicans, who were so sullen yesterday, came out and tried to bribe my companions and me with a pair of pretty horses that we had admired yesterday, but this only inclined me against them rather than for them. Then a quarter of a hundred women and children came and they succeeded by their lamentations to induce us to suspend the loading of the corn. They maintained that this was all that the families had to live on until the next harvest.

As we volunteers knew well enough how much was necessary for one meal but did not know how much would be needed for eight or nine, I decided to ride to headquarters with one of the Mexicans to speak with the officers themselves about the matter, while the wagons were to wait for my return. As it was getting late, we rode rapidly toward the town; and as darkness was about to set in, our horses were foaming in front of the quarters of our officers. My companion presented his case with Mexican cunning. And the officers were already inclined to believe him and to issue orders not to disturb the corn, when an old Mexican and Deaf Smith stepped forward and said that the present inhabitants of the mission had always been the most bitter enemies of the Americans and that San José concealed a proportionately larger amount of corn than was necessary for the families, as they had sold large quantities in San Antonio every year and that their present conduct was pure hatred for the army.

After both sides had spoken, I received instructions to take only three loads thereof and to leave the remainder with the families.

The Mexican was overjoyed to get off so easily and to receive such a good price for the three loads. He was so elated that he spent the night doing the fandango. I, however, mounted my horse and, with my gun before me, trotted off toward the mission. Since Comanche signs had been seen several times during the past few days, I cautiously looked in all directions; I definitely cherished no desire to let myself be scalped. While my whole attention was thus focused and watching for various objects as they appeared from time to time, I rode forward on a wrong road which, although the distance seemed long, I did not notice until I was frightened by a powerful noise caused by thousands of cranes flying up from a pond just as I rode out of the prairie into the forests along the banks of the San Antonio. The flapping of their wings and their loud, repulsive, confused quacking caused such an uproar that my usually gentle horse made a violent jump to the side. Trembling all over and snorting intermittently, it stretched its head forward to determine the cause of the nocturnal disturbance.

Evidently I was on the wrong road and, therefore, obliged to turn back. After I had returned to the prairie I decided, after wandering around a while, to pitch camp for the night in the tall grass. After I had hobbled the fore feet of my horse, as usual, and had spread out one of the blankets on the grass, I threw the other one over myself and over my faithful gun in order to protect both from the heavy night dew; the pistols and the saddle served as a pillow. But barely had I wrapped myself up so comfortably, when several shots at close distance caused me to jump up again. Speedily my warhorse was saddled, and cautiously I rode off in the direction where just then another shot had fallen.

I might have been barely a hundred yards away from my camp, when a dark object that I soon recognized as the steeple of San José rose above the forest before me. In a few minutes I again joined my comrades, who had worried about me and who, since I had promised to be back with them by midnight, had sent me signals.

Next morning, with our welcome provisions, we entered San Antonio where all the troops, reinforced with a new company from Mobile, Alabama, also called Greys, were holding a grand parade at which Major [Robert C.] Morris was commanding officer.

At the same time it was decided today to march off to Matamoras on the 30th of December, and everyone who wanted to take part in the expedition was instructed to be ready by that time.

Half of our company and a smaller part of the others remained back to protect the fort in San Antonio, and the rest of us, including four Germans, joined with the Mobile Greys under Captain [David N.] Burk[e]'s command, since we did not like at all a military life that was too quiet.

25 Inhabitants of the countryside.
26 Tobacco wrapped in dry corn leaves.

CHAPTER ELEVEN

The Departure
for Matamoras

~

THE THIRTIETH OF DECEMBER ARRIVED, and we took leave of our friends who were to remain here, never suspecting that they would fight sooner than we and that this would probably be the last time that the Greys would shake hands in a brotherly manner.

The cannon thundered a last farewell after us, and we camped the first night on the Salado [River] only six miles from the Alamo. It was the same place where General Cos and his troops—and a few days later a troop of Comanches—had camped.

On the second day we marched through the deep, densely forested valley of the Cibola [Creek], and again, as further up where we had crossed it the first time, practically the whole stream had disappeared, and only a little brook wormed its dwindling way down the channel. That night we camped at Seguín's plantation that lay on the approximately eighty foot high bank of the San Antonio River.

Juan Nepomuceno Seguín followed his father Erasmo Seguín's lead of friendship with the Texans. The Seguín ranch near San Antonio was a favorite stopping-off place for Texas travelers and also the Volunteers. Juan fought at the Storming of Bexar, and then joined Travis at the Alamo. An expert horseman and cavalry captain, Seguín was sent out with a plea for reinforcements. As lieutenant colonel Seguín, he commanded San Antonio in the post-war era. He was elected to the senate of the Republic of Texas.

Art by Jefferson Wright,
Archives Division, Texas State Library, Austin.

We left the plantation the next morning and marched down on the left bank of the river toward the little fort of Goliad, which with La Bahía, a little town, is about 105 miles from San Antonio. We decided, therefore, to await reinforcements and then to undertake a major strike on Matamoras. Colonel Johnson and Major Morris were in command, but in reality it was [Dr. James] Grant, the beloved Scot, who led us, in spite of the fact that he constantly refused to be regularly elected.

The sixth day showed us again the waters of the same stream that pushes its way between the Alamo and San Antonio. On the right side and about a mile from the ford lay La Bahía and a little higher up, the little fort, Goliad, which a few Texans under [Philip] Dimmit had recently captured from the Mexicans.

For a few days we lay on the left side of the stream, where we drove up several herds of horses and selected the best ones for our use. Here we followed without success a small group of Indians that had attacked several ranches.

Finally, on the ninth of January, we marched through the deserted streets of the town, and only occasionally one could see the wrinkled face of an old Mexican looking out of the little loopholes that served the log cabins as windows. The larger buildings were deserted and their inhabitants, also, had taken refuge on their ranches along the wooded banks of the San Antonio at the beginning of the war, where they decided to await the results of the war; others had openly treated us as enemies and they had hurried off to the Rio Grande to move against us with the invasion of Santa Anna's first mercenaries.

Our numerous assurances that we had taken up arms only to protect the nation and the Mexican confederation and that no Mexican would be compelled to bear arms in the war for freedom, availed nothing; even Colonel Grant, who had lived a long time in the northern provinces of Mexico and who had at least the appearance of being highly respected by the inhabitants of that section, urged them in a friendly manner to unite with us and to shoulder the muskets for the general welfare and to defend their herds and homes united with us against the oppressions of Santa Anna; but everything was in vain. They either moved away or lurked around, only to report faithfully our plans and movements to the usurper.

We here met a Doctor Bunsen from Frankfort on the Main, who had recently arrived with a company from Louisville, Kentucky, to participate in the storming of Matamoras. Also a certain Patten of the same place was in his company.

The total number of our troops now stood at six hundred men, and we were waiting only for gunpowder, lead and provisions to be ready to march. But these articles were to appear any day, and as one period after another passed by and we were, meanwhile, obliged to lie idle, a general feeling of ill-will broke out among us against Governor Henry Smith, who let the army lie idle here under all kinds of hardships. Instead, if he had supplied us with lead and powder, we might now have had Matamoras, which the enemy, since he knew our intentions, fortified more strongly each day.

Many, dissatisfied with the hesitating government, had already directed their steps northeastward back to their homes. But we had not considered that it might be as difficult for the provincial government to get moneys together as it was for us; not one citizen had paid in any money for the purchase of war supplies, and those supplies, which the generous citizens of the States had bought and gathered, were still en route by sea. The only mistake of the government was that no proclamation called upon the people to support the army. The collection of supplies would, no doubt, have been sympathetically supported everywhere, as everywhere the volunteers passed through the country, the colonists gave us from the best of everything that they had in the house and placed their herds at our disposal. Never could we ever induce the owner to take pay for them.

The army had now melted down to approximately 450 men. If the army were not to break up altogether, something had to be done to occupy the active, fiery spirited men.

In a general meeting it was decided to march to Refugio [pronounced Ray-foo-ree-o], thirty miles nearer our destination, and to wait there no more than eight more days. From the dispatches of the governor we could hope that certainly within this time a considerable detachment of volunteers from Georgia and Alabama under Fannin, who now was colonel, and a large consignment of supplies for the expedition would arrive. We left only a small occupation force in Goliad in order to guard the cannons and to restore the fort as much as possible. I cannot fail to mention here one of the most peculiar cannon of Goliad. It was a two-pounder that the Mexicans fastened on the back of a mule and used in the pursuit of the Indians.

The army directed its march toward the mission of Refugio, where it arrived two days after leaving Goliad. Like the mission buildings of San Antonio, the mission had been inhabited by Spanish monks whose object it was to Christianize the Indians. Now only the high, decayed walls and the weatherworn roof gave evidence of the Christianizing zeal of the Spaniards. Not only in the spiritual realm did the priests desire to rule, but they also desired to have physical power. Trickery and force of arms were alternately used against the wild and numerous inhabitants of the prairie. The Comanches tell even now of a frightful scene where around eight thousand of their tribe were killed.

Scattered about the church were the little houses of [James] Power's Irish colonists, who had only recently settled here. The place was located on an elevated prairie; and because health and contentment of the inhabitants beamed from their features, I believed that the climate here was favorable to Europeans. The splendid, fresh, green meadows on which numerous herds of cattle were grazing—each colonist owning at least from two hundred to five hundred head—made this little town one of the most pleasant in the former province of Texas.

Towards the southwest the Rio Blanco ripples down between tall rocky bluffs. It begins to be navigable for small craft within a half mile of here, from where it rushes toward the thick forests of Copano Bay. The tide of the bay drives the fresh waters of the river far back into the level country at regular intervals. Thousands of water birds swim about on the rising and falling waters, while there are countless numbers of fish in the water that come up into the country with the flood of the tide, and most hurry back out into the bay again with the ebb. The dense forests are alive with beautifully feathered southern songsters, and the pecking and knocking of the flocks of wood-peckers untied with the constant gobbling of the turkeys reveal to the hunter a hunting ground which cannot be surpassed any-where in the world. When one passes out of the dense forests that seldom permit a friendly ray of sunlight to pass through, up into the countless small savannahs [treeless plains], he discovers a country that is covered from November to May with countless groups of wild geese, which walk about unafraid among great herds of wild horses. Cattle and deer appear not to be any more afraid of the coyote or the large wolf than of any other wild life. One is charmed with the richness and fertility and the grandeur of the southern climate, and few would care to wish for them-selves a more beautiful paradise than this one.

The dwindling tribe of Carancahuas [Karankawas] seldom make inroads into this rich region in which their fathers, once a mighty nation, chased the fallow deer and peacefully enjoyed the wild honey mixed with roasted game; but those times have disappeared and that region abounding with game is void of people; their bones are bleaching on the prairies with those of the Comanches, their eternal enemies. The Carancahua tribe, which now counts only approximately thirty to forty men, now roams only near the lagoons and on the low, narrow islands of the Gulf along the Texas coast, where they take the redfish and the buffalo fish for their daily need out of the waters of the roaring sea.

It was in this lovely region, called by the Mexicans the El Dorado of the West, the army pitched its camp a little below Refugio during the latter half of the month of January, 1836. Here we waited in vain for several days for the arrival of fresh auxiliary troops and for messages of news from the governor, but neither appeared. We had already decided to leave without further delay on the morrow for the town of Matamoras [later spelled Matamoros], one hundred and sixty miles distant, when General Sam Houston,[27] the commander-in-chief of the Army, suddenly appeared in our camp. The various companies immediately assembled and surrounded the military leader, already renowned from Niagara Falls to the Rio Grande. His patriotism, his democratic views, and his liberal actions had won for him the general love and trust of all Texans, and he deserved them. Difficult were the problems he faced. He was to quiet down the restless heads, concentrate their forces, and prepare them for the work that had to be done with the approach of spring. The whole plan, to create a completely independent state, now stood clear and in the brightest colors before the mind of every citizen of Texas. The Mexicans, instead of supporting us in our efforts to throw off the yoke of tyranny, preferred to join the tyrant; and enormous preparations to destroy the settlers in Texas were being made by Santa Anna, eagerly supported by the priests. There was no other way open to us; either separate from Mexico and establish a new republic, or else leave all our property in Texas and flee over the Sabine into the States.

"Comrades!" began General Houston, "it is with pleasure that I find myself in your midst again after such a long separation, and I notice with astonishment that the keenest anticipations that I had of the patriotic spirit of the army, in reality, have been even surpassed. Comrades, we must seek to maintain such patriotic fire and not use it up where it will be of no benefit. Soon, friends, I believe, soon will the enemy under Santa Anna raid our peaceful savannahs, soon will their bugles urge their

*General Sam Houston,
the commander-in-
chief of the army.*

soldiers to our destruction; but that mighty word—freedom—
will inspire us, the thought of right, and of religion, of wife and
child, will make us heroes. And, disregarding the superior
number of the enemy, I hope that our army will defeat his purpose on the foaming Guadalupe; and before the next summer,
the flag of Texas, the true symbol of freedom, will wave in all
the ports of the land. But to be victorious, citizens, it is necessary
that we stand united, and that we extend our hands to one
another in firm union. Our weapons will be victorious—separated we shall lose.[28]

"You intend to take Matamoras. I praise your courage. But I
must candidly tell my friends that this plan does not please me;
I see no advantage that can emanate from it; I see only an
unnecessary sacrifice of the blood of Texans for a town that can
have no value for us and that lies beyond the border of our territory. If the enemy is to be harmed, let us await him and let his
forces, fatigued by long marches and privations, feel the work

of our guns. Let us prove to him what a nation can do which is united. Though weak in numbers, it will rise up en masse and boldly speak out: 'We want to be free'. Let us show them that when nations rise up for the cause of justice, the Almighty will carry the banner. But I see, comrades, by the expressions on your faces, the disapproval of my opinion; it is, however, my judgement; I want to act only in the interest of the new fatherland; but my voice is only one, that of yours is—to Matamoras. Well, then, to Matamoras be it. But at least wait a short time until the troops from Georgia and Alabama land, and, united with them, what power of the enemy can withstand us?"

The Artillery-Captain Pearson stepped forth and spoke to the army:

"Comrades! As much as I respect General Houston, I cannot approve his suggestion. We already have lain idle here too long and the consequence is that the larger part of the army has left us in disgust. Too long we have waited in vain for munitions; in vain we looked for reinforcements from day to day that the government had promised. It would be for nothing that we would stay here longer, hesitating, idle, enduring the hardships of a campaign. If we shall endure, let us be acting, and I herewith call on all who are in favor of an immediate departure for Matamoras. Colonels Johnson and Grant and Major Morris are in favor of the expedition and will participate in it. Once more, let us not hesitate longer, and, all who endorse my position, be ready at noon—to leave for Matamoras!"

These two speeches, coming one after the other, called forth various feelings, and as the army had voted decidedly for the storming of Matamoras, it was only Houston's eloquence and popularity that induced the larger part of the army to wait and to begin the march in conjunction with Fannin's reinforcements.

The Old General [Sam Houston] once again stepped forward to give us another sample of his eloquence, and I will try to write down a brief excerpt from his speech:

"Comrades, Citizens of Texas!

"Once more I come before you, and it is with the most fervent desire that this time my words will find general approval.

"Our proclamations to the other states of the Mexican confederation, asking them to support us in our struggle for the restoration of our former rights and for the protection of the Constitution of 1824, have, as you all know, been without results. Even many of the Mexicans who live between the Sabine and the Rio Grande have disdainfully forsaken the cause of freedom, and have not only denied us their support but also united themselves with the troops of Santa Anna and, as enemies, waged war against the land. Others have gone beyond the Rio Grande in order to smother us by combining themselves with the next best power. Still others have remained on their plantations on the banks of the forested rivers apparently to idly observe the war. These, comrades, are for us the most danger-

The Mexican federation of its states and territories.

Art by Terreblanca, 1828. In Alessio Robles,
Coahuila y Texas . . . and Weber,
The Mexican Frontier.

ous, because he who is not with us is against us. Also, from the otherwise liberal inhabitants of Zacatecas we have observed no movement in our favor. No other help remains for us now than our own strength and the knowledge that we have seized our arms for a just cause. (Hear!) Since it is impossible to call forth any sympathy from our fellow Mexican citizens and no support is to be expected from this side and as they let us, the smallest of all the provinces, struggle without any aid, let us then, comrades, sever that link that binds us to that rusty chain of the Mexican confederation; let us break off the live part of the dying cactus[29] that it may not dry up with the remainder; let us plant it anew that it may spring luxuriantly out of the fruitful savannah.

"Nor will the vigor of the descendants of the sturdy north ever mix with the phlegmatic attitude of the indolent Mexicans, no matter how long we may live among them. Two different tribes on the same hunting ground will never get along together. The tomahawk will ever fly and the scalping knife will never rest until the last of either one tribe or the other is either destroyed or is a slave. And I ask, comrades, will we ever bend our necks as slaves, and quietly watch the destruction of our property and the annihilation of our guaranteed rights? No! Never! Too well I know my people. The last drop of our blood would flow before we would bow under the yoke of these half-Indians. (Hear!) On my journey through the province I have had opportunities enough to learn the wishes of our countrymen. All of Texas is for separation. Even some prominent Mexicans who are living among us are preaching loudly that we should sever the bond that binds us to Mexico. 'Texas must become a free and independent state,' is the general word.

"A general convention of the representatives of the people will be held at Washington [on the Brazos] on the first of March of this year. It is the duty of the army to send several representatives; and I hope that my comrades will elect only men who will vote for our independence, who will fearlessly proclaim our separation from Mexico. And what they decide upon, comrades, we will defend with force of arms.

"My friends, I must ask for a few moments more of your attention. There is general complaint about the negligence of the government in supplying the troops with war materials. But to eliminate the causes for this complaint lies beyond the power of the governor. Ship loads are on the sea, and only unfavorable northwest winds have prevented their running into our harbors.

Possibly even now they may lie safe in Matagorda Bay, and the citizens will rush to deliver the cargoes to the army."

Loud applause greeted the popular general as he left the spot where he was standing, and all his friends and old comrades heartily shook hands with him.

However, a small detachment of seventy men, including the whole artillery company, insisted on immediately advancing at least to San Patricio [named for St. Patrick], forty miles nearer Matamoras, a decision they carried out that very day. They left us under Johnson, Grant and Morris, besides taking two pieces of artillery to immediately fortify San Patricio, while Colonel Grant with a small detachment intended to scout the western border and purchase horses on the Rio Grande for the whole army. Bunsen and Langenheim were with this expedition. On their departure we wished them good results on their undertaking and hoped soon to see the steeples of Matamoras united with them.

After General Houston's departure, our two companies, the Greys, crossed the river and camped two miles from Refugio not far from the plantation of a Mexican named Lopus [Lopez] who showed astonishing interest in the war for independence. We were soon to discover that he was a traitor. From here we made excursions into the surrounding forests and prairies and waited with great anticipation and longing for the arrival of Fannin, who was to land with his troops at Copano [pronounced Có-pa-no], fifteen miles away.

The remainder of the army was quartered with the citizens of Refugio and came over to us only when they wanted to catch fish and turtles. The other time they spent catching and breaking-in wild mustangs that ran about in small groups on the prairies between here and the bay.

As it was necessary for a small guard to go down to the coast to wait the arrival of Fannin and to immediately inform the army of his appearance, four other Greys and I volunteered to attend to this post for a week, which was approved. We immediately equipped ourselves. A young hog that we had killed constituted our main store of supply. Besides, however, we had a small quantity of dried beef, a small amount of corn-meal and a little coffee and sugar. Thus equipped we proceeded on our journey, our baggage and provisions being packed on one horse.

Although the ground was very dry, high sage-like grass covered the level country down to the bay. Groups of mesquite bushes and small tress concealed the coyotes, which were found here in large packs. They were not shy in the least. Surprised to see a caravan of this kind moving through their quiet domains, they left their retreats and trotted in rows a short distance away along side of us with their interesting heads constantly turned toward us. A hurricane-like wind was roaring from the Gulf over the prairie toward us. We would have liked to load our horses with wild geese that often came within reach of our pistols, but on account of the storm, they would not venture out of the tall grass.

When we were still eight miles from Copano, we could hear the roaring of the surf as plainly as if we had been in front of the foaming waves. Anxiously we hurried forward to get the first glimpse of the majestic mirror of the bay, which we expected at every turn of the road around a point of mesquite forest. But we constantly deluded ourselves. None of us had ever been in this region before. As we were just walking down a little hill that was uncommonly overgrown, we amused ourselves by setting the grass on fire. Barely had the flames taken hold when they rushed forward with amazing rapidity. Within a few minutes they disappeared beyond the hill, which we had just come down. The black stripe before us and the just as dark cloud of smoke that accompanied the fire indicated to us that the mighty fire column would soon pass our comrades at the mission. The screams of the frightened flocks of birds died down again. The thundering of the waves sounded ever clearer. We had just stepped out of a group of trees in that immense prairie that lies all along the coast of Texas.

The winter-bleached, open plain on which we now rode was encircled on the north by forests, while in the far distant east and west it rose to meet the moving sea of clouds. But to the south roared raging waves, whipped by the hurricane-like winds against the sandy shores of the bay. A lonely, one-story, wooden building, which had formerly served as warehouse for the goods of the people moving to San Antonio, stood on this incredibly beautiful shore.

Years ago the inhabitants of this heavenly landscape had left their lonely habitation. The only human beings that still frequented this place from time to time were the fishing Carancahuas or possibly [French colonizer Henri] Castro with his Lipans, who occasionally roamed this far but whose colony actually extended only to the right bank of the Nueces.

It was in this old warehouse that we established our quarters, and in spite of the winds sending fury on this stable but trembling building, we had soon started a merry fire on the wind-protected north side of the house and prepared dinner.

The first evening approached, and with the disappearing sun the howling of the storm died away. As it was very sultry and as we would rather sleep in the open than in houses, we lay down on the gallery. After we had stacked all of our belongings at our heads and placed our guns as usual under our blankets, we slept splendidly in spite of the roaring surf that rolled over Copano's beaches.

Towards four o'clock in the morning we were awakened by a strange noise, but we could see nothing that might have disturbed us. We were on the point of lying down to sleep again when we saw a number of dark figures at some distance on the prairie slowly approach us. In an instant, our guns were ready. Not a sound escaped our lips; no movement betrayed we were

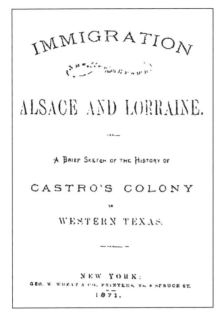

IMMIGRATION

ALSACE AND LORRAINE.

A BRIEF SKETCH OF THE HISTORY OF

CASTRO'S COLONY

WESTERN TEXAS.

NEW YORK:
GEO. W. WHEAT & CO., PRINTERS, No. 8 SPRUCE ST.
1871.

*Henri Castro of Paris France —
a Texas empresario of great
importance — carried on
colonizing in the manner of
Stephen F. Austin following
Austin's death in 1836. Historian
Amelia Williams wrote, "He is
more comparable to Stephen F.
Austin than is any other Texas
empresario." Castro was
responsible for first civilizing the
Texas land west of San Antonio,
pushing the Texas frontier
westward toward the Rio
Grande.*

awake. If we were quiet in comparison, our unknown enemies must have been dead—not the slightest noise revealed their movements through the dry grass, and still the group was approaching us. Suddenly the deadening lead took flight from our guns, and in a few seconds everything had noiselessly disappeared. We jumped up and approached the place to which we had fired. Although we were sure that we had hit, we found nothing.

The night was so exceedingly beautiful and we were so thoroughly awake that we sat down on our spread-out blankets near a small group of aloe plants and gazed out on the still restless waves that occasionally threw a fine spray over us.

The morning explained to us the adventure of the night before. Not very far from us lay two dead wolves, the victims of our guns. But imagine our consternation when we returned to prepare our breakfast and found that all of our provisions with the exception of the meal had disappeared. Even the coffee lay

spilled out about twenty
steps away. Imagine our
rage. Certainly each one
resolved henceforth to shoot
at every wolf that crossed
his path and not be as con-
siderate of them as we had
been the previous day.

But in order to get
breakfast we had to use
some other means besides
rage, especially as we had
no inclination to cut beefsteaks from the hind quarters of the wolves. Conse-
quently two men were sent out to hunt game, while I and
another went down along the bay for half a mile to secure a
load of the oysters that had gathered there in mighty colonies.
When we returned, the hunters had already brought in a turkey
and two ducks, and in a short time the fifth man, in spite of the
wolves, had prepared a brilliant breakfast that could not have
been served better by Jacob Astor in New York.

For eight days the clear open forest, the coasts of the bay,
and the water supplied us with fish, oysters and wing-game of
many kinds.

---

[27] Formerly senator in the States and also a one-time governor of Tennessee.
[28] United we stand; divided we fall.
[29] The Mexican coat of arms is a cactus with as many leaves as there are
states in the confederation.

CHAPTER TWELVE

Fannin's Landing

~

BY THE SEVENTH DAY, we had given up all hope of seeing run into the harbor the little flotilla that we had so anxiously looked for. During our watch period, we sat on the shore and looked at the undulating bay's enormous waves, the billows not breaking, however, before reaching the beach. This is how one generally sees the sea just before or immediately after a storm. Then one sees with amazement the water in terrible battle with itself, while great quietness prevails in the atmosphere.

But we didn't watch in vain. Just then there rose up out of the water on the southeast horizon what appeared to be two grey little clouds; to the eye they seemed man-made. As they approached us the mist disappeared, and the images of the little clouds turned out to be two proud and slender frigates that were speedily dancing toward shore under a light southwest wind in full sail on the rolling waves. From the openings (firing slots) the cannon thundered toward us a friendly greeting from Fannin's Free Corps, and their threefold "hurrah" greeted their new home.

One of our comrades rode in full speed over the prairie toward Refugio to announce Fannin's successful arrival. He arrived just in time to contain the dissension and discontent that had been occasioned by inactivity and would have led to the total dissolution of the army in a short time.

After a few hours the larger part of the troops were busy on the shore or on the waves, landing the supplies that they had brought with them.

Among the few companies I must mention here that excellent Georgia battalion under Major Ward, whose members were all herculean and muscular figures. But the best ones were the Red Rovers, well formed native sons of Alabama. All were dressed in brown hunting shirts and trousers and were armed with pistols and guns. Dr. [John] Shakleford, their captain, was respected by all as their father, because he was the only aged man [age 46] among them. His son and his [two] nephew[s] shouldered their guns also for the sake of our just cause.

It was ten o'clock at night and the bustle was not over yet. The entire shoreline was lighted with many watch fires, and instead of the howling of the wolves that in the previous night had roamed the savannahs, one could now hear the steps of the relieving sentinels and occasionally loud, hearty laughter from a group sitting around a campfire. But suddenly four riders on foaming horses from Refugio rode through the outposts. They brought dispatches from the government according to which all Texans should elect representatives today for the first national congress to meet on March 1, 1836. [The "Convention of 1836" that wrote the Texas Declaration of Independence and the Constitution of the Republic.] Since only two hours remained for holding the election,[30] the work proceeded rapidly, and by twelve o'clock we elected by an overwhelming majority candidates who favored independence.

The next three days were spent unloading the supplies and transporting them up to the mission. Shortly thereafter the frigates

Colonel James Walker Fannin.

turned their prows toward the sea. While the little cannon of
Fannin's people fired them a farewell, the star-spangled blue
field, the flag of Uncle Sam, waved wishes of good luck from
the slender mast-head down to the single star that beamed from
the light blue flag that led the Georgia battalion to the mission.

A few days after Fannin's arrival in Refugio, all of our
hopes were disappointed. The prospect of marching to Matamoras had disappeared, and many left the army again. Fannin
would have been glad to take part in the expedition, but he
feared—and he had reasons to—that he would not lead the
command if the generally very popular Colonel [James] Grant
was present. He, therefore, feigned other reasons and
remained steadfast in his decision to await the enemy on this
side of the Rio Grande. Consequently he marched to Goliad in

order to fortify the place and to make preparations for the spring campaigns.

That part of the army stationed at Refugio prior to Fannin's arrival had dwindled down considerably and remained as before in its old quarters. Captain [Amon Butler] King's company alone, that played a heroic role next spring, had melted down to thirty-one men.

The Greys marched to San Patricio to inform that little advanced detachment of the army of the present state of affairs and to induce the men not to expose themselves longer to the danger of being cut off from us; and should they still be unwilling to follow us, to induce them to at least put the cannon under stronger protection, either to turn them over to Fannin or to wait for the government to give orders about the cannons.

Our march led us over a high prairie that was strongly overgrown with mesquite bushes and on which many varieties of cactus covered large stretches of now very dry ground. Frequently we saw the neglected herds of cattle belonging to the former inhabitants of Irish descent who, practically all good Catholics, had moved over the Rio Grande in order to avoid coming in contact with a host of heretics like us.

Here also, as everywhere else, exceptions were to be found. An especially noble example of patriotism was displayed by a noble individual of this nation. Mr. Fagan placed his whole and not insignificant crop, and several hundred cattle, at Fannin's disposition without any prospect of ever receiving any pay for them, as it was possible only for a Texan to hope that we would be victorious.

As a warning to the lonely wanderer, several crosses stood on the side of the road. Beside the crosses rested the bodies of several Mexicans who had fallen under the scalping knife of the Comanches or the Lipans.

On the second day after leaving Refugio, late in the day, we arrived at the little, though neat and orderly laid-out and built,

San Patricio where, as mentioned earlier, only Irish lived.
[Town was named San Patricio (St. Patrick) Hibernia for the
Irish patron saint.]

[F.W.] Johnson and Grant with the rest of them had taken
possession of a few vacant buildings. Although many other
houses were unoccupied, we preferred to throw up our quarters on the edge of the forest that bordered the Nueces [River].
As we were very tired, our old companions soon had a row of
lively fires burning; and not satisfied with providing us with
provisions, they would not allow others to do the work of
preparing them, a custom practiced in general in the San Antonio army.

The next morning we were awakened to go hunting, as the
whole densely wooded Nueces valley seemed alive with
turkeys. Their cries sounded from every direction.

By nine o'clock approximately forty of them were in our
camp, besides several rabbits. These were the first real rabbits
that I had seen in America; they are fully as large as those in
Europe, but they have much brighter hair color than the European ones, as is the case with the smaller species that one finds
in the States.

The scenery was beautiful. While the left bank of the Nueces borders a perfectly level plain covered with a growth of
mesquite bushes, the opposite one revealed, after we had passed
through the dark forest of the valley, a cheerful, hilly region.
The prairie was decorated in places with groups of live oaks
and other varieties of trees. And at the foot of a chain of hills lay
a bright narrow lake whose waters rippled with fish. The Mexican government had turned over this region to a German so
that he might establish here a colony of his countrymen. The
disturbances in Mexico and then in Texas itself prevented the
execution of this plan.[31]

Colonel Grant had already bought a large number of horses
and was willing to leave for the Rio Grande in a few days to

supply the whole army with even more fresh horses, as they were unusually cheap on that river.

On the third day after our arrival at San Patricio we received news from Matamoras [Mexico]. The citizens of that city were hoping we would appear. Then they would seize their arms and drive out General Cos, who was now commander there. Since so many contrary reports from there had come to us, we did not trust them. Although Colonel Grant tried to put us into a position with approximately one hundred and fifty men to attack the city by night, we considered it such a foolhardy undertaking that we could not pay attention to it for a moment. We would not rely so easily on the persuasiveness of the inhabitants on the other side of the Rio Grande as Colonel Grant really did. This gullibility was Grant's only weakness.

In vain we tried to induce him and his little division to retreat. Since we were aware of their bitterness toward Fannin, we proposed returning to our old San Antonio; but not one man was willing to follow our advice. And after a few days we were obliged to leave with only the cannon. At the same time Grant and Johnson rode off with their units, however, in different directions, through the mighty Tamaulipas prairie to their destination, the Rio Grande. They left us with the promise they would follow us within six weeks with enough horses for the whole army.

Nothing of importance transpired on our march back to Goliad, where we arrived the beginning of February. From Goliad we wanted to march back to San Antonio to meet there with our companions who had remained behind. Fannin's commanding the army remaining at Goliad did not please the free principles of the Greys.

However, we were obliged to stop there for a while at least, as Fannin would not give us of his provisions except for the period of time that we remained in his place. He assured us, however, that he was shortly expecting the arrival of two ships in the Lavaca Bay that were being loaded in New Orleans with all kinds of supplies. So we remained and began busily with Fannin's troops to fortify the fort which, with the cooperation of several Polish officers, soon took on the appearance of a fortress; and except for treachery, the Mexicans would barely have succeeded in taking this fortress from a Texan garrison, even though small. It lay more advantageously than the Alamo and was not spread out so much.

Our business was now to demolish the low buildings around the fort under whose protection the enemy could approach unhindered quickly up to the walls, and to destroy the four- to five-foot-high and three-foot-thick hedges. To do this destruction, we used wind and fire. After a few days the artillery had an open view all around.

[30] At 12 o'clock sharp, the lists are closed at elections.

[31] This area is still free and the land is the property of the government. I wouldn't know of any stretch of land more suitable to Germans; the climate is healthy, cool, and beautiful. The soil is rich and a navigable river is nearby, as is the Corpus Christi Bay from where the farmer can transport his products to any market. Also, we must mention the proximity of the Mexican border, in the direction of which significant trading is going on.

CHAPTER THIRTEEN

The Opening of the Battle of 1836

IT WAS TOWARD THE LATTER PART OF FEBRUARY that dispatches arrived from the government and from New Orleans newspapers that told us of the defeat of the Blues who had sailed to Tampico.

General [José Antonio] Mexia, who during the battle of the individual [Mexican] states of 1833, had fought against the destroyer of the Constitution of 1824 [by leading an uprising against forces of Antonio Lopez de Santa Anna], had been forced due to Santa Anna's numerical superiority to clear the field and, with the loss of the battle, to flee from Mexico. Living in exile in New Orleans since that time, he was hoping that Mexico's lucky star would rise again some day and he determined in that event to draw anew the sword for his unfortunate fatherland. But he wouldn't have to wait long for such an opportunity.

Santa Anna personally gave him the opportunity, in that he pardoned General Mexia and sent him thirty thousand dollars

José Antonio Mexia, in June 1834, while serving as a member of the Mexican Senate, led an uprising against forces of Antonio Lopez de Santa Anna and was exiled from Mexico. Even earlier he had accompanied Stephen F. Austin on Mexia's Expedition.

with which to purchase arms and other war supplies in the States for the campaign in Texas. Mexia was to return with these to his home. 'Tis true, Mexia bought arms, but not to deliver them to Santa Anna and become a traitor to his country; but, on the contrary, to use them to equip several new companies that were gathering in New Orleans. With these he sailed on two schooners to Tampico. His purpose was to once again raise the tri-colored flag from there for the restoration of the Constitution of 1824, and from Tampico to act in conjunction with the Texans. He was influenced in coming to this decision by several Mexican army officers who were in secret correspondence with him and who promised him on their word

The flag that flew over the Alamo had three colors, green, white, and red, the same as the flag of Mexico, implying the desire for allegiance to Mexico if the Constitution of 1824 were restored.

of honor to go over to him with the troops under their command immediately on his arrival.

After the Blues had drawn down the sails outside of the well-known, dangerous Tampico sand bank, they waited for a small boat that was just coming down the stream from the town to tow over the foaming banks the unknown schooners, which it took for freighters. Soon they became in charge of the boat and directed the pilot to take the ships upstream and to cast anchor immediately in front of the city.

But they had barely gone half way when the schooners suddenly stuck fast as the pilot either unknowingly or intentionally had driven out of the channel and on to the sand bank.

Just opposite lay a little fort that commanded the river from which a boat was now coming to examine the schooners. The officers and men of it were immediately taken prisoners; and since everything was now revealed, an immediate storming of the fort was undertaken, which capitulated in barely a quarter of an hour.

All of Tampico was alarmed over the attack of the men who were believed to be Texans; and as Mexia and his troops, completely fatigued, arrived at the city during the night, everything had been prepared to confront them.

The battle continued until the dawn of day. The garrison had concentrated in a single position, and if Mexia's enticers had kept their word, Tampico would have fallen. Being either low or cowardly, they forgot their promises, and instead of going over to join the attackers, they opened fire on the attackers. After sunrise the attackers were on their way back to the little fort to return to Texas or New Orleans. But many were missing, and in another article in the *New Orleans Bulletin* we read where twenty-nine men of the Blues were shot on Santa Anna's order during the early part of February.[32] They had lost their way on land in the countryside or in the streets, and in this manner fell into the hands of the enemy. Two Kentuckians, when they saw that they were going to be shot, jumped forward against the soldiers and fought a desperate fight. But it was in vain. And although they wounded several, they were finally overpowered and, though heavily wounded, shot.

This was the prelude to the tragedy that was enacted on the western prairie during the next spring, when the Mexicans revealed the true color of their character.

From these reports we saw what fate awaited us if— through negligence or dissension on our part— the enemy should surprise us. The most advantageous time to march was now, arriving as the fresh grass was coming out abundantly. However, our widely known northwest storm, aftermath of winter, still blew across the prairie.

More bad news came a few days later. [Francis (Frank)] Johnson himself with the four remaining men of his detachment arrived from San Patricio. Five days before they had returned from the Rio Grande with several hundred beautiful horses and, as before, took up their quarters in the now completely vacated town. As the trip had somewhat strained the horses, they were turned out on the green meadow during the night and guarded.[33] Near midnight, as the guards sat unsuspectingly on their horses, they suddenly were surrounded by several hundred mounted Mexicans, who shot them down without mercy after the guards had defended themselves like mad, as several of the enemy subsequently admitted.

At the same time, the fatigued troops in the town were awakened out of their deep sleep by the enemy bugles sounding the signal for the attack. Several hundred enemy soldiers galloped through the streets with incessant shooting, calling out: "Viva Mexico! Down with the Americans! Death to all Texans!" They went into the scattered houses in which our people were quartered. A large group of the enemy now surrounded the log cabin which was occupied by twenty-two of our men, whose position was revealed by the still flickering fire in front of the door. Although the little house was surrounded by at least twenty times as many of the enemy, Johnson and five other men rushed out of the house and broke their way through the line. Only one of them fell and was killed; and when the enemy gave way and broke the circle in a cowardly manner, the remainder of our men rushed out onto the plains and headed in the direction of Refugio.

For several days they lived on cactus of various varieties with which this prairie especially is covered, as they had either forgotten or lost their ammunition in their haste.

Those who remained defended themselves in desperation. Already many were wounded, but they still continued to fire vigorously on the again encircling enemy, whose musket balls in conjunction with balls from the artillery punctured by the hundreds the walls of the log cabin. Suddenly there was a lull on the enemy's side, and those who were ordained to die could breathe freely again. A short stillness set in, interrupted only by the yelling of the distant Mexicans who were driving together the frightened horses. Then a Mexican officer stepped forward and offered the surrounded ones mercy if they would surrender without further contest. Since they had nothing to risk, several stepped forth; but Pearson and the others declared they would rather die fighting than surrender and be at the mercy of such enemies. But barely did the unfortunate ones stand before the house when a volley from the enemy wounded several and killed one. The others fled back into the house that they had just left, and all were now determined to sell their lives as dearly as possible.

The firing continued through the whole night, and only when the sun rose did the guns quiet down. Only occasionally did a single bullet coming from a crack in the block house knock down from his horse a Mexican countryman as he raced by.

Toward eight o'clock the blowing of the bugles indicated the arrival of a high officer, and soon thereafter several of the

enemy appeared with a white flag before the log cabin that protected the few still living heroes, and requested an interview.

Hope never seems to completely leave the human heart.
Practically all the wounded Texans again trusted the sham
promises of the enemy and soon stood among their ranks. But
only for a short time; before noon their bodies, full of holes,
watered the soil of the prairie with their blood.

Only two of them [William] Langenheim, the tall
Brunswicker, and a young Creole from Missouri, who spoke
Spanish, were saved for other sufferings.

32 Among them were several Germans.
33 Bunsen was among them.

CHAPTER FOURTEEN

March 2, 1836

ON THE FIFTH OF MARCH we received invigorating news from the General Convention at Washington [on the Brazos].

On the second of March our first congress had solemnly proclaimed the independence of the former province of Texas from the Mexican confederation and declared that the district lying between the Rio Grande, the Sabine and the Red River from this day would take its place among the nations of the earth under the name of the Republic of Texas.

Today was as stormy as was the jubilation that swept through the colonies, and the new star that waved over Goliad for the first time today trembled on the blue flag. But barely had it waved from the walls in its splendor for an hour when suddenly a new attack of the storm hurled the flag, star, and staff in a terrible whirl down into the fort. This was in fact an evil omen. But what state, just springing into life, will not have to battle against reverses for the sake of independence? After a short time the blue banner again waved among the raging elements. The storm soon abated, and the departing sun gilded the purple clouds that revealed the last traces of the departing storm on the western horizon.

The beginning of the new month brought us many important events. A new government with [David G.] Burnet as president and Lorenzo de Zavala, a Mexican, as vice president was installed. General Houston issued orders to destroy the fort at Goliad and also the Alamo, and for the troops immediately to withdraw behind the Guadalupe, as Santa Anna was said to be on the march to Texas with twelve hundred men!

Houston's orders probably reached Goliad in time, but not the Alamo, as a messenger

Left: Lorenzo de Zavala, 46, was elected ad interim *vice president of the Republic of Texas on March 2, 1836.*

Right:
David Gouverneur Burnet, 48, was elected ad interim *president of the Republic of Texas at the Convention of March 2.*

from there advised us that the garrison there, composed of 150 men, was already surrounded by several thousand Mexicans and had been summoned to surrender by Santa Anna. However, they indignantly rejected this. The courier reported that the blood-red flag waved above the enemy's camp, and the 150 of our men urgently asked for aid from Fannin and Houston. Houston, with five hundred militia, camped at Gonzales further up on the Guadalupe.

Another order from General Houston gave us the alternative of either retreating behind the Guadalupe or, if it were the wish of the army, to march on to San Antonio. In the latter case his troops and ours were to unite forty miles on this side of the Alamo at Ceguin's ranch [Erasmo Seguín's near present Floresville]. At the same time he observed that it was the wish of the militia, united with Fannin's unit, to rush to the aid of the force at the Alamo.

But Fannin was inclined neither for the retreat nor for the march to San Antonio. On the contrary, he would rather face the enemy in the fort of Goliad as fortified by him. In Goliad he held undisputedly the first position, which rank, however, he would have had to resign if he combined with the main Army. Our efforts to induce him to march to San Antonio were fruitless. In vain we pictured to him the fate of our brothers. Nothing could change his ambitious determination; he remained at Goliad. Often one could clearly see how ambition and contradicting feelings battled within him, and during one of those moments he gave orders to march to the Alamo. We camped on the other side of the stream and expected to break camp for San Antonio the next morning. Suddenly we heard the words: "Back to Goliad! The larger part of the troops prefer to defend the fort."

From where Fannin derived his conclusion that the Volunteers were not inclined to rescue the lives of their brothers in the Alamo was not explained to us, and without taking the vote of the army, everybody went back to Goliad.

The Greys moaned and complained about the fate of the besieged ones for whose reinforcement they had been on the march but were then detained by Fannin. Soon it was too late as Santa Anna in person closed in around the Alamo with seven thousand men, and every day the enemy moved closer and closer around the decaying walls of the Alamo. The garrison already had gallantly repulsed several attacks. Even if they could hold out for a short time, it was apparent that they would finally succumb. At the beginning, to be sure, it would have been easy to fight their way out during the night, but they did not wish to leave the walls that we had so honorably taken away from the enemy during last year's campaign.

At the risk of their lives, one or two came daily through the enemy lines and brought us the pleadings of the garrison and especially the private letters of [William B.] Travis, the commander, and letters from [James] Bowie and [David] Crockett.

William Barret Travis of South Carolina and Alabama, commander of the Alamo when it fell on March 6, 1836.

Archives Division,
Texas State Library, Austin.

James Bowie.

These two renowned backwoodsmen of North America begged the volunteers at Goliad to help save the Alamo.

As said before, Fannin could not be moved to evacuate Goliad, and he still believed that the besieged forces, if they wanted to, could surely withdraw. This is the only thing that I can say in his justification. I cannot believe that he feared to face the miserable and partly conscripted hordes of Santa Anna in conjunction with General Houston.

Another message of horror came to us from the southwest. The last three men of Grant's little detachment rushed into our fort and brought us details of the destruction of that gallant

David Crockett.

The Bowie knife.

Scotchman and his men. As they were returning home with approximately four hundred beautiful horses, their detachment of thirty men was suddenly attacked. On each side of the road were heavy thickets that converged toward each other a little ahead of them, where an opening of about one hundred feet remained. They were in the act of driving through here when several hundred enemy lancers streamed forth from the thicket, and without paying any attention to the riders, gave immediate chase to the horses. But Grant, who did not want to lose the horses and who had seen unbelievable examples of cowardice in these half-Indians, drew his sword and attacked the enemy at least ten times as strong as he. The guns of our troops immediately sent a number of the enemy to the ground. After the pistols also were fired, there was nothing left for them to do but to withdraw from the confusion and reload and attack again. The commands of Grant were drowned in the general noise and only a few could carry them out.

It was a terrible confusion; the hundreds of horses that were wild, as it were, became frantic hearing the firing and stampeded across the dry prairie[34] enveloped in a cloud of dust. With the exception of Grant, the Texans, who had no other arms than their guns, pistols, and Bowie knives, were now busy warding off the lances of the enemy. Woe unto them who fell slightly wounded from their horses, or otherwise did not sit firmly in the saddle and were thrown down! Woe unto them, as the whole herd of wild, panting, half-mustangs galloped over them and battered them to pieces.

The number in the troop of Texans got smaller and smaller. One after another, pierced by the lances, they disappeared under the all-destroying hooves. Only Grant and the three men who brought us the news appeared on the outside edge of this terrible whirlpool, and they would have been free to take flight if Grant, who saw several of his men still battling against enormous odds, had not rushed back into the whirling mass of confusion. Frantically he meted out stroke after stroke to the cowardly hirelings— he wanted to save his companions or die with them. Everything gave way before this gallant one as his Scottish arm and his Scottish sword whirled around, dealing death to the enemy.

After the other three men with him had loaded, they rushed after their leader to support him, but they had not reached the battling mass, when suddenly—Oh, pity!—the lasso flew through the air and, falling, looped the body of the noble Scotchman, who strove to throw off the claws of death. He struggled in vain, and with a "hurrah" from the hellish breed, he sank, torn from his steed, and disappeared like his comrades under the hooves of the foaming horses thundering away in a cloud of dust. Consternation pierced the hearts of the three that were approaching; a moment they stood still and gazed after the disappearing mass. Then all three, without saying a word, turned their horses toward the northeast and rode in full gallop along the road toward San Patricio.

Here they found the enemy already in possession of the town. Since it was dark, they rode right through between the outposts and did not discover their error until the bullets of the enemy guards whistled about their heads. Barely had they time to take another road when the bugles of the enemy sounded the alarm. But the good, faithful horses again strained their already exhausted strength and carried their riders safely and quickly far out on the open prairie, from where they again galloped away after a short rest. And after two days they rode slowly into the gates of Goliad.

The day after they came in, a considerable consignment of flour arrived in Lavaca Bay, and on this and the following days about eight hundred cattle were slaughtered, from which the meat was cut in long strips and dried. Great quantities of supplies were to be accumulated to avoid any suffering in case of a long siege.

A detachment of one hundred and twenty men went thirty miles down the San Antonio river to fetch a large quantity of maize that the planters there wanted to turn over to the army and to protect them from the restless Indians who (stirred up by the Mexicans in Texas) were making occasional raids. Our sleep on the plantation where we remained for the night was interrupted by Fannin's cannon, the pre-arranged sign that he was to send us if he deemed it necessary. We marched during the whole night, and by nine o'clock the next morning we had covered the thirty miles. Nothing of particular importance, however, happened. Only a few scattered enemies appeared in the vicinity of the fort.

A few days before, Captain King's company (which was, as previously stated, composed of thirty-one men) had been ordered down to Refugio to protect several families that had requested Fannin's aid against the Indians on their journey to

Goliad and the colonies. But these soon sent news that they were surrounded in the church by at least one hundred and fifty Indians and Mexicans and requested immediate help from Fannin.

The Georgia Battalion under Ward, therefore, was dispatched; but just as it arrived at Refugio, King was marching over the little Rio Blanco to pursue the enemy that had slyly fled. Ward also, who had heard of a little fort that was said to have been erected by the Mexicans and Carancahuas five miles from Refugio, departed the next morning to the designated region to destroy it. But as he found nothing suspicious, he returned to the mission. Barely had he re-entered the old church, when approximately six hundred cavalry of the enemy and a long twelve-pounder appeared on the opposite bank of the river and immediately began to bombard the church.

Toward four o'clock in the afternoon the enemy received several hundred infantry reinforcements which, like the cavalry, had come from San Patricio. The church was now completely surrounded, and several efforts to take it were bravely repulsed. But the Mexicans remained in possession of the low houses of the settlers that stood in moderate distance, and the Mexicans did some damage which caused the besieged to make several break-out attempts. Soon the buildings that were so dangerous for the Texans were enveloped in destructive flames.

During the whole night the Mexicans kept up vigorous fire. But barely had the midnight hour passed when the Georgia Battalion marched unnoticed through the encircling enemy line. It did not march off toward Goliad but, on the contrary, toward the sea coast, where they soon lost their way on the broad prairies.

The morning revealed to the Mexicans that they had wasted their powder during the night. They were on the point of leaving for Goliad to storm this fort in conjunction with Santa Anna and the remainder of Urrea's troops from San Patricio, when the unfortunate King and his company appeared on the opposite bank of the river. As he noticed the enemy and was at the same time noticed by the enemy, he took a favorable position in a little dense forest and defended himself with incomparable gallantry against the Mexicans and Indians that pressed in on him from all sides. Even to this day one hears them speak of King and his people with horror.

In vain General Urrea offered them honorable capitulation. Until now, however, surrender was out of the question, and the departing day saw the gallant defenders as victors. But when darkness set in, the little troop slipped through the tall grass and past the enemy posts. And they already believed themselves to be safe, when suddenly a hellish war whoop of a Carancahua broke the stillness of the night. In a few moments hundreds of Mexicans surrounded them, and further fighting would have ended with the destruction of all, although King was ready to fight to the last moment. But the repeated assurances from the officers present that they would be treated respectfully finally caused them to surrender.

The next morning, however, their bloody corpses lay about on the high banks of the Rio Blanco. Mexican bullets had murdered them, and the butt-ends of the muskets of the soldiers horribly smashed the skulls of any quivering bodies so that the brains spattered about.

Of King's unfortunate company only two Germans were saved, by a German also, a Prussian, who was an officer in the enemy artillery. His name is [Lieutenant Colonel Juan José] Holsinger, and he will be mentioned again later.

At this time the Mexicans living in Texas were sneaking from one camp to another. Where anything was to be gained, they served as spies. Nothing was sacred to them. This time, also, they were the first to bring us the news of King's destruction. But we hesitated to accept as true any information emanating from such sources.

34 The stretch of area between the Rio Grande to about several miles from the Nueces is desolate, dry, and lacking in water, and the traveler encounters only a few small brooks between San Patricio and Matamoras.

CHAPTER FIFTEEN

The Fall of the Alamo

FANNIN'S LITTLE ARMY MELTED more and more; we heard nothing further from the detachments that had left us. Enemy cavalry often appeared in sight, and Colonel [Albert Clinton] Horton and his thirty horsemen already had several skirmishes with them.

No courier appeared from San Antonio; the Alamo was too closely surrounded, and it was now a matter of impossibility to pass unnoticed through the numerous posts of the enemy.

Soon after King's battles and murder we received news from General Houston at Gonzales that did not leave us in any doubt about the unhappy fate of our comrades in the Alamo. The dispatch announced:

"The signals that some of my men were in the custom of receiving every morning at sunrise from the unfortunate Travis and his comrades have died away. It is possible that all our heroes are buried under the debris of the Alamo, whose walls were too dear to them to turn the trophy of the previous campaign back to the enemy. The

213

next point of the enemy attack is the walls of Goliad, and may the army there consider the strength of forces surrounding the walls. I, therefore, beseech you once again to make a speedy retreat and to unite with the militia behind the Guadalupe. Only if we are united will we be in a position to achieve anything. Furthermore, it will be impossible for me, in case the detachment at Goliad is besieged, to stake the fate of the Republic on a single battle in such an unfavorable position for our troops as are the open prairies. Therefore, once more, Colonel Fannin, move to behind the Guadalupe!

Sam Houston."

A little detachment of thirty militiamen had fought their way in broad daylight through the enemy lines surrounding the Alamo, and a few days thereafter the main attack began. After Santa Anna, the Napoleon of the West as this miserable braggart called himself, had been repulsed several times with severe losses, he took refuge in infamous trickery which consisted of his requiring several Mexican women to secretly sell poisoned food to the besieged ones. Trafficking food, although in secret, had taken place up to this time between the people of San Antonio and the besieged men. Consequently the latter did not at this time suspect the hellish plan. But soon some felt the effect of the poison, and presently death rolled through the veins of those who had eaten the food. Fortunately only a few had to suffer as only a small amount had been consumed up to then. But the gallant Bowie lay dying on his bed when the bugles from without sounded the signal for the attack.

Among the seven thousand to eight thousand men in Santa Anna's army there were twenty-five hundred men composed of criminals of the lowest kind who were being kept under the watch of the remainder of the army which, however, was not composed of much better elements.

This host of gallants was placed in front, and behind them were the cannon and the bayonets of the other soldiers. Those who were still in shackles had their chains removed, and the blood-red flag was placed in the hands of those who were about to die.

Santa Anna now stepped out in front of this herd that, clothed in rags as they were, with the Napoleon of the West in the lead, looked more like a bandit corps than an army.

"Mexicans!" he cried as he passed along the lines. "Mexicans! Today is the day you shall show the rebels the spirit that you have already proven to us in the fatherland. Today is the day that shall make you free and guiltless again if you will scale yonder walls of the Alamo and plant the flag that leads you on to the holy walls of the church; but today is also the day when your eyes will behold the blue heavens above you for the last time if the blood of the dogs behind the walls of the Alamo does not flow, and if your flag does not wave from the church instead of the star. As sure as your work is bloody, you shall surely fall with the cannon placed behind you and the bullets of your comrades if you don't do your job. Look behind you and behold the thousands of bayonets and consider the few in front of you. A bold attack and you are free.

"I know that you are courageous, and for that reason I am letting you do your own leading. But I shall follow for your protection. Consider once more, your freedom is at stake. Forward! Viva Mexico!"

The cannon joined the call, and the bugles accompanied the weak applause of the prisoners on whose features could be seen deathly fear. In despair they rushed forward against the cannon of the Alamo that immediately spit forth volcanic flames, and their grapeshot raised havoc in the ranks of the attackers. Two times the Mexican attackers turned to flee, and two times the artillery of their brothers struck them to the ground in groups. In despair they stormed forward once more to scale the walls, but only a few succeeded. Around the walls the dead human bodies were stacked up in layers, and over these Santa Anna now led the charge with fresh reserves. These also gave way before the now small group of defenders. But urged on anew, the troops rushed forward again. On the opposite walls just then appeared another detachment of the enemy. The wall was completely unguarded and their passing over could not be prevented by the Texans because of the shortage of men. Attacked from all sides, one little group of Texans after another fell and died the death of the hero.

Only David Crockett and six other men were still fighting when the corps of Santa Anna's troops passed over the walls. And since the last of the Texans had six to maybe eight loaded muskets lying beside them, these men heaped a pile of corpses around them. But finally, shot down by the bullets of the rejoicing enemies, they too fell.

Everything had quieted down and the dead men were lying about in the fort, when suddenly a man waving his arms wildly appeared on the ruins of the flat buildings and all alone defied the enemy. Wildly he cried: "A few minutes, only a few minutes, you bloodhounds, will you rejoice in the fruits of your victory, and then you shall fall victim to our vengeance!" With these words he fired at the moving mass and then looked rigidly down on the other side, where a single Texan, Major Evans, bleeding from many wounds, was rushing wildly toward the powder magazine with a burning torch in his left hand. He had not been noticed by the enemy, and with triumph the man on the wall followed all the movements with which Major Evans approached the magazine. The Mexicans stared in horror at the raging man without shooting at him. Swiftly he ran along on the old decaying walls, and from under his feet rolled the old masonry to a depth of approximately forty feet below.

Then did they first notice the wild man with the untamed flickering torch, without being aware of the danger that threatened them. A moment later the ruins of the Alamo covered the

The fall of the Alamo.

Mexicans and their victory. But before Evans could rush into the death-bringing magazine, he was pierced with a bullet and fell to the ground. A loud cry sounded down from the building; and as if he himself wanted to ignite the powder with the torch, the shattered body of the last fighter was hurled with a mighty force among the blood-thirsty enemy.

Colonel Bowie, who was lying on his death-bed, was stabbed by orders from General Cos. Two thousand, two hundred Mexicans covered the battlefield, and scattered among them lay the 180 men of the brave garrison.

Finally, but unfortunately too late, did Fannin decide to follow Houston's instructions. The affairs of the republic stood in a critical condition. San Antonio was lost; the volunteer army was practically destroyed; the enemy army of eight thousand to

Death of Bowie.
Art by Louis Eyth. Daughters of the Republic of Texas Library at the Alamo.

ten thousand men strong was in the land; there was no prospect for aid in case of a long siege; nor were there enough provisions. These were the important reasons that led Fannin to consider to evacuate and destroy Goliad. But so tenaciously did he cling to the walls of Goliad that he, in doubt, several times changed his already-issued orders.

CHAPTER SIXTEEN

The Battle of Coleto

~

UNDER THE LEADERSHIP OF COLONEL FANNIN we began on the 18th of April, 1836, our retreat from the demolished and partly still-burning Goliad, for whose fortification we had all worked with great zeal. A stack of dried meat from almost seven hundred steers and the remainder of our meal and corn was set on fire, and columns of smoke from them ascended to the cloudy sky.

All the artillery with the exception of two long four-pounders, a regular mortar, and a small mortar were spiked and left behind when we left the ruins at eight o'clock in the morning. Nowhere was there a trace of the enemy, only their spies, who for several days had revealed themselves westward toward San Antonio. The number and size of the provision and ammunition wagons that we took with us were too large and the power to move them was too small; so before we had gone half a mile, the way was strewn with objects of all kinds, and here and there a wagon was left standing or knocked to pieces. The rest of the baggage remained standing a mile from Goliad on the romantic banks of the San Antonio or was dropped in haste into the clear water of the river.

Chests filled with musket provisions or the belongings of soldiers disappeared into the water. All the horses and oxen were used to transport the above-named artillery, two wagons, and the powder magazine. In this way we went slowly forward without even getting to see an enemy.

Our route led us through one of those charming landscapes where little prairies alternate with thin forests of oak without any undergrowth. Frequently we saw herds of cattle grazing on the luxuriant grass; and immense herds of deer looked with amazement at the little army wending its way through the stillness of the west. The noble Andalusian horses, that had their beginning here with the horrible conquest of Mexico by Cortez, stampeded away in close formation over the undulating prairie, and long after they had disappeared one could still hear the rumble of their fleeing hooves.

Eight miles from Goliad begins a considerable treeless area known as the nine-mile prairie. It was in this prairie that the army had wearily advanced from four to five miles by three o'clock in the afternoon. I and a few of my friends who were bringing up the rear-guard were about two miles behind with instructions to keep a watchful eye on the forest, which was several miles to the left of us. Since not the least trace of any enemy had shown itself so far, we rode on without a worry, until we accidentally turned around and noticed at a distance of about four miles a figure in the area of the forest through which we had just come that looked like a rider on horseback. Since, however, it did not move, we came to the conclusion that it was a tree or some other lifeless object. Without taking further notice of it we rode on. A quarter of an hour might have passed; and as our army at a distance of one to one and one-half miles was moving at a snail's pace ahead of us, and as we did not wish to catch up with it, we decided to halt a little while to graze and rest our horses. Only now, as we looked about the immense prairie to enjoy the beauty of the scene, did we see behind us near the edge of the forest a long black streak on the plain. It was impossible for us to see what it was. A few thought possibly they were large herds of cattle that the settlers were driving eastward out of reach of the Mexicans. But this seemed improbable as all of those that stood on the side of the Texans had cleared the region west of the Guadalupe, since they would rather lose everything than to further bear the yoke of Santa Anna. As we looked more intently and observed the disturbing object more closely, we noticed a motion and a twisting in the dark mass that grew larger and larger and, in proportion to its approach, became clearer all the time. We could no longer doubt that it was the Mexican cavalry following us in full gallop! Hastily we mounted our horses and dashed off at full speed to our comrades to prepare them for the encounter with the enemy. The news was received with a hurrah. Everything was at once prepared for battle. We proceeded as rapidly as possible, albeit very slowly, in a square formation. Fannin, our commander, was a courageous and spirited warrior, but as commanding officer who should act with independence, understanding, and decision, he was totally unfit. Instead of trying to reach the forest one mile away for the sake of our safety, where the Americans and the Texans would be invincible, he decided to offer battle on an unfavorable, open terrain.

The Mexicans sped up and at a distance of from five hundred to six hundred yards gave us a volley from their carbines, to which, however, we paid no attention as the bullets flew in respectable distance over our heads. Only occasionally a bullet would whiz up entirely exhausted as if it were breathing its last breath and strike the ground in front of us without even knocking up any dust. Only one, an innocent little thing—the marksman probably never suspicioned that he was so close that he could kill a person—whistled through between me and the man next to me and tore off a part of the cap of my friend Thomas Camp who, after me, was the youngest man in the army.

We remained completely passive and let the enemy approach. They fired volley after volley at us as they came nearer. Our artillery officers, mainly Poles and tall, fine men, patiently waited for the time when they could reply to the unholy greetings to advantage. The moment arrived, our ranks opened, and the artillery hurled death and destruction among the enemy. Their horses reared up wildly from the confusion of battle and terror.

The effect of our fire was frightful. Herds of horses were running about without riders, while others were wallowing in blood and kicking about furiously. The resulting confusion to some extent retarded the attack of the enemy, and consequently we began to move forward again. But we could do this undisturbed only for a short time as we were soon threatened with a new attack. Fannin ordered a halt in spite of the fact that his attention was called to an enemy corps that was pushing through the forest to our left, which probably intended to cut us off from the woods ahead, while the detachment in the rear of us only aimed to detain us. Either Fannin did not grasp the danger of the situation or his ambitious nature held him back, because someone else had discovered the maneuver of the enemy before he did.

Finally, after we had repeatedly protested to him in vain that it was imperatively necessary for us to get to the woods, the Greys felt obliged to indicate to him that they would march off alone. But now it was too late. The enemy already appeared on the elevation ahead of us, and we had no choice but to fight our way through them or else give battle in our then most unfavorable position. Fannin was for the latter; and before the captains, who had assembled for consultation, could reach a definite conclusion, the countless bugles of the Mexicans from all directions sounded for the attack. The cavalry itself rapidly advanced from all sides at once, not enclosed ranks but in broken formation and with yelling and constant firing.

Their wild cries, with which they sought to intimidate us— because they could not do it with their guns—stood in clear contrast with the composure of our people, who waited for only the best opportunities to use their guns. The thunder of our artillery soon came in rapid succession, and the cannonballs flew devastatingly among the enemy. As the attack of the cavalry had so far been fruitless, all of his forces, since the infantry had just arrived, were now put into motion by the enemy, and we were attacked from all sides at once. Besides this, cooperating with the Mexicans were three hundred Indians of the tribes of the Carancahuas and Lipans crouched in the tall grass on the left of us toward the San Antonio River. We did not become aware of this contemptible and—on account of his hidden position—dangerous enemy, until a number of our people had been wounded by their bullets. Whereupon we sent a few loads of grapeshot into the tall grass. That freed us from them a moment, as they hastily fled in every direction.

Meanwhile the enemy infantry, that had combined with the cavalry, advanced step by step with constant but irregular firing. Now we also made use of our guns and sent well-aimed shots into the advancing hosts. We were soon enveloped in such dense smoke that we were occasionally obliged to cease firing and to advance slightly on the enemy in order to see our sights. The whole prairie as far as one could see was covered with powder-smoke, and thousands of lightning flashes quivered through the dark masses accompanied with the incessant thunder of the artillery and the clear crack of our rifles. Among them sounded the scattered bugle calls of the Mexicans, encouraging the men to battle. From time to time our grapeshot hailed death into the ranks of the enemy under the majestic roll of thunder. I do not believe that a coward was to be seen on the battlefield at this moment. Who has time in such tumult to consider his own life! Who is not inspired by the lusty blowing of the bugles and the thunder of the cannon? One pays no attention to death that reaps its harvest. All his senses are dulled. One sees nothing, one hears nothing except his enemy, and only partially does one hear the commands of the officers. That is the way it was with us. As the dense smoke only occasionally permitted us to see the advancing troops, we stepped forward to meet the enemy. Foolhardily, several of us stood in his midst and fired.

I myself had gotten so far ahead in the general tumult and fired so incessantly that I did not notice how I stood right among the Mexicans. Everything was confusion and it seemed as if we were shooting each other down for pleasure. When I discovered my error, I hastily went back to my position, and besides, my rifle's ignition-tube was stopped up. On my return to my comrades, I stopped at each fallen enemy and took their often loaded musket, and fired the living muskets.

But how did things look in our camp? Many of our people were either severely wounded or killed. All of our artillerymen with the exception of one Pole had fallen and formed a wall around the now silent cannon, which were no longer effective as the range was now too close.

The whole battleground was covered with dead men, horses, guns, and all kinds of objects. I did not spend much time in looking at the battlefield, but ran about to try out the guns of the fallen ones, as quite a while probably would have been necessary to put mine in order again. I searched a long time before I found a usable one, as the damp, almost wet, air had made practically all unfit for use. Fannin himself had been wounded three times. The third bullet had penetrated through a waterproof coat, a summer coat, the trousers, a pocket in the overcoat in which he had a silk handkerchief, and into the flesh. But strangely enough it did not tear through the handkerchief; and as he pulled it out, the bullet fell on the ground. Only then did he feel the pain of the wound.

It was now between five and six o'clock. So far the enemy cavalry had tried in vain to drive its horses against us, because the terrible effect of our artillery and gunfire brought all their efforts to nought, and they had to retreat.

Their infantry also was compelled to follow without waiting for the signal to retreat, and our cannons, now operated by the Greys, sent their parting greetings after them.

Some seven hundred and forty enemy soldiers lay on the prairie; but we had lost about the fifth part of our men. With the exception of the slaughter at San Antonio, this likely was more than ever before had fallen in any Texas battle.

Meanwhile the enemy remained in possession of the little elevation and seemed willing to renew the attack the next day. The night that we had so anxiously looked forward to came soon after the close of the battle, but it was to be no period of recovery for us. A fine rain was falling and spoiled the remaining good guns that we still possessed. Every moment we expected to be attacked by the enemy, who had posted themselves in three detachments around us. The first was placed toward Goliad; the second, on our way to Victoria; and the third, to our left and equally far from the other two so that they formed a triangle. Their signals indicated to us their exact positions. Under these circumstances it was impossible for us to retreat without being noticed. No other way lay open to us than to spike the cannon, abandon the wounded and all the baggage, set our guns in order, provide ourselves with sufficient ammunition, and fight our way through the enemy, that is, through that detachment that blocked our way to Victoria. If we could only reach the forest we would be safe, and then no power that Mexico could muster would be capable of a successful fight against the Texans. The Greys would rather sacrifice a part of their forces for the young Republic than to knowingly leave their whole force to the gruesomeness of the enemy, upon whose honor and humanity we could not rely.

Fannin, however, was of another opinion. Was it possibly the three not very serious wounds that had exhausted his spirit and gallantry, or was it the groans and wails of the dying—as practically all of the wounded would die because the enemy here also used mainly copper bullets—or was it the hope that our advance guard, which had reached the woods before we noticed the Mexicans, would return with help? Only from the thunder of our artillery could they infer that we had been attacked, and then, as the echo hummed through the forest, it was too late for them to reunite with us since, as stated before, the Mexicans had surrounded us. They were thus also cut off from us. Consequently they could not do anything except to ride hastily to Victoria ten miles away and to lead the militia there (erroneously reported up to six hundred men) to our rescue.

Fannin constructed his plan on this hope, and in vain we pleaded with him to use the darkness of the night to cover his retreat. He decided to remain and wait until eight o'clock in the morning. If no help should appear by then, we could beat our way through the ranks of our contemptible enemies by day; and if we could not be victorious, we could, at least, die fighting.

"Until then," he said, "Comrades, grant my words consideration; listen to the cries of pain of our brothers whom the skilled hand of a surgeon can save from the hands of death! Are we willing, are the Greys of New Orleans, the first company to enter the field for freedom, willing to leave their wounded brothers to horrible death that the barbarous enemy has sworn to them? Friends, once more, I beseech you by the patriotic and humanitarian feelings that live in your hearts, do not forsake the helpless ones here. At least give them protection until the break of day. If no help is here by that time, fellow citizens, do your duty; I will follow you!"

We felt the seriousness of the moment and the heavy responsibility of our plan and hesitatingly remained. Sadly and without consolation we stared into the night. What awful choice; to leave our friends and brothers to certain death, or to sacrifice ourselves for them! Our hope for reinforcements from Victoria was very weak, as we were not convinced of the truth of the rumor that militia were present.

But we resigned ourselves to our fate, to wait for the next day. Meanwhile our few vehicles, dead horses, and other solid materials were laid up around our camp as breast work in case of another attack.

The groans of the dying friends and enemies near and far were heartbreaking. With shudders we heard their moanings and the hollow noises of the construction of the breastworks as they sounded through the black night across the dark savannah.

At regular intervals the signals of the enemy sounded toward us. Otherwise everything was quiet, not even a breath of air moved. Only the cold misty rain helped to stiffen the half dead bodies of our comrades; while others, who were burning with horrible fever perhaps caused by poisoned copper bullets, were pleading in despair for water—only a swallow—only a drop.

But there was not a drop to quench them; we had nothing to give except our heart's blood. God alone could help. He heard, He saw everything, and helped. A fresh rain cooled the bodies from without; and with the gradual disappearance of the outward heat, the terrible inward fever subsided also.

To combat the stiffening of my own joints, I walked up and down in the camp, while I cast useless glances into the impenetrable darkness.

No rescuing sound could be heard from the east, no star was to be seen on the horizon, no hope flickered in the heart. Words in broken German awakened me from my thoughts.

"Friend," it said, "lay this carpet bag under my head for me!"

I did so and asked in German the name of the unfortunate comrade.

"I am—a German," was the answer. "Oh," he continued, "I would gladly—gladly—have fought—ten more battles for Texas—but it's over—with my labors—I'm done, my countryman—I am dying—my name—Eigenauer from—Lauterback—friend, if you ever get home again—think of me—my old mother still lives—write—I died—for Texas, write I died—for Texas, write her—my country—all—all—"

He had to be silent; death sat on his tongue. Three bullets had passed through him after he lay bleeding on the ground. I heard his last groan—and I went out—toward the enemy.

Black figures not very far away passed by me from time to time. They were the Indians, who were carrying off the fallen enemies to conceal from us their real loss with the coming of day. Gloomily I wandered about, and only with the breaking day did I return to camp.

Everybody was already awake in our little fort. Quietly and expectantly our looks wandered over the forest wall from where our expected rescuers were supposed to come forth. But with the advance of day our hopes, on whose fulfillment Fannin had yesterday believed so faithfully, began to disappear. Doubt after doubt rose up like thunder clouds, as to whether the entire report that there was a large number of militia at Victoria had been false, since it is difficult in such thinly settled country to receive quick and reliable news.

The artillery of the enemy that had not yet arrived on the battlefield yesterday was now planted in position this morning with the detachment that blocked our way to the woods. Our labors during the night were now in vain. The enemy commanded the elevation, and our breastworks were useless as enemy artillery could now reach every nook and corner of our camp, a circumstance that hadn't been noticed yesterday in the heat of battle.

We could not remember ever having seen Fannin, usually so gallant and at times almost rash, so undecided as he was during the last eight days. Especially since yesterday it seemed that one plan after another passed through his head. The sheer number of those plans seemed to confuse him and to hinder him in his usually prompt manner of reaching a decision on a given matter and putting it into speedy execution.

The groans of our wounded had now ceased. They had died either from their wounds, or from the cold and wetness of the night, or the rain had somewhat alleviated their pain. Scattered far and near about our camp lay dead Mexicans that the Indians either had not found or could not carry away. A few of our men went over to view the dead bodies of the enemies, and not very far from us they found the banner of the Mexican army under a pile of dead riders and horses and brought it into the camp. But no rejoicing hurrah came over our lips. All knew that the deciding moment, that was to decide life and death, was soon to strike. The flag was thrown without a thought on the debris of our camp.

It was approximately seven o'clock when we had given up all hope for reinforcements and had assembled to decide on which manner to attack the enemy and on how we could beat our way through, when suddenly the Mexican artillery bellowed out a good morning to us and grapeshot whistled through and over the assembly, which at once caused us to decide to attack the detachment on our road with our guns and Bowie knives in order to get to the forest. Everything was in readiness; even some of the severely wounded would rather die fighting than be helplessly murdered.

Look! Unexpectedly a white flag, the sign of peace, rose before us and stopped us from moving. Being suspicious, we still wanted to carry out our plan, but Fannin's command stopped us in our tracks.

New hopes had arisen within him to save the men, who had been placed in his care and who were in this desperate situation because of him, even if it be through honorable capitulation.

Three delegates of the enemy approached our camp, two Mexican cavalry officers and a German who had worked himself up to colonel in the artillery and had won the favor of Santa Anna. He was, if I am not mistaken, from Mainz and originally a carpenter. He probably possessed mathematical and architectural talent and had offered his service to the German-Mexican Mining company which, however, had not been accepted. Later he went to an English mining company and was hired by it and sent to Mexico. Here Santa Anna noticed his talents and had him build the beautiful castle Mango de Clavo for him. Through the construction of this castle that completely filled the expectations of the owner, Santa Anna got a very high respect for the knowledge of the builder (which in reality was only average) and employed him as an engineer in the army, where he was later advanced to Colonel of Artillery.

This German, [Juan José] Holsinger, was the only officer of the three who could speak English. The English conversation proceeded, however, in very broken English, so it was necessary first to translate our negotiations into German and then back into Spanish.

After long negotiations Fannin finally agreed that we should surrender all of our arms, that our private property should be respected, that we ourselves should be shipped through Copano or Matamoras to New Orleans and set free, and that, as long as we were prisoners of war, we should receive the same rations that the Mexican army received. Upon our word of honor, we obligated ourselves not to fight hereafter against the then present government of Mexico.[35]

After the Mexicans had ridden back to [General] Urrea, the commander of the Mexican army, to complete the ratification of the treaty, we stood around our colonel suspiciously.

The united volunteer Greys from New Orleans and Mobile protested loudly: "Forward! Is this the way that Fannin fulfills his promises? Is this his gallantry? Has he forgotten Tampico, San Patricio, and the murder of our brothers in the Alamo? Has living in Texas a long time not acquainted him with the character of the Mexicans? Never will the Greys agree to a capitulation that will remove them from their precious new fatherland. Even if the Mexicans were to keep their word this time, it will be the Greys who will not feel themselves bound by the terms of this capitulation. Citizens, comrades, we now appeal to you. You do not yet know the false character of the Mexicans. You have not yet had enough dealings with these barbarians to be able to judge them accurately. Believe the Greys; surrender, capitulation means in the Mexican language to die. If it shall be to die, let us die fighting for Texas, a sacrifice for freedom. With us hundreds—thousands—of the enemy will fall, and possibly we will succeed in breaking through their ranks, although they are probably ten times as strong as we. Think of the few of us who succeeded in taking San Antonio away from them. Two hundred and ten men against two thousand! Why should we not at least now risk the battle?"

Thus we spoke, but our speech had missed its purpose. The prospect of soon being back in the States again and of reentering upon their former conditions of life moved the other troops to give preference to the capitulation. Certainly the life of a soldier in the wilderness is difficult, and the privations that he must endure are many. But they did not know the charm of the life that the prairies, teeming with game, offered them. Like the red Comanche, one could hunt all seasons of the year. No worries about shelter, food, and clothing stress the fantastically dressed ranger. Everywhere he finds nourishment in abundance, and his few remaining civilized necessities are earned with the gun. Happy as he freely roams through the splendid west, he seldom sees the villages. But when election day approaches, when the highest officials of the land are to be elected, *then* the ranger stands with his fellow citizens to cast his vote in the best interest of his country.

It was, therefore, useless to talk against such inclinations. They decided gullibly to sign the capitulation, and the Greys and a part of the Red Rovers, who still held to their former position, were obliged to yield to the majority and like the others hand over their guns.

Inwardly deeply humiliated, which showed itself on our faces, we walked up and down in our camp, casting angry looks at Fannin and the others who had voted for the capitulation. Some sat lost in thought with eyes fixed stark on the ground and envied those who had died during the battle. Despair could be seen on the features of many of the men, who only too well foresaw our fate. Especially one American named [Edward Isaac] Johnson [of a prominent Cincinnati, Ohio family] stood out because of his anger. Gnashing his teeth, he stamped on the ground. Thick clouds of smoke from his glowing Havana cigar twirled about his head. Like the smoke from a steamboat, cloud after cloud streamed from his mouth, as these puffs of smoke came out. Denser and denser did the cloud mass become until it seldom revealed his head, in which it seemed a horrible plan was now being fabricated.

Curiosity had brought many Mexicans into our camp, and in company with the Greys they wandered over the field which was covered with debris and corpses. They glanced nervously at the stern Greys infantrymen, whom they had feared all the time, as if they were still afraid of them. However, their enemy, the Greys, who had driven their dried-up soldiers from house to house in San Antonio, stood now unarmed.

Now of course they looked down with contempt on the spectacle of having prisoners of the Texan army. Never before in their lives had they been so fortunate to experience a thing of this kind.

Group after group of the Mexicans crowded over into our camp to see the pretty guns that we had surrendered. Everybody was in fervent emotion—one side was possessed with the malicious joy of victory, and the other side, the Greys, felt shameful despondency. Suddenly a light flashed through the misty morning, a dull bang followed, and a terrible jarring of the air was combined with it. And then deathly stillness fell over the prairie, which was again covered with wounded men.

Impenetrable, suffocating smoke held down by the damp air rolled heavily over the dark green prairie. The horses of several of the enemy officers reared up wildly and, frantic with fear, rushed out with their stupefied riders in uninterrupted speed. The horses ran into the safe distance with ruffled up manes and flying tails. All of us had either done so ourselves or were thrown to the ground by the concussion and, after a while, still half stunned, we went toward the place where the explosion seemed to have broken loose.

The powder magazine had disappeared; only a part of the lower framework remained. Around the place lay several men wounded, although not severely, and about fifteen yards away from the wagon lay a black body that barely resembled a human being, who was still alive but not able to speak. It was burnt charcoal black like the color of a Negro, and it was impossible to tell who the unfortunate one was. Our eyes wandered around searching; the roll was called and the missing man was Johnson. [Refer to Book I for Johnson family details.]

No one had noticed him before. Was it an accident or was it really his plan to kill himself and as many Mexicans as possible at the same time? At what he considered the favorable moment, he must have ignited the gunpowder storage keg. But as the lid was not locked, the main force of the detonation went upward, and in this way the terrible plan missed its purpose.

The confusion was not over yet and the rage of the Mexicans had not subsided when suddenly we heard a clear signal of alarm, and the enemy hastily assembled their troops. Soon there was an explanation for this movement. Our true advance guard appeared in the forest together with all the militia that Colonel Horton could get together in the short time. The report on which we had built our hope was certainly untrue, that is, that there were from six hundred to eight hundred militia at Victoria. Instead, there were from thirty to forty men who were waiting for Fannin's arrival and who now appeared under Horton's leadership, altogether forty-odd men, with the firm decision to help us.

"But what fright took possession of us," said the brave Horton later on, "when we gathered what had happened from the position of the Mexican troops on this fateful morning!! We stood in astonishment and were undecided what to do, when suddenly the war-like bugle notes of the Mexicans sounded. No time was to be lost; quickly we had to counsel and just as quickly we were ready. If Fannin had so far forgotten his duty by surrendering, we were obliged to save ourselves for the Republic. Now was the time when Texas needed our arms and our guns. All of our volunteers were now either taken prisoners or were murdered. Consequently we turned our horses and speedily galloped back to Victoria to unite with Houston's troops at Gonzales."

As Horton and his men fled, the Mexicans hastily pursued, but without results. Safely the former reached the dark densely forested banks of the Guadalupe and disappeared in the familiar forests, which saved them by receiving them into their dense foliage of from ten-to-fifteen feet high cane reeds, and the enemy dared not follow them.

If our troops had arrived a half-hour earlier, we would have frustrated the bloody catastrophe that soon followed, but it was written otherwise in the book of fate. The volunteers were to die, that Texas might step forth from her really precarious position with greater splendor. A sacrificial offering had to be made for freedom in order to fire up anew that spirit that was for a while slumbering so carefree, especially in the hearts of the settlers. It was necessary to execute a bloody act to demonstrate the difference between the blessings of a free system of government and the injustice and presumption of a tyrannical absolute government such as Santa Anna had introduced by the overthrow of the liberal Constitution of 1824 and its conversion into a centralized governmental system.

---

[35] This would not have been a problem since the government in Mexico changed almost every year.

CHAPTER SEVENTEEN

The Imprisonment

AT TWO O'CLOCK WE RECEIVED ORDERS to return to Goliad and await Santa Anna's answer that was to designate the port through which we were to be shipped to New Orleans.

We, therefore, left the battlefield where the day before we had victoriously defended the rights of freedom, and in the evening by the clear light of the moon we entered the old church of the still-smoking fort, our prison quarters.

Fort Goliad and the town of La Bahía lie on the right bank of the San Antonio River, and at this place the banks are rather high and barren. The fort and the city lie about thirty miles from the river's mouth in Espiritu Santo Bay and from fifty to sixty miles from the main waters of the Gulf of Mexico. The whole region on which the town stands is composed of white broken sandstone through which the water has washed deep furrows. Toward the stream barely a twig or tree is to be seen to soften the dead view of this desolate place. A number of stone houses, that are always only one story high and resemble boxes turned upside down and painted white more than they do human habitations, project like high walls out of the surrounding huts, which are built of unhewn tree stems set up perpendicularly and finished with mud. As viewed from the opposite bank of the river, this view has something of unusual interest. After one has traveled for months through the ever green and fruitful forests and prairies of the West and has searched in vain for sights of antiquity, with the exception of San Antonio and its missions, the stranger sees sprawled out before him a town, whose location is uncultivated, but whose style of architecture makes a very favorable impression from a distance. The houses that rise one over the other in terrace formation on the slopes of the high banks remind one of the ruins in the Arabian desert, especially when the scorching sun of the south shines down on them, and the eye is unable to endure the blinding glare.

Even higher than the city toward the east, Fort Goliad lies on a plain. It consists of a rectangle about twelve hundred feet long and one thousand feet wide enclosed by a wall, in part, seven feet high and provided, largely by Fannin's command, with bastions at each corner. On the south side is a gate, over which was built construction that formerly contained on one side the guard room and on the other the jail. On the north and opposite side of the fort, in the direction of the San Antonio, stand the ruins of an old church with a flat roof on which had been placed several small cannon. Westward from the church there is a row of one-story buildings of equal height, also constructed with flat roofs. From the left bank, as I have stated before, the town and the fort has such a desolate and yet such a highly interesting position that we were agreeably surprised when for the first time we came around the point of the forest and saw the place before us in all its beauty. On the opposite and left side of the San Antonio lay the ruins of the old Spanish mission of *Espiritu Santo* in the middle of a densely wooded region. At our feet lay the clear San Antonio River. Toward the right and left were dark forests. Before us lay Goliad and La Bahía in their blinding sand. And behind these toward the southeast, south and southwest lay an immense prolifically green prairie on which the great herds of cattle and horses of the inhabitants of the town quietly had grazed before the outbreak of the Revolution. It is worthy of note that only the small spot on which the town stands has sandy soil, while all around the soil is overgrown with a rich growth of grass.

Nobody had yet entered the fort when, after an absence of thirty-five hours, we arrived here from the battleground. The Mexicans evidently feared a concealed mine or some other scheme to cause them injury. Consequently we were the first ones to enter the desolate ruins again, but as prisoners, and were stuffed into the old church for the night. Literally stuffed, as we stood so close man to man that it was possible at the most for only one-fourth to even sit down. It was well that the inner room of the church had a height of thirty-five to forty feet. If it had been lower, we would have suffocated. As it was, the air remained fairly fresh.

Thus the first terrible night passed away. A burning thirst had taken possession of us. Parching with thirst, we called violently for water, but only around eight o'clock six of our men were instructed to go to the river. The first load disappeared like a single drop on a red hot stove. Only after the vessels had been filled and emptied three times was our thirst slaked, and we awaited the moment when we would be released from this dungeon and be given nourishment. But our hopes were in vain. We received nothing but water toward evening and the second frightful night broke in upon us. The heat was much greater and more suffocating than the night before. Many slept while standing, as the bodies were pressed so close against one another it made it impossible to fall over. Some of the smaller men who were fortunate enough to cower on the floor could rest at least for a short time. The awfulness of the damp atmosphere that prevailed here was suffocating, and it was possible to endure lying on the floor for only a short period. The next morning finally appeared, but with it still no liberation from this deathly dungeon. Our breakfast, as before, consisted of water. Strong guards stood at the side doors, and the main entrance was guarded by a barrier of several cannon, but neither the sharply load muskets nor the cannon could suppress our rage. Fannin's men loudly demanded the fulfillment of the terms of the capitulation. They clamored for food and demanded to see the commanding officer, or they would not consider their lives too dear to sacrifice them for their rights.

The colonel of the *Battalion de Tres Villas* appeared immediately after these protests in company with Holsinger and assured us that he would do his utmost to drive up some steers and butcher them for us, as they themselves were not supplied with the least of any other kind of provisions and had not issued any rations to their own army in two days. Although we knew that this was untrue, we promised to remain quiet until evening. Since the cannon at the door were loaded with live ammunition and the men were standing by with burning torches to suppress the slightest movement among us, I am convinced that it was intended to exhaust our patience, to provoke us to the limit, and then, when we should venture to obtain justice with force, to fire on us with grapeshot and then to kill the rest of us with the bayonets. In this way Santa Anna and his henchmen could later have announced that they were compelled to shoot us down in order to save their own lives. In fact they were the first to violate the terms of the capitulation, and a disturbance among us would have been perfectly excusable. If it really was Santa Anna's plan to murder us in this way, the commander at Goliad did not have enough courage to carry it out.

That evening at about six o'clock we received beef: however, at the most, six ounces to the man and much larger promises for more as soon as more cattle could be driven up. Now we had meat but it was raw, and we had neither fire nor room to cook it. With a few small pieces of wood that lay about in the church and a little paneling that we tore from the walls, our resourceful comrades soon had two, although very small, fires going as the heat and thirst was almost unbearable with these.

On account of the smallness of the fires, only a few at a time could roast their meat. And before they all could have gotten through, the whole night would have passed away. Consequently those farthest away from the fires renounced their claims and ate their meat raw, an example that was generally imitated as the fire only added new miseries to the other privations of the body.

After we had spent another night in distress like the former two, the command to vacate the church was finally given, not to march away but to exchange the roof of the church for the open skies and to take a position within the walls under heavy guard.

Facing us were several companies of infantry that were ready any moment to shoot us down, in case one of the many sentinels that stood around us should give the alarm. At the large built-over entrance of the fort stood four pieces of artillery, although they were not directed at us. It was raining lightly as we were leaving the church. In spite of that our condition was considerably improved since, although we were still close together, we could at least get fresh air. Today also we did not get anything to eat, and we began to give away our things and also our little money for something to eat. For this the soldiers charged enormous prices, so that a man, not a really hungry one, for about ten dollars, could eat tortillas. It is a delicacy made of corn, salt, and water and baked in the form of a little pancake the thickness of the back of a knife cooked on a hot tin grill or even on the open coals with constant turning over and over. This is done after the corn has first been soaked in suitable lye, then pounded to pieces by the artful grip of a *señora* aided by two stones and finally freed from its mealy mass. According to my opinion this is a discovery of the Mexicans, and the aforesaid tortillas would probably make a very good grade of leather if passed through a better machine than the women of Mexico. But what doesn't taste good when one is hungry? Trousers, shirts, and other articles of clothing quickly disappeared among the greedy and half-civilized Mexican soldiers, whose only good trait of character is that they divide with the poor what they steal from the rich. To steal is natural with them, and they do it even when they are not in need. Consequently travelers who travel through the northern states of the Mexican confederation must be very watchful not to lose one or more of their horses every few weeks. First a hired-man, that one usually takes along for a servant or a guide, will disappear with one, or possibly a ranchero,[36] who probably has thousands himself, may entertain himself by stealing one and driving it into his own herd.

It was about four o'clock when all the wounded from the battlefield were brought into the church and into a few small buildings. The number totaled approximately two hundred men, including about thirty of our comrades.

The enemy army was without physicians. Consequently Doctor Shalefort [Dr. John (Jack) Shackelford] and another of our men had to serve as surgeons, an Englishman and George Voss of Hamburg, as assistants, and Joseph Spohn, a young attractive Creole from Louisiana, as interpreter. These alone had permission to go about freely, and also to see Fannin and Chutwick [Joseph M. Chadwick, acting adjutant general], a young cadet of West Point from the States, and they had a room to themselves.

On the fourth morning we each received three-fourths of a pound of beef that we roasted on little fires. Just as we were busy with our meat, one hundred and twenty new companions in misfortune appeared to our surprise under heavy guard. They were the troops of Major [William] Ward who, after wandering about in the completely unknown prairie for eight days, surrendered on the same terms, after hearing our capitulation.

Twenty-six men of Major Ward's troops, all carpenters, had remained at Victoria on command of Holsinger, who indicated he needed them in getting the artillery over the river as the Mexicans were of no value at heavy work. Although we barely knew each other, we sorrowfully shook hands as friends. Ward, who now saw how wrong it was not to have obeyed Fannin's order to return to Goliad at once, did not wish to leave his companions in this sad condition into which his ambition had brought them, and shared the privations of the imprisonment with us instead of living in the room with Fannin, where he was at first directed.

When I think of that time, my hands involuntarily clinch together; and gnashing with fury I would like to delete the time that has passed since that day, and lead my comrades against the cannons and bayonets of the Mexican devils that I might not die unavenged.

The next morning, the fifth of our imprisonment, all Germans were called out by Holsinger, the Prussian; however, I did not step forward but remained with my friends, the Americans, as I was determined to share everything with my companions in sorrow. And in my opinion differences of national origin were out of the question, as equal feelings and equal misfortunes had united us. We felt no difference. We were neither Englishmen nor Germans nor Americans; we were one nation from the time that we entered Texas together. We were Texans.

This was not just my opinion but also that of all my friends and my fellow countrymen who, like me, also would have done, in proud feeling of independence contemptuously rejected Holsinger's offer to take service with the Mexicans as artillerymen against our dear second fatherland, Texas. What a disdainful offer! It could emanate only from a creature like Holsinger that we should offer our hand to destroy a young nation that was fighting for its rights, for the rights of humanity!

"No," answered Mattern, "if you would leave me the choice between a brilliant position in Mexico or a life in the mines among the criminals, I would choose the latter rather than that this arm should do service in the suppression of freedom! No, Colonel, I thank you for your courtesy, but our views are different! Our spirit advances with the times, but yours and that of the priesthood battle in the opposite direction. It is in vain, your time is past. The people know that they are the ones who have the right to make the laws."[37]

The last words were not heard by Holsinger as he turned around to walk away. He felt displeasure but he could not force himself not to admire the spirit of our man Mattern.

On the sixth day we each received the third and last ration of one pound of beef in the fort. All of our things had passed over into the hands of the Mexicans, and we possessed possibly only a few precious objects which, however, did not escape the greedy glances of the enemy soldiers who tried by every means and tricks to entice these away from us also, to steal or to simply take away, as we were not permitted to follow them through the guards. Naturally compensation was out of the question as was consideration of our complaints.

From me they stole one of those large, pretty, woolen blankets which are made in the mountain lands of Mexico and are completely waterproof. But they also had an enormous price. Mine, that I had bought for ten dollars twelve to fourteen days ago from a Mexican spy that we had captured, was probably worth from forty to fifty dollars. In the center of these blankets are openings for the head to pass through, the sides of which are usually surrounded with either stitched or worked-in garlands. The four outer corners are ornamented in the same way. If the ends of these covers, especially the finer ones that are usually white, are gracefully folded back so that the right side falls over the left shoulder, this ornament makes a very good impression on many a fantastically dressed ranchero or officer. Besides that they are light and warm. In vain I asked Holsinger to have mine sent back to me. He answered that was not possible because I as a prisoner would have to put up with many things. During the afternoon I had the pleasure of seeing my poncho wrapped over the body of the same villain to whom I had paid ten dollars when he was our prisoner.

In order to attain their greedy purposes more easily, our customers came and acquainted us with the highly gratifying news that we would all be shot. Very humanitarian of them to give us an opportunity to sell the few things that we still possessed in order to sweeten our last days.

"What good will it do you?" they said, "in a few days you will be shot anyway."

But we could see through their plans and it helped them very little, as we could but believe that the enemy officers, even if they should be unscrupulous enough to do such a deed, would be restrained for the sake of their honor since they would be called liars and murderers before the world. Christians, we knew, they were only in name, but they held just that much stricter to the forms of Catholicism.

We were momentarily expecting a courier from Santa Anna, who was just then making preparations to pursue Houston. General Urrea had crossed the Guadalupe right after our capitulation. He accomplished this because the militia had evacuated Victoria without firing a shot.

Probably from six hundred to eight hundred men were now at Goliad, including men of the previously-mentioned *Battalion de Tres Villas*. The name of its colonel, who was also the commander of the fort, has slipped my mind.

On the seventh morning at about nine o'clock the Mexicans brought in another one hundred prisoners, volunteers from New York under Colonel Miller, who were captured immediately after their landing at Copano. Since they had not heard anything of the arrival of the Mexicans in Texas, they believed themselves perfectly safe and went in boats, on account of the shallow water, to the land area one-half mile away without arms. Barely had they arrived at the shore before they scattered, glad to set their feet on solid ground again after a journey of several weeks. Suddenly hordes of the Mexican cavalry rushed out of the mesquite timber, through which the road to Refugio winds, and attacked them; and before they could recover from their astonishment, they were prisoners. They received other quarters outside of the fort and in addition were permitted to move about freely. In order that they could be recognized by the soldiers, they wore broad white bands around their arms. From Colonel Miller and especially from Joseph Spohn and George Voss we have the report of what transpired at Goliad after our departure.

The night approached without our lips tasting any food except the refreshing water from the San Antonio River. Terrible hunger must have been raging within the unfortunate ones, who, disregarding the same, were in good humor and so full of hopes that they were planning what they were going to do after their arrival at New Orleans. Others were picking the little flesh here and there from the bones that we had thrown on a pile to burn several days before our retreat. They were namely bones of the eight hundred steers from which we had cut the meat that we had then dried and later burnt.

---

[36] *Ranjero* - inhabitant of the countryside.

[37] This was first written in 1844; in 1848 revolutions all over Europe arose after the [Prince Clemens von] Metternich era. He was a diplomat in charge of the Congress of Vienna of 1815, after Napoleon, and he presided during this time, when feelings of freedom and nationalism erupted, but then the aristocracy reasserted itself. The French Revolution in 1789 was followed by the era of Napoleon. Napoleon put the aristocracy back in power and called himself Emperor. [Although this edition of Ehrenberg's book is dated 1844, he mentions events of 1848, four years later.]

CHAPTER EIGHTEEN

The Murder of
the Prisoners

THE MORNING OF THE EIGHTH DAY came with many clouds. Had the enemy not changed our condition, we either would have forcibly freed ourselves or ended our imprisonment in death. But things happened otherwise.

While grey clouds covered the horizon, not the slightest motion occurred on the surface of the earth. On the prairie lay a damp sultriness capable of inciting feelings of misgivings even among those who had nothing to fear, whose own horizon was clear. How much did our imagination depict the impenetrable future with dark visions or pictures that were all too soon to be realized! A courier with Santa Anna's decision about our fate probably had arrived during the night!

We looked forward to the news anxiously and keenly hoped, in conformity with orders, to break camp immediately for Matamoras and to greet the free, blue Gulf there, to cut through its foam-covered waves, and, finally, to sail up the mighty Mississippi, that father of the rivers of North America, to the city that we had left seven months before with great and joyous enthusiasm. Bright as well as dreary glimpses into the future alternated in rapid succession.

One vision was that from now on we were to view the battling nations at a distance, without ever being participants in the contests between freedom and despotism. This was a sad picture, but several of us, including myself, saw a more dreary one ahead of us. We already imagined ourselves in the mines of Mexico, heard the clatter of chains about us, and saw ourselves compelled like criminals to bring the ores to the light of day. Viewed from another standpoint, even from here, a hopeful side showed itself, as we still had hope and the right to take up arms again for Texas and to fight again under the banner of the young republic. If we should ever get back, we would be bound by no oath, no word, and no capitulation.

The cannons that had formerly guarded the entrance were turned around during the night and directed at our quarters. Apparently they were heavily loaded with live ammunition. On the other side of them stood the artillerymen with burning torches ready to fire at the first signal.

In front of us stood several companies in dress uniforms which were very shabby and made of the coarsest material. The soldiers did not have the least bit of camping equipment with them which, however, most of us did not notice, as they usually had little or nothing to take with them. I believe that I can frankly state that not one of the Texans noticed this.

At last an officer stepped among us with Santa Anna's orders in his hands, but he did not tell us any more than that we were to march off at once. This was at eight o'clock in the morning.

Where to? To Copano or to Matamoras? This was not revealed to us, and we were left to guess about this.

A short time was needed for us to make our preparations to leave this place of misery, and in a few minutes we stood in position two men deep, with the exception of Colonel Miller's detachment which, as previously stated, lay outside the fort. Furthermore, Fannin, the physicians and assistants, the interpreter, and the wounded were missing. They were later to be taken to New Orleans by a shorter route.

After the roll had been called for the last time and after the last echo of the oft repeated "Here" that accompanied the calling of the different names had died away, the order to march was given. The Greys marched through the dark gate. They were under the command of First Lieutenant McMannemy of the Greys of Mobile. Strangely enough, both captains had left for Houston's headquarters on company business a few days before the retreat began.

Outside the gate we were approached on each side by Mexican soldiers. Like us, they had been placed man behind man to form two rows. Thus enclosed, we marched forward. We had almost four hundred men and the enemy at least seven hundred, not counting the cavalry that was swarming about on the prairie in small detachments.

From now on I will give an account of my own experiences. I'll also tell of adventures according to other already named sources. These sources are not any less reliable than mine, I can assure you, as three and sometimes even more eye-witnesses told identically the same account, and since the Mexicans did not deny the stories told by our people.

Quietly the column marched forward on the road toward Victoria, contrary to our expectations. Where they were going to take us in this direction was an object of general speculation. Most of us seemed to think that they were taking us to an eastern harbor in order to ship us to New Orleans from there, which basically would be the same, and it would be even nearer and better for us this way.

The intolerable silence of the usually talkative Mexicans and the sultry heat accelerated the nervous expectations and stress we all felt. This death march, as one can really call it, often reminds me of the bloody scenes that I was to witness at that time.

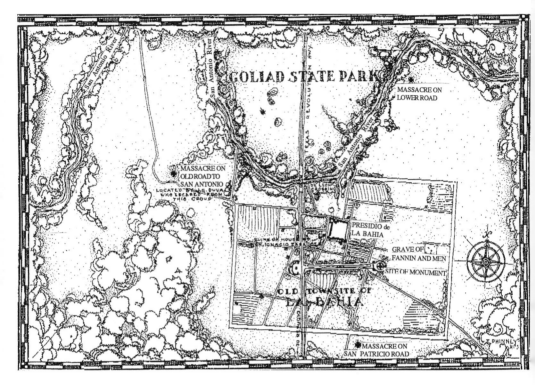

*During the death march, the Greys were divided into three groups, as
indicated above. The town of Victoria lies northeast of Goliad.*

Anxiously I looked back to the rear part of the column to
see if Miller's people were marched off at the same time with us.
But imagine my astonishment when neither Fannin's men nor
the last captured Georgia Battalion was to be seen! They had
separated us without our noticing it, and only the Greys and a
few of the colonists were marching in the detachment I was in.
I glanced over at the escort and now I first noticed their festive
uniforms and the absence of camping equipment. Bloody pictures rose up in my mind, including events at Tampico, San
Patricio, and the Alamo. Then I thought of the character of our
enemies, their duplicity, their banditry, and their exultation in
bloody deeds. All of these prepared me for the worst, and there

were moments when I was on the point of telling my companions of my suspicions.

But never-dying hope kept me from doing this. I visualized the future in brilliant colors and, absorbed in this thought, I continued to step forward. The pictures showing our probable fate became livelier in my imagination, and soon the possibly happy ones of the future exchanged places with the painful ones of reality. The next moment I threw my few remaining articles to the Mexicans, out on to the fresh green prairie, so that I would be unfettered in my moves, should I have to run in case of emergency.

Probably a quarter of an hour had passed since we had left the fort, and not a word had passed over our lips nor over those of the enemy. Everyone seemed to have dropped into deep reflections. Suddenly the command of the Mexican sounded to march off to the left from the main road; and as we did not understand, the officer led the way himself. My companions in misfortune still carelessly followed the leader. To our left a little five to six-feet-high mesquite hedge extended straight to the roaring San Antonio River about a thousand yards away. The river's clear waters are at right angle to the hedge and push through thirty to forty foot tall bluffs that rise almost perpendicularly from the water on this side. Our steps were directed down the mesquite brush and toward the river, when suddenly the thought seized every one: "Why in this direction?" This and the presence of several mounted lancers to our right, to whom we had previously given no attention, confused us. We also noticed that the line of the enemy between us and the hedge that had remained behind was now lining up on the other side so that they formed a double file here. Unable to comprehend this movement, we were still in a maze when a "Halt!" was commanded in Spanish. It ran through us like a death sentence. At that moment we heard the muffled rolling of a musket volley in the distance. Naturally we thought of our companions who had been separated from us and evidently led off in that direction.

"Remember Goliad!" March 27, 1836, General Santa Anna's troops massacred Colonel Fannin and more than 300 Texan prisoners-of-war.

Astonished and confounded, we looked at each other and cast questioning glances first at ourselves and then at the Mexicans. Then another command—"Kneel down!"— rang out from the lips of the Mexican officers. Only a few of us understood Spanish and could not or would not obey the order.

The Mexican soldiers, who stood only three steps away, leveled their muskets at our chests and we found ourselves terribly surprised.

We still considered it impossible to believe that they were going to shoot us. Had we known, what wouldn't we have done desperately in order to sell our lives more dearly! If we had been compelled with unarmed hands, we would, like Winkelried, have grasped onto the bayonets of the enemy; and many a one of our murderers would have let his life bleed away on the green carpet of the savannah. Even a usually fleeing coward will become courageous when he sees certain death before him and all hope of saving himself has gone. Then raging fury drives him forward to throw himself on his enemy and in the attack of despair to pull the enemy with himself into destruction.

Only one among us spoke Spanish fluently, and those words seemed incomprehensible to him. He stared doubtfully at the commanding officer as if he wanted to read on his features a contradiction of what he had heard. The remainder of us fixed our eyes on him to thrust ourselves on the threatening enemy at the first sound from his lips. But he seemed, as we were, possessed of the unfortunate hope that this order was merely a threat to force us into Mexican service. With threatening gestures and drawn sword, the chief of the murderers for the second time commanded in a brusque tone, "Kneel down!"

Sounds of a second volley thundered over to us from another direction, accompanied by confused cries, probably from those who were not immediately killed. This shocked our comrades out of their stark astonishment, which had lasted around five or six seconds. New Life now animated them, their eyes flashed, and they cried out:

"Comrades! Listen to that shooting! It is happening to our brothers! Hear their cry! It is their last one! There is no more hope here—the last hour of the Greys has come! Therefore—Comrades!—"

A terrible cracking sound interrupted him, and then everything was quiet. A thick smoke slowly rolled toward the San Antonio. The blood of my lieutenant was on my clothing. Around me my friends quivered. Beside me Mattern and Curtman were fighting death. I did not see more. Deciding quickly, I jumped up and, concealed by the black smoke of the powder, rushed down along the hedge to the river.

I heard nothing more and saw nothing. Only the rushing of the water was my guide. Then suddenly a powerful sabre smashed me over the head. Before me the figure of a little Mexican lieutenant appeared out of the dense smoke, and a second blow from him fell on my left arm with which I had tried to ward off or parry the blow.

I had nothing to risk and everything to gain. Either life or death! Behind were the bayonets of the murderers, and before me was the sword of a coward who blocked my way to the saving stream. Determined, I rushed upon him. I had to go forward and—the coward took to flight in characteristic Mexican gallantry. Now the path was open, and the point of my escape was near. Another few moments passed. The smoke rolled like a black thunder cloud over to the other side, and I stood with rapidly-pounding heart on the rocks at the edge of the water. As the water flowed at my feet, behind me the hangmen were pursuing.

Like a corps from hell they came after me, but with a yell "The Republic of Texas Forever!" I threw myself into the rescuing floods.

Swimming slowly toward the opposite bank and being prodded from time to time with poorly-aimed bullets the enemy was sending after me, I swam through the current of the saving river. However, another victim was to fall due to the Mexicans' barbarity, namely, our faithful large dog who had accompanied our group from the beginning to the end, and who now jumped into the waters after me to share my pleasures and sufferings with me in my flight through the unknown prairie. He had already reached the center of the stream when the Mexicans made a target of him and although they seldom hit, the faithful friend, wounded, disappeared under the waves.

Arriving on the other side of the river, I looked around once more to where my comrades were bleeding, while the bullets of the still-firing enemies whistled about me. The hellish exultations of the enemy, mixed with the cries of pain of my dying brothers, sounded over to me. What feelings took possession of me here!

I was saved. I saw my enemies, threatening, standing on the opposite bank. The scene of the butchery seemed like a dreary dream, and yet I witnessed the terrible reality before me. As by a miracle I was saved from certain death, and only now, after all danger was over, I began to tremble.

I had read of crimes of the most terrible kinds, but I never could have attributed to a people who called themselves Christians infamous deeds of this type, to shoot down with devilish delight prisoners who had surrendered themselves with trust of oath and word of honor.

The inhuman, cowardly, blood-thirsty race of people, these desecrators of religion who parade their religion and who pretend, as the only path to salvation, to worship Christ who commands to love the enemy and do good unto him! But such is the weakness of Catholicism. Instead of giving its followers moral strength and an invigorating, rational faith, it blinds them with outward display of splendor and gives coarseness and immodesty full freedom, and absolves every crime from punishment, for money and feigned atonement.

I cast another look and a farewell to my dead companions and then turned to flee. I had to hasten if I didn't wish to fall into the hands of the lancers who were now on this side of the river less than half-a-mile below me.

I threw away everything that I could spare, as the water had made my clothing considerably heavier and, unfortunately, in the haste, my diary also, that I had kept up to this time. Provided with only the most necessary clothing, even without coat and cap, having lost the latter in the stream, I entered the forests and prairies of the heavenly west.

CHAPTER NINETEEN

Fannin's Death

THE ACTION HERE WAS OVER; the horribly mutilated bodies of the warriors of Coleto Bay lay on the green slaughter grounds in the vicinity of the walls of Goliad. They were naked, as the Mexicans had completely plundered the dead bodies of the men.

But the last act of the drama had been enacted inside the fort, as follows:

The wounded lay groaning in the old church, and all of those who were not seized with a raging fever, as is usually the case with those who are struck by copper bullets, heard the murderous volleys that struck down their comrades. In a rage they tried to free themselves from their bandages in the hope that by bleeding to death, they would anticipate the devilish enemies and rob them of the triumph of digging into the hearts of the dead.

After the last shot had been fired outside the walls, the curtain rose for the second to the last time and the orders of the commanding officer of the enemy reached the ears of the wounded:

"All Texans come out!" he said, "and the lightly wounded bring the heavily wounded into the center of the fort."

Those who were not disabled immediately rose in resignation to step before the judgement seat of Almighty God on the same day with their brothers to ask for justice. But nothing could induce them to bring their dying or raging comrades to the place of murder, and only the attendant, Voss, who had hopes of not being shot, helped the brown murderers carry out the dying ones, several of whom died before they reached the fateful spot. Barely had they been thrown onto a pile when the order in Spanish was given—and another bloody heroic deed of the *Battalion de Tres Villas* was finished.

Not a word was said to indicate to them that they were going to die. Not a minute's time was granted them to ask the mercy of God. Without any previous preparation they also were murdered by the disciples of the Jesuits.

Fannin himself now stepped forth from his prison and Joseph Spohn was at his side. With indescribable sadness he looked at the still-bleeding bodies of the wounded. Deeply he regretted that he had not hastened to the aid of the fallen garrison at the Alamo, or that he had not sooner followed Houston's orders to retreat to behind the Guadalupe River. Tears of deepest sorrow ran down his cheeks during the slaughter of his true and faithful comrades. They were not the tears of cowardice—not the fear of approaching death! No, no, they were due to the unhappy fate of his brothers. Fannin was too courageous to fear death and to cry about it like a child. No, they were the bitter tears of repentance and of compassion that moistened his cheeks.

He had composed himself when he left his prison, and in spite of his strongly inflamed wounds, he advanced with a firm step to his executioners.

Having arrived at the place of execution, he drew out his costly gold watch and handed it to the leader of the Mexicans who had the orders to shoot him.

"Sir!" he said, "divide the worth of this watch among your people. Tell them to aim well—here." He covered with both hands the region where his heart was to beat only a short time longer. "Tell them here, sir, is where I wish that their bullets would drill through me."

Then Joseph Spohn placed a white sheet of cloth over Fannin's eyes, and a few moments later as the smoke had cleared away, the Colonel lay on the ground with a shattered head.

The drama had ended.

Joseph Spohn, who was saved afterward, sat on the carriage of a cannon and stared at the corpses of his comrades. He barely noticed the bloodthirsty looks that the triumphant enemies cast toward him.

I must mention one more scene. As was already said, Dr. Shackelford was taken from our midst to serve as a surgeon. It was now impossible for them to get along without him, and in order to save him, he and another American were forcibly concealed under buffalo hides in the tent of an officer.

Imagine the feelings of a father whose only son and beloved nephew came to such a horrible and treacherous end. At every volley, at every shot, the unhappy father groaned: "My son—my son—my brave Red Rovers, all, all are murdered—Oh it is horrible! Shackelford has robbed the citizens of Alabama of their sons—Alabama is bereft of its sons! No, not orphaned, there are still enough men in the state—how I want to go there," he continued at short intervals—"I will go there—I will speak—they shall shudder—the stones shall soften—The Union must shoulder the guns—old Shackelford will call through the States: Citizens! Americans! to arms!—to arms!—the blood of our brothers cries for vengeance from the prairies beyond the Mississippi—To arms! is the call, like the old weak doctor [Shackelford]—to arms!" Several shots fell, and he continued in indescribable pain: "Oh my son-my only son—my nephew," he wept. "My sons! yes all! all you Red Rovers, you were my children—

I was your father—you loved me as a dear father—and now?" a long pause, but then again, throwing the buffalo skins from him in despair: "Ha Red Rovers! Children! Countrymen! What shall I tell the people of Alabama! What shall I answer them when they ask the doctor for their sons? Where shall I hide my face, when they point at me with their fingers—that is Shackelford, they will say—the Red Rovers are dead, but Shackelford lives!" Beside himself with pain, he fought with the strong carpenter to get on the outside. "Let me go—let the old father die with his sons—let me—but—I have the right—I want to live— live—to call the States to war—my call shall sound from the Gulf to Niagara Falls and from the Mississippi to the seas—we will—yes, we want to get revenge—bloody revenge will we have."

He continued to rave in this manner for a long time, and his companion in misery had a hard time to keep him inside the tent.

But soon the usual serene quietness lay again over the prairie. The quiet was occasionally interrupted by the creaking of the ox carts of the enemies that dragged the pale, naked, bleeding bodies to a funeral pile where they were only partially cremated. On the next night packs of wolves assembled at the place of execution, where they could be seen gnawing on the partly burnt bodies. On the following day black vultures swarmed around the corpses, around the wolves, and around the ruins of Goliad. Cawing, they prophetically announced the overthrow of the Mexicans.

CHAPTER TWENTY

The Flight Through
the Wilderness

MY GOAL WAS TO GO WEST TOWARD SAN ANTONIO, but only to deceive the enemy, as my real direction lay east-northeast toward the Brazos River. But after I had wandered through the wilderness for about two hours I struck a little brook that meandered off to the San Antonio River. I walked into it, as it occurred to me that it would obliterate my trail, and walked in it for a while.

It was strange that not the slightest fear had taken possession of me, and I moved on foot forward as courageously as if I were walking through the charming surroundings of mighty New York. Serious thoughts floated about in the sea of my feverish imagination, and as the American coast for the first time appeared before the fleet of Columbus, so the future rose up before my soul. The Greys had fallen but I was alive, the only one (as I thought) saved by the Almighty to inform the world of this infernal deed. In my imagination I already saw how the troops and the old general himself would listen with shuddering and rage to the tale of this infamous deed. I already heard the solemn vows one brother made to another, the father to the son, and the son to the beloved father. I envisioned the bandit army annihilated or fleeing across the Rio Grande. And in the background, the victorious lone star rose anew in its splendor over the prairie. Splendid dreams—It was the prophetic spirit that tore open the veil of the future. It granted a deep look into the dark book of fate.

Exhausted from walking rapidly, I lay down in the tall grass on the bank of the little stream, and after I had noted the direction in which I was to go, I closed my eyes. Deep dullness filled my mind. No terrible dreams, no feverish fantasies, no pain from my light wounds, no fear, nothing hindered the refreshing repose that overtook me for the strengthening of my mind and body.

For the first time in a long time, a stormy sea of clouds, remnants of a hurricane, rolled over the skies, and a fine rain was falling on my face when I awoke at night. The tall grass on the hill waved in the wind, and the undulating outlines of the elevation appeared as if a band of Mexicans or a troop of roving redskins were sneaking over the hill. I listened, but as I could not hear a human sound, I correctly concluded that I was in error.

I stood still to recall the map of the Republic, so that I could take the proper direction; it took only a few moments and I was ready. Northeast seemed to me to be the best direction. But what point of reference was I to take as a guide in this dark, starless night? The only one available was the wild motion of the clouds, but it was not a good one. Consequently I chose the rain, that struck me on the right side of the face, as a guide.

My arm hurt very much and was at first so stiff I could not move it. But the penetrating rain soon softened the swelling and cooled the heat. It also alleviated the pain that was raging in my head. Toward four o'clock in the morning I found an inviting cave in the treeless bluff of a bayou that I had to cross. Exhausted, I lay down in the cave and soon fell into a deep sleep, from which I did not awake until about nine o'clock in the morning. It had ceased raining, but the several-feet-high mesquite grass wetted all my clothing. Toward the right a line of forest extended to the Guadalupe, the first stream on my wanderings that I had to strike and cross. Therefore I turned my steps toward the section covered with oak trees, where I had the advantage of not having the grass as high as it was on the prairie.

The whole evening after I had left the woods I wandered through one of those regions where the traveler sees nothing but hills covered with waving grass. Not a tree, not a bush, not even a cactus (that is found nearly *everywhere* in the west) emerged in the endless monotony. From my feet all around and out to the cloudy horizon, I appeared as the only living being. No herds of deer grazed here, no gobbling turkeys passed through the prairies and no song of a bird interrupted the serene quietness of the solitude. During the winter this region must be covered with geese, but a month ago they had begun their great journey north and to the waters of the Mississippi.

Disregarding the loneliness and filled with dauntless hope, I went forward with long steps, constantly and almost unconsciously whistling a favorite march.

Toward five o'clock I heard what sounded like subterranean thunder, and soon I saw a herd of wild horses on the horizon speeding over a hill. They came in close formation directly toward me and stopped about one hundred and fifty yards away and gazed at me in consternation. At the loud signal of a fleet-footed mustang, the whole herd of about three hundred dashed away with flowing manes in the same direction from which they had come. Soon they had disappeared behind the hills where I was directing my steps. Finally, as I reached the highest of these hills, I saw before me the wooded banks of the roaring Guadalupe. Soon I reached the thin forest and, true to my course, stepped confidently forward under the post oak trees. I expected momentarily to see the stream where I planned to spend the night. The night approached, and I crossed several roads I dared not follow as Urrea's army was ahead. Only in the dense forest was I safe from the Mexicans, even if not completely from the scalping knife of the roaming Carancahuas or Lipans. However, I had little fear of these as they attack only when there is something to be plundered.

The second night after my flight had already set in, I prepared my bed from Spanish moss that, hanging in long festoons from the trees, indicated the nearness of the stream. But I still could not hear the roaring of the water.

Toward midnight a majestic thunderstorm, such as an inhabitant of the north has no idea of, awakened me. A powerful, foaming current rushed down the ravine in which I was lying, and half of my body lay in water. This was a warning not to sleep in a ravine in the future. I jumped up and sought shelter under a powerful pecan tree, where I was to some extent protected from the rain. After half an hour the moon and the stars looked down clearly from the blue skies through the tops of the old oaks and hickories, as if the whole night had been quiet and pretty.

Spanish moss hangs from trees in South Texas.

I tore fresh moss down from the gigantic limbs and prepared a new bed. Although I was soaked to the skin and did not have a very good bed, I soon went to sleep as soundly with the calling of the whippoorwill as if, beginning with sundown, I had lain between cover and mattress under a roof in the colonies. When I awoke with the sun, I could barely move my left foot. Practically my whole left side was stiff, and as I moved forward, I experienced a cutting pain in my hip. After walking for a quarter of an hour, the pain disappeared and, strong and vigorous again, I swam across the turbulent Guadalupe, where I had just arrived much to my satisfaction.

During the first half of the day my wanderings led me through the rich, prolific, densely wooded bottoms of the stream, where it really was not easy for me to follow my course. But, in spite of all obstacles, everything went well. I was guided partly by the bark of the trees and partly by the sun shining down from the clear sky which, however, is not a very good pilot during the mid-day hours. During the afternoon I entered the prairie that sprawls between the Guadalupe and Lavaca rivers, and while I was there, was surprised by nightfall.

As I again found myself on a treeless, recently burnt off, plateau, I placed my pilgrim's staff in the ground in such a manner that its upper point indicated the direction in which I intended to go the next morning. If it should be cloudy weather the next morning, I would at least know my direction.

But the entire next day was pretty, and I roamed through a heavenly region. Countless little prairies, tree courses, and islands grouped endlessly, alternating one with the other. Barely did I pass one far projecting point when new points, new forest lines, and new archipelago projections of dark green islands would appear. Dark blue lines of forests appeared on the almost darker horizon. Now, too, the region began to have more signs of life. Small herds of horses and cattle (that often wander far away from the colonies) grazed on the spring green of the savannah along with countless deer.

With the exception of the first day of my flight, I had not experienced the slightest hunger, in spite of the fact that so far I had eaten absolutely nothing. Neither did I experience any appreciable decrease in my strength, and while I hoped to see the black forests of the Lavaca momentarily, I moved forward to the beat of our favorite march.

Although my stomach showed no craving for anything except clear water, which I had found in abundance so far, I believed it best to give it something to do, and in view of this decision, I picked some green leaves while walking along and tried to make a frugal meal out of them. But it was "no go" as the Texans say when a thing will not go. The early spring in this region does not offer the white man the least thing with which to satisfy his hunger if he is not provided with a gun, while the region west of the Guadalupe is filled with cactus which if necessary can keep one from starving.

On the fifth day the sun rose again clear and bright in the deep blue sky, and very early it sent its almost burning rays down on the lively, changing landscape.

A trip through the Republic may be compared to a trip through the art gallery of the new museum in Berlin. As one hurries through the rooms from one creation to another, so one wanders almost carelessly in the paradise of America from one park to another, and only then is the eye, dulled by the ever fresh beauties of nature, pleasantly surprised when it beholds the sandy beach, the raging surf, and the waves of the Gulf of Mexico.

Meadows and islands of black forests lay about me. Numerous herds of horses, cattle and deer stared at me as I walked past them. Many a flock of turkeys marched around in procession and observed me with misgiving, while the sand grouse trumpeted its monotonous morning march. Anxiously my eyes hung on the dark forest line ahead of me, where I hoped to find the clear Lavaca. Without worry, I continued my journey this morning on a broad wide path that meandered off in my direction between the islands. Since yesterday not a drop of water had passed over my lips and, panting for water, I looked around for a sign of a spring or little stream. My eyes scanned the end-less expanse to the right and to the left, but they could discover nothing of promise. My hopes were fixed on a projecting forest and the road I was following led toward it.

I had to throw away a small turtle that I found on the road because I was lacking any tools for opening it. Not a single stone had I found on my flight, and I constantly wandered on a reddish brown soil which was dark, nearly black, in the valley of the Guadalupe.

I almost despaired of ever reaching the dark forest and I could clearly perceive how my strength and my courage were leaving me. Slowly I dragged myself forward, and my active fantasy was the only driving force for my very heavy feet.

It was about noon when I rounded the forest projection and in front of my veiled eyes another immense plane flickered up; islands and prairies, deer, horses, and cattle tumbled and swam about in front of my eyes, and miles away it seemed to me that a forest was again stretching its black arm out to the west—

I stared out into the glowing prairie. Confused, my eyes beheld a rolling landscape, and—I collapsed.

About twenty steps from me stood a majestic live oak tree under whose dark gigantic branches a whole battalion could find protection from the hot rays of the sun. I saw it as I fell, but I was not able to drag myself to it. Neither did I care to, since it seemed that if I was to die, I wished not to do so parching with thirst under the perpendicular rays of fire that fell from above, but rather to breathe out my confused spirit as soon as possible. My eyes rolled like balls of fire in their sockets, and there was a beating in my forehead as if it were being clubbed to pieces.

As I surmised, it was evening when I awoke, since the sun set deep and bloody on the horizon. I was somewhat refreshed and dragged myself to the shady oak. Once more I closed my eyes to spend the night here and to push forward anew with the early morning. However, after an hour, as the unbearable thirst would not allow me any rest, I opened my eyes again and believed that the night was still hanging over the prairie. But, Oh horrors! High and clear hung the sun, a sea of flames in an unending field of indigo. Not the refreshing night but the glowing day was before me, and I must have slept almost eighteen hours with my wild fever.

But if I were to save myself from an unavoidable death, I must get away from here to search for water, and my only hope was the black arm [of the forest] reaching toward the west ahead of me. I staggered forward. There was no shady tree, no bush, no twig on my way. Nothing but an endless waving flowerbed lay around me. At last I reached the border of the forest. But there was no trace of water; everything was dried up. I probably would have been eaten up by the wolves here, if I had not soon discovered (at a far distance out on the mighty treeless plateau that lay before me) a clear blue lake, whose opposite bank seemed to be enclosed with dense forestry and several plantation houses.

Seized with new courage, I stepped forward in spite of the unexplained question how a person was to come upon a lake here when none was charted on any map of the region. I staggered forward, and only the hope of reaching the water gave my nerves new strength. Again the sun burned down on my feverish and moss-enveloped head. The waves on the blue plain quivered and blinded my longing vision. The buildings on the edge of the forest stepped forth more and more out of their misty veil, and with every approaching step the outline of the inviting mirror changed.

The region now began to take an unusual aspect, similar to that which borders the sea. Thick, strong grass, reed-like growths, palmettos and other things covered the dry earth, which now took on a wave-like appearance. I had just walked over one of these waves and was standing on the crest of another and directed my eyes anxiously toward the lake. But what hellish delusion! What awful deception! Where was the lake with its quivering waves? Where were the settlements that I had seen so plainly? Everything, everything had disappeared. Terrible! All hopes were momentarily destroyed.

I could not and would not believe it; I peered to the left and stared to the right, but discovered nothing. I turned my gaze back to where I had come, fearing I had gone around in a circle in a fit of fever. I saw the islands that I had recently passed. Again I looked to the region where the blue water had appeared, but nothing was to be seen. The grasses trembled and vibrated, and even the rays of the sun that fell on the prairie quivered. The houses of the settlers had disappeared. Dreary forests appeared before me and, in front of the mighty forest, several massive moss-covered live oak trees stood like the out-posts of a great military camp.

I threw myself like an insane person on the prairie, buried my face in the earth, and broke the hot rays of the sun by cover-ing my head with a handful of grass. But I could not stand it long this way. Raging fever rolled in my blood and pounded in my head. In despair I would have put an end to this earthly suf-fering, but the necessary means to do this act were lacking. Feverishly I jumped up, and Oh what joy! Dark clouds like the many chains of the San Saba mountains were stacking them-selves one over another in the east. A fresh Gulf breeze blew out of the same direction, and with new courage and hope I walked on toward the dark forests again.

A fine rain soon fell and refreshed the surrounding cre-ation. Fresh and green, the grasses and plants lifted their heads that had been hanging sadly downward before, and out of the timbers great numbers of horses and cattle that had gone under the shady trees during the singeing noonday sun, drifted out on the prairie. Their great numbers and the various cattle brands[38] indicated to me that I had reached American colonies. But where and which was impossible for me to say. I believe that I had covered from eighty to one hundred miles in a straight line, but I could not depend on this assumption since I had never traveled in the coastal lands east of the Guadalupe.

The rain had almost completely relieved my thirst and fever, and fortunate it was, for the terrible heat in my veins would have killed me in another night. I wandered until nine o'clock through the thin forest, and I felt rather sure to find a stream in its depths. Being exhausted, it was necessary for me to look for a campground at this hour. I soon found a dry forest creek on whose banks I gathered some moss for a bed. Since I found that the sandy bed of the creek was still damp, I dug a hole about eighteen inches deep in its bottom in order to get a good drink in the morning from the water that would collect there during the night. I then threw myself on the moss and slept until the crowing of several roosters awoke me the next morning.

[38] Marks by which the ranchers know their herds.

The Colonies

A MIGHTY GULP OF THE PRECIOUS WATER that had gathered in my spring during the night was my morning's refreshment, and then I looked around and discovered that I was within a hundred yards of a large plantation. The orderly condition of the fields, the fences and the buildings, and the large quantity of poultry was to me a sure sign that the enemy had not defiled this section with his presence. My heart beat with joy on seeing a human habitation again. Happy beyond description on being near civilization again, I walked with new strength to a clear stream, to my left, whose crystal ripples murmured over a gravel bed. Once more I slurped the most precious of all drinks and then went across the stream without entering the plantation, as I was convinced that the buildings were vacant and that the inhabitants had destroyed their food and fled toward the east. Besides that, I expected to find some more plantations on the other side of the stream. And so it was. When I stepped out on the prairie from the strip of woods about one thousand yards wide, I discovered eight or ten farm buildings on the rolling rim and numerous herds of cattle roaming about. The places were alive with poultry, but not a sign of a human being was to be seen. Everybody was gone, far away, to escape the murdering bands from Mexico.

Every convenience that human beings could wish for their comfort was at hand but, with the exception of corn, there was not the slightest trace of any food. Everything had been concealed or destroyed.

On my honor, I assure you that I wasn't hungry or else I would have hunted the poultry. But a number of eggs looked so inviting to me that I ate about a dozen raw since I could not start a fire. After this meal I fell into a sound sleep on a pile of cotton. Being refreshed, I felt for the first time after my flight a gnawing hunger. As I searched through the buildings another time for food, I found two names written with charcoal on one of the doors, one of which was the name of my friend, Thomas Camp.

Up to this time I had been firmly convinced that I was the only one to have been lucky enough to have escaped the massacre. But here this name showed me that others had escaped and were already ahead of me to inform the world of the infamous murder at Goliad.

Delighted, I sank down to thank the Great Spirit. In the rejoicing of my heart I could have kissed and embraced all of humanity with the exception of Santa Anna and his henchmen.

I searched in vain for food. All that I could find were the remnants of dried beef that were left on the rods when the beef was hastily cut down, together with a few little sacks of seed hanging on the wall of one of the sheds. I took these sacks along with all the remaining beef that I could find, hung them around my neck, and thus equipped, I proceeded on my journey. I had also improved my wardrobe. A large, grey, so-called Kentucky felt hat, that cast a shadow about three feet in diameter, now sat on my head instead of the moss cap. Thus I was able to proceed in shade. At my left side hung a canteen, that I had borrowed, well filled with water, together with the grey helmet from my friend, the absent planter, and my name as debtor was written on the door on the side of the other two names.

It was as hot as yesterday, but under the grey felt hat, I marched as if I were under evergreen live oaks. Ahead of me lay, as I presumed, the forests of the Navidad [River] from five to six miles away, which merged with those of the Lavaca. I crossed a great, green, oval meadow on whose borders all around one could barely see the many homes of the colonists. On the great plain itself was seldom seen groups of live oak trees. The bustle of the animals now left the woods in spite of the very hot sun to eat the new springtime grasses.

The angry, blood-red face of the sun god had just disappeared behind layers of clouds on the horizon when I stood on the crest of a prairie elevation within a thousand yards of the timbers of the Navidad. I noticed two horsemen but was in doubt of their nationality. The sudden sound of military music and the appearance of a troop of dragoons around a forest projection indicated to me that Urrea's entire division was advancing!

I took only one look, and I dived down into the tall grass. I crept toward a small, dense tree island and concealed myself at the foot of a magnolia tree in some vines and Spanish moss. Here I determined to wait all night.

Barely was I finished when the enemy put out sentries, and my whole island domain was within enemy lines. By the way, to behold this from my retreat was not a pleasant matter. However, I was consoled by the fact that nothing could be done about it, and I anxiously looked forward to the coming of night.

Darkness finally enveloped the green savannah. Hidden by tall grass, I now crept out between the sentries that stood from fifty to sixty yards apart. The watchful blue uniforms, who suspected no heretic in their vicinity, stepped together, three in a group, and were merrily chattering, probably about the large amount of loot that they expected to carry back to Mexico. I had a strong inclination to grab the musket of one of these men. But I was liberal hearted and, besides, the musket was such a contemptible weapon in the eyes of the volunteers that even the men who carried it fell heir to its contempt. In our opinion as well as that of the inhabitants of the Free States of North America, it was a weapon only fit for hirelings (mercenaries). I, therefore, followed my course and was soon out in the open again, where I could walk like a human being.

But now by all means I had no choice but to hold counsel with myself about a number of things that crossed my mind, in the same manner as when I crossed the prairie. The first question was: Where am I? Then: Had I gone forward in my contemplated direction? Was this forest area the Navidad? Where would Sam Houston probably be? What should I do now and what course should I take to reach the Texan army? After much debating back and forth, I decided to direct my steps toward Washington [on the Brazos] where I had some chance of encountering the army of liberation. It was my definite opinion that this would be the best course that Houston could take in his retreat from the Colorado to the Brazos, as the deep, almost impenetrable, forests that covered the rich valley of the red Brazos would be the best terrain for the backwoodsmen to give the firm of Santa Anna and Company a little demonstration of their marksmanship. The next question was: Where was Washington? And could I depend on my skill to work my way through the wilderness and also avoid the redskins at the same time? Vividly I remembered that awful day when I, with a thousand curses and filled with fire from within and fire from without, fell unconscious to the ground. But I also remembered that the eastern part of Texas was more densely settled and contained larger forests than the western area. With these thoughts I went forward, when I suddenly came upon a plain road which I followed without thinking.

After going a few miles, I came to several plantations that stood from two to three hundred yards from the road, but I lost not a moment and hurried on along the road with new life. After I had wandered for about six miles, I found myself between two large cotton fields that spread out on the sides and before me as far as I could see in the pale light of the moon. Black timber surrounded the field, and on the opposite side lay a number of dark mounds that I took for the outlines of residential and other buildings. Cautiously I left the road and went slowly through the dry, rattling cotton stalks. Several times I stopped and listened, but not a sound of a living being could be heard in the houses. Only the owl carried on a wild confusion with his companions in the nearby forest. On approaching nearer, I could recognize among the considerable number of buildings especially the Negro quarters, the mighty cotton gin, as well as the blacksmith shop. It was evident that this was the property of a rich colonist.

Something dark moved in the shadow of the gin and cotton press. I listened but could not hear a sound. I advanced a few steps nearer, when suddenly the whole creation seemed to wake up. A terrible flapping of wings and a wild confusion of cries sounded all around me. Countless shrill cries filled the air and an endless cloud of wild geese rose up into the sky, darkening the moon and the scenery surrounding me. Quacking constantly, they flew around several times toward the edge of the forest, roaring like a storm when they flew over my head. Finally, however, they settled down on the other edge of the field. The pickled [drunk] army of the dictator [Santa Anna] could not have given me greater fright than the wild flight of these feathered heroes, especially as I had thought that these annually welcome guests had already left for their flight north.

The presence of these creatures here substantiated my former conclusion that neither friend nor enemy resided in the houses. Without further hesitation I now stepped among the buildings, between which stood a number of shady chinaberry trees. Hundreds of chickens and turkeys were roosting on the branches. In the pretty garden surrounded by fig and peach trees lay large groups of snoring hogs, and through the yard walked a herd of cattle that looked at me as if they had not seen a human soul for years.

As I entered the dark door of the main building, something came toward me noisily, walking over the wooden floor that was covered with carpets. I jumped to the side, behind the door, and a totally white mule walked majestically by me. He looked out of the door like an imperial excise officer [border guard] during bad weather, raised his head to the moon and commandingly brayed, demanding quiet, so that the whole plantation trembled. I took a deep breath and landed him a powerful blow with the door, and now the scare was on him. As if possessed, he dashed out through the frightened cattle, and his fading form finally disappeared in the dark woods.

I walked through several rooms and noted great disorder everywhere. Tables, chairs and beds lay scattered about. Everything indicated that the inhabitants, like all the colonists living west of the Colorado [River], had taken flight with the greatest haste. The set table stood in the spacious, elegantly, for Texas almost aristocratically, furnished dining room. The dishes contained untouched meals that needed nothing but warming. But a soldier who has had no cooked food for fifteen or sixteen days is not very particular, as the Texans say. And anything that satisfies hunger is first-class for a patriot. In fact, it was excellent beefsteak. Since I had suddenly become a rich plantation owner, I seated myself real comfortably at the table and arranged the dishes of food in order. I emptied one pan or plate after another, and in a short time the ghostly appearing moon looked sadly with me on the clean, empty, shining tablecloth.

Everything would have been good if I could have brought fire from heaven like Prometheus, or if I had had a confidential acquaintance with the redskins such as I had a few years later. If my somewhat too patriotic fellow-Texans could have suspected that a poor devil from Fannin's butchery was going to arrive here practically starved to death, they certainly would not have destroyed all the food and would possibly have left a gun and a little powder and lead. They had destroyed everything in their rage. Only the barns were filled to the roof with corn, but the mills were gone. Consequently the enemy could not use much of it, and neither could I.

If I remained here, I would in reality be no better off than I would be out in the prairie. I would either have to eat corn with my donkey, who still looked suspiciously at me from the side, or daily chase the poultry with a club and eat the captured game raw like the Indian-like Hungarians did a few years ago in Vienna, when they appeared in the guise of American cannibals (who a thousand miles west of Philadelphia ate each other!) and tore living chickens to pieces and devoured them before the very eyes of the good-natured people of Vienna.

After giving it considerable thought, I decided to slip around to the camp of my neighbors six miles away and try to get a fire-brand from them. If I should succeed in doing that, I would not exchange my abode here for the Arcade or the Bishop house in New Orleans or for the Astor house in New York because, in my mind, there was nothing more to be desired than freedom.

With a box half filled with ashes, I stole down the Navidad—it really was this little river that bordered on one side of the plantation—under the protection of the forest along the waterway. I pressed over the cultivated fields of several squatters, and just as I was about to step out of some bushes, I found myself directly in front of a Mexican outpost. I hastily withdrew and tried my luck at several other places. But wherever I approached, I found a closely picketed chain of sentries. I consequently returned without results to my plantation.

On the next day I made another attempt, hoping that the enemy had broken camp and moved on. But I was wrong. The same thing transpired the following two days, on the last of which I almost was captured.

Disappointed hopes and the many fruitless marches to the camp of the enemy had made me bold, and instead of walking along in the difficult but secure forest, I threw away the ash box angrily. I now believed that the Mexicans intended to settle down here in one of our richest colonies, which made it look very gloomy for us and especially for our independence. I now tried to figure out what could be done and how far away the Colorado [River] probably might be, and also thought about other matters. But I could find no satisfying answers to my questions. And then, my heavily loaded donkey and another mule, and two Mexicans heavily armed with carbines and pistols, came panting around a forest corner about four hundred to five hundred yards away. The donkey brayed. The mule and Mexicans looked flabbergasted in astonishment. And then one of them with a mustache looking like horns saw in the distance something dark, namely, my insignificant self, sink into the tall grass. With a frightful "*éste carajo Americano*" he with his carefully hesitating companion rushed forward and circled the spot where the dark object had disappeared. They did not trust the situation and tried to take a shot at me from a distance, as if somebody were there, in the words of the cautious one.

But I stole slowly toward the forest, carefully bending to the side the blades of grass that stood in the way. I was particularly careful not to show my head. I was already forty to fifty yards away when the one with the whirling mustache was still firing at the spot where I had disappeared. Suddenly, however, I heard some noises that confused me. I looked up a very little and ran hastily to the woods, in case more of the blue coats should appear. Instead of that, I saw my donkey and his noble companion going off in a full trot, paying no attention to the load on his back and braying loudly. My Mexicans pranced after them. And their long drawn out "Mu-u-ula [Mule], mu-u-ula hio mu-u-ula" sounded most charming under these circumstances. I did not contemplate long, but rushed away with long steps that Hopping Johnson barely would have been able to surpass. I marvelled at the fleetness of my feet, and soon I again entered my natural domain, the jungle. "Texas forever!" I cried again after I escaped the blue coats for the second time.

CHAPTER TWENTY-TWO

Urrea's Camp

~

"LUCKY TO ESCAPE! Lucky to give them the slip! Like the fox when the trap snaps shut in front of his nose!" Happily at home again, I observed. Now I sat among immense piles of cottonseed[39] stacked up in the gin, like a cricket in his closed-up hollow. I could expect the enemy at any moment to come for more provisions, as the loads of corn on the enemy's mules came from my plantation.

Thousands of plans crossed through my mind, but they exploded as quickly as many a steamboat had exploded on the Mississippi. I wanted to go to Washington [Texas] but I did not know where it was located. Neither did I know where I was, nor where [General] Houston was. Neither could I play the role of a settler until the republicans came back, not only because I had no fire but also because it was not safe here. I worried and schemed a long time. At last a bold idea came to mind, namely, to go directly into the Mexican camp, to present myself to the general as a traveler, to solicit his protection in this unpopulated Texas, and to sail to the army of my countrymen with the first favorable wind.

This was, indeed, a weird idea. However, that same evening I was on my way. It was already dark when I walked through the line of Mexican outposts, who were very eagerly calling their "*Alerta*" to each other, yes, in fact, so eagerly that not a soul noticed how a member of the accursed rebel army wandered through their watchful chain.

Close to two thousand men lay before me, and the prairie covered with watch-fires lay like a dark star-spangled-sky before me. I walked through the rows of Santa Anna's heroes sitting around the fires. They were a true picture of comfort as they sat there with crossed limbs cracking pecans, cooking *caldo* [soup], smoking cigarettes, or playing cards for their wages that the Napoleon of the West had owed them no telling how long. Some were cursing us heretics and others were innocently enjoying a mental plunder of the city of New Orleans. They were determined to punish this city in an exemplary manner because of the sympathy that it gave to the Jewish Texans,[40] and the city on the Mississippi could congratulate itself for having escaped without being burned to the ground. In passing, I wished them good luck on their journey. "Go to it my boys," I said and walked on through the irregular fires to a few tents on a slight elevation near the forest, where I expected to find the headquarters.

A group of jolly women sitting in front of a tent attracted my attention. They were busy shelling corn for a noisy herd of mules. Several bold-looking men on horseback surrounded the herd of mules that was fighting for something to eat. With incessant cursing and other long drawn-out words, and using the whip, the men tried to establish calm among the restless mules. If quiet came for a moment, a hail of curses were repeated so that the noisy revolt began anew. A great enjoyment for the Mexicans!

I stepped closer to the women. And the fire must have strangely illuminated me, because the ears of corn fell from the hands of the *señoras* in fright. I do not know whether it was I who looked so frightful or whether it was only my tremendous grey Kentucky felt hat. At first they looked at me in surprise, but when they heard my "*Buenos noches,*" they cried as if in one chorus "*un carajo Americano,*" [a damn American - actually an even stronger reference than damn], our usual title. I bowed very respectfully to the *señoras* and thanked them for their very flattering welcome with a few courteous Spanish words I knew, and then asked for the location of the general's tent.

"*Capitán,*" they called to a little Mexican on a horse. "*Capitán,* come here quickly, *un Americano!*" The captain came up and looked at me with his one weak, black eye. The other one had been shot out by one of [Philip] Dimitt's men at the [October, 1835] capture of Goliad. He demanded to know what I wanted from him and how the devil I got here.

The man looked so barbaric, his face was so overgrown with whiskers, and he spoke such horrible English that a more courageous heart than mine would have lost courage. But for some time I had become so strangely indifferent, that I looked him so calmly in the eye as if an old acquaintance of mine stood before me.

"My courageous captain," I answered, "You see here a perfectly peaceful traveler, who has something of importance to tell the general."

"Something of importance? Importance, *señor?*" he asked, staring at me in excited curiosity. "But," he continued, "have you appetite, *señor?* — probably are hungry—drink a cup of cocoa.—Come, let us talk—come—but—*señor,*" measuring me from head to foot. "You do not look—as if you had—anything of importance, I mean—but if you know anything—I would gladly like to know something of importance."

"Sir," I said, "I have things of importance for a general but not for a mule-*capitán*; but in spite of that, I will drink this cup to your health."

The mule-*capitán* felt himself flattered that I at once titled him *capitán* in the presence of the women, as he really was only a lieutenant in the group that had just been fed.

"*Señor*," he continued more considerately, while I enjoyed another piece of cornbread, "do you know we soon go to Washington to whip the damn Yankees. You no be one of them? I see kinky hair. Are you not, *señor*, of black and white blood?" [Mestizo]

"I can not say, *señor*, that I have the honor of being related to the black gentry. But I presume you are—hm?—"

"Right, *señor*, right—but you look so brown—your hair so woolly, *señor*"—He shook his head.

"Do you mean Washington in Texas?" I interrupted him, "I presume that Mexico will not wish to tie up with Uncle Sam?"

"We want to beat Uncle Sam, *señor*. We want to drive him out of America, and all blacks shall become free men, *señor*."

"Very humanitarian, sir, I wish you good luck on your journey. But by the way, if I may be permitted to ask, my brave *capitán*, who so disfigured your noble features, and who had the inexcusable impudence of knocking out your eye?"

"*Señor*," he answered solemnly, "*un carajo Americano* [a damn American], sir, when we were at Goliad. *Señor*, we were playing good Christians like we often do. A plot—the bandits—the *Americanos* saw us over the wall, *señor*—Saw us peaceful—That made them mad, *señor*. They shoot—my companion falls—me, *señor*," he added gnashing his teeth. "They shoot out my eye—and I want to get my fusil [a light flintlock musket], *señor*. The bandits—the Jews—come over the wall on one side, and the *Mexicanos* depart on to the other. Now, *señor*, I not be strong enough to fight all. I leave my fusil and go over the wall and run to Matamoras, *señor*, with one eye." He took a deep breath and continued, "My wife, *señor*, will not have man half-blind. She takes another man. I can do nothing. *Padre* say, she is right. He forgives my sins for three years for nothing—very kind. But it was not very good—Had I a fusil, I would have shot myself, *señor*."

"Nonsense, *capitán*, don't be a fool. You are still as fine a fellow as ever marched in his own boots. What, commit suicide?

Possible likeness of Ehrenberg.
Art by José Cisneros.

Shame! A man like you speak of shooting himself, and all that because of a petticoat who flutters with the wind and changes colors as if to out-do the lizard.[41] Well, *capitán*, I thought the sons of Mexico were too courageous to talk like that."

   "*Señor*, I courage enough have—I no shoot myself—went to General Cos—say to him, I am a patriot—tell him, I have fought at Goliad—tell him I was last one to run away, tell him lots more, *señor*—Cos sends me to [Brigadier] General [José] Urrea—he make me leader at Tamaulipas—but in Texas, *señor*, have become *capitán des mulas*—have a very good salary, *señor*, but have not yet received anything. The *padres* have said that we will get much, and Santa Anna has said that we will get very much—and Cos and General Urrea have promised us great piles of *doblóns* [doubloons] and *pesos* in New Orleans and Philadelphia, *señor*, we going there. You do better going with us—get rich—awfully rich."

Martiny [Martinez?], a nice little adjutant of Urrea, just now passed by in company with another officer. I remembered him from Goliad and knew that he had been reared in the States and that he spoke English very well. I jumped up hastily and followed him.

"*Señor, señor*," cried the commander of the mules, "you not want to tell me the important news—the important news, *señor*?" But I acted as if I did not hear him and asked the adjutant where I could speak to the general.

Surprised to see one of the rebels here, he looked at me and asked from whence I came, if I were one of Fannin's men, or if perhaps one of the rebel army, and if I had possibly deserted.

At first I had an inclination to play the role of a deserter, but I could not persuade myself to carry such a disrespectable name for even a few weeks. In order to forestall any further questions, I told him that I would report only to Urrea in person and that all further questioning would be useless. This had a powerful effect.

However, he was very friendly and observed that the general could not now be seen for half an hour as he was eating his supper, and that I might meanwhile go with him to his tent to ingest something warm.

I still had an appetite and could easily manage an adjutant's helping as the Mexicans eat very little. And as our people are accustomed to say: they eat like canary birds, quarrel like sparrows, consist of skin and bones like the crane and run like a horse when they perceive gunpowder behind them.

Beefsteak and *frijoles* is an excellent meal for a person who had tasted nothing warm for fifteen to sixteen days with the exception of a cup of cocoa. But what surprised me the most was the excellent beefsteak, without which neither Americans nor Texans can live anywhere, and suffer like an alligator that shrivels up out of water.

Then I ate my helping in good Yankee style in about five minutes, while the two officers took over half an hour to question me, after which time we broke up to see the general.

Three mustached people sat on traveling trunks around a table that was still set with a simple meal. The first one to attract my attention was a black-brown individual with an extremely small face which compared to the broad brimmed hat like the head of a peacock to its tail, and what of the face that was not concealed by the shadow of the broad brim of the hat was obscured by a heavy mustache over the lips and a dark beard under them. His sparkling, little eyes cast piercing glances at the entering Texan. I at once recognized him as the death messenger who brought orders for our execution from Santa Anna to the commander of Goliad—at least we believed that he had brought the orders from San Antonio.

On the side of him sat another notorious individual, a Mexicanized Rhenish-Prussian, really quite a noble fellow, and already known to us from Fannin's capitulation. I mean the notorious [Lieutenant Colonel Juan José] Holsinger. With him, as with all the Mexican defenders of the fatherland, the most important and dignified thing was the aristocratic, yet barbaric-looking mustache that was nicely twisted to a point. And I marveled that a carpenter [engineer] had risen so high after I had seen his twisted beard and also that he should be able to create such a noble decoration as these usually would grow only on noble skin. The paper that lay before them held bold drawings made by Holsinger's hand—too bold, it seemed to me, for the hand that executed them. His constantly moving mouth entertained the officers who were sitting nearby. In spite of his explanations, they looked at the plan as if everything was Greek to them.

The third, finally, was a five-feet, ten-inch tall rather pale-looking man. Only a small amount of beard was discernible on his face and his eyes (that did not sparkle as fiery in this proud descendant of Spain as those of the little half-Indian death messenger) wandered from the drawing on the table after a time, and then his eyes pierced the adjutant and me. General Urrea—for it was he himself—addressed me in a very friendly manner, asking who I was and what I wanted. As I could speak very little Spanish, he asked me what other languages I could speak, and I answered: English and German. He paused for a moment and then spoke with the other two. But it was so rapid that I could not understand a word he said. Whereupon Holsinger addressed me in a very angry manner and directed me to answer his questions to the minutest detail. "First," he began, "from where do you come? Who are you? What in the devil are you doing here? And what do you want from us?" He then was silent, however, first warning me not to say anything but the strictest truth.

"On question number one, Colonel, I must answer you that I am a citizen of the North American Union, and that I stand under the protection of the twenty-four stars which, I believe, stand in unshakable bonds of friendship with their southern sisters and, I hope, are worthy of the confidence of Mexico." Here I took out a pocket knife and began to whittle as Yankees do when something important comes up, so that my emotions would not reflect in my face.

Holsinger mumbled, "Very well. Very well spoken." He smiled and translated this part of my examination.

"On the second," I continued, "I can only answer, and I hope that it will be sufficient, that my name is X. X. and that I was born in a land called Prussia."

"Prussia? Prussia? I thought you were a Prussian. Prussia

stands in good relationship with our republic. I am, therefore, not surprised that you are a Prussian."

I acted as if I had not noticed his suspicious remark but continued to answer the third question. "Quite a while ago a kinsman of mine disappeared from his home. We have never been able to find any trace of him. And it was only in the year 1834 that I was informed by a German newspaper editor in Cincinnati by the name of Hartmann that my lost uncle—or at least a gentleman by that name—was in Mexico and was employed by the English Mining Company at *Real del Monte*. Since for a long time I have desired to cross the high plains of the Tlascalians and to see the battlefield and place where Cortez gave the world an example of his bloody courage when he destroyed Montezuma, I set out last summer when I was in New Orleans and went with a schooner to Matagorda Bay, where I bought a mustang in order to proceed by horse from then on. I began my journey in July but soon became ill with the chills and fever. I did not get well until late fall. That season, as you know, Colonel, is not good for traveling on account of a shortage of grass for the horses. During the winter I remained with Mr. Williams,"—the name I invented for the owner of the plantation where I had been staying—"who lives about six miles from here. Last March I took another fever, the so-called bilious fever, and I cannot say how long I was laid up. Neither can I remember anything except that the plantation owner came to my bed one day and told me that he and his family would have to leave the plantation at once; but since he had no light wagon in which to take me along, he would be forced to let me stay here for a while. I should, however, be without fear, as his good old black servant, Jack, would come within three days and get me. I saw him enter, I heard him speak, the kindly Williams, I saw him set food near my bed, I felt the warm grip of his hand, saw him leave—but I did not understand anything. I again fell into feverish dreams and must have lain there a very, very long time, until a few days ago when I recognized my sad situation. After I had eaten a little of the practically dried up food, I felt somewhat refreshed and decided to wander over to the houses of the neighbors. But all the houses to the right and to the left were deserted, and I did not see a human being until I stood in the center of your army."

"A very touching account, Mr. Prussian," said Holsinger, and translated the last part thereof with ambiguous smiles to the general.

"The fourth and last question, Colonel, is easily answered. I come to you as a man in need who asks nothing but the sympathy of his fellowman. I am through, Colonel. Kindly ask General Urrea's permission for me to accompany his army to the next inhabited region."

The trio had a long debate. The mustaches were thoughtfully rolled. Martiny was questioned, and I personally had to endure the penetrating looks of first one and then the other and, at times, of all three.

"Now, Mr. Prussian," Holsinger finally began, stroking his beard, "this is a very nice little story, and I must admit on my honor that it has touched all of us. But we do not believe a word of it. Then every Yankee could come with his false pretenses. Consequently this time, the unadulterated truth, for you know that we are not joking. Also, where is the army of the rebels now, and are you not a spy?"

"Spy, sir," I responded hastily. Composing myself again, I answered, "I am not thinking of playing such a role," but I asked, "what did you say of a rebel army?"

"Do not take on a disguise," he continued, "the Texans I mean, where are they?"

"I do not know a word of them, much less why they are called rebels."

The colonel was surprised, the general was much surprised, and the death messenger more surprised. They looked at each other, debated, shook their heads and shrugged their shoulders.

"Have you never heard of the name Fannin?" asked the colonel, "But the whole truth," said he with his eyes drawn together in a threatening manner.

"Fannin—Fannin," said I, rubbing my forehead slowly, "Fannin? No—no—I think, never."

Again the trio consulted each other a while. Then they were silent and so steeped in thought that not a joint moved. The polished beards were gripped in the hands as if these important parts of the Mexican officers were in danger. The Texan incognito sat there quietly and, while whittling figures, speculated on what the *mustachios* would bring forth next.

Suddenly, it seemed, a great thought struck Holsinger. Unceremoniously he released his mustache that he had been holding with both hands. In doing this, however, he brought it into such disorder that he was obliged to pause to put it into order again. He first spoke in a loud tone in Spanish to General Urrea and then in German to me, while the other two men rubbed their hands between their knees.

"Now, my dear Prussian," he said, giving his mustache another artificial turn, "I presume you know the name of your uncle in Mexico."

"On this point I can fully inform the colonel," said I, "my uncle is *Señor* Antonio X. X. in *Real del Monte*, twenty-two leagues from Mexico," and continued to whittle slowly and innocently. Without hearing another word, the inquisitor turned to the general and informed him of the correctness of my answer. Holsinger knew the whole mining personnel, or at least the officers, as he was formerly counted among the latter himself.

After another little conference in which, as I believed, they mutually expressed their doubt about my statements, the inquisitor addressed me another time and, after assembling all the dignity that his black mustache would permit, he said in a fear-inspiring tone, "Listen, professed Prussian, do you not know that we shoot everyone we find in Texas?"

"Uncle Sam, sir, would very much take that amiss," I said, sticking to my story with the greatest composure. "Uncle Sam, sir, is not to be trifled with, especially when some of his component parts are concerned, because every citizen is a part of the republican colossus."

The colonel translated this into reckless Spanish, indignant that I should have dared to threaten the Catholic priestly authority. Urrea heard the boisterous translation and smiled a little; but the death messenger set his mustache in order, doubled his brown fists and struck on the table so that the dishes rattled; and this blusterer slung curse after curse at me in such rapid succession that the sum total sounded like one long, drawn-out word.

Urrea, for whom things seemed to get too warm and who had remained passive up to this time, arose, looked around, and his majestic figure alone commanded silence, but a single look and a calmly spoken word with a well-sounding voice at once destroyed the anger and the raging of the other two. I heard a number of slowly spoken words with which he ordered Holsinger, among other things, to take care of me for the night. The manner of the half-breed had appreciably changed in typical Mexican fashion even before Urrea ceased speaking. His barometer had fallen and corresponded with that of the general.

As I was leaving the tent, the general called to me in Spanish, but very distinctly, whether I was hungry, and before I could answer, the young adjutant and I had to sit down at the table. The young man was Urrea's favorite and, although he was very young, received favors above all the other officers. During his stay in the Union he had absorbed the infatiguable spirit of "the brother Jonathan" and had acquired knowledge that likely none of his comrades could demonstrate. Withal he possessed such a lovely character and had such a fine, tender appearance, that he was irresistible.

Honestly, it was time that the hearing came to an end as I barely would have been able to carry on the masquerade much longer. My only means of salvation was my whittling, which concealed my feelings and gave me such a composed, careless manner that it surprised the three.

As Holsinger assured me, my hearing was to be continued the next morning. But my fellow German must not have been able to bring that about. When I came to Urrea, I found out that none of that would happen, and that the general was very friendly. He ordered Martiny to give me one of his suits [uniform]. And even the Rhenish-Prussian, to avoid seeing the horrible Kentucky felt hat, gave me an officer's hat nicely decorated with gold braiding. Around ten o'clock the next morning I was, without previous notice, confronted with several Texan prisoners, none of whom knew me with the exception of one. This one was Jack Rees, who like me had succeeded in escaping from the massacre but was later likewise compelled to surrender on account of the shortage of food. A wink from me cautioned him, and we stared at each other's faces like two figures in a wax cabinet. But the inward joy at seeing another comrade who had been saved threatened to break our assumed masks. I passed this last trial also, walked free through the Mexican lines and lived in the tent with the general, who seemed to take special pleasure in the little Prussian, as he now called me.

As I went through the camp the next day, I saw Holsinger's cook from Hamburg, by the name of Gansen, whom the colonel [Holsinger] had rescued at Refugio. He had belonged to King's company, and as the men were to be executed, Holsinger had thrown an artillery coat over him and had pulled him out of the confusion. The heroes fell and a scoundrel was saved, who at the Fannin massacre, as Martiny told me, had offered his unrequested services, to turn the cannons against his own comrades. However, Urrea was indignant at the insolence of this man, which is saying much, and ordered him to leave the cannon at once and to attend to his kitchen duties. To this fellow (whom I didn't know any further than that he had once been one of our men), I confided my fate as I was glad to see that another of our unfortunate companions had been saved. He also was very happy, pressed my hand, and gave me the advice to act as if we had never seen each other, which I promised. However, it did not make much difference to me as I was of the firm opinion that I was out of danger. As I entered General Urrea's tent that afternoon, he smiled at me, threatened with his finger and told me that he had discovered who I was.

"Well, General, your assumption or rather your knowledge is correct, and I cannot and will not further deny it. But I would be grateful to know from what source you have your information."

"Your countryman has not acted as was becoming of him," he answered, "but the little Prussian need not be concerned. He, to whom Urrea gives his word, may rest easy."

I was inclined to ask him who gave Fannin his word on the Coleto, but wisely held my peace.

"If the little one asks it," he continued, "he shall at once have a horse and a pass to Matamoras, and from there he can go wherever it pleases him. But it would please me if he would remain in Texas until the close of the campaign, which can now be considered as practically ended, and then go with me to Durango; if he should not like it there, he will be at liberty to choose another place."

"Thank you very much, General, for your kind consideration. I would rather remain in Texas, but allow me to observe that it does not appear to me as if the campaign were nearly ended. In the first place, the Mexican troops are not nearly at the Sabine; and in the second place, I do not believe that the militia of the land will forsake all of their property without trying a battle. The backwoodsmen, General, are no cowards, and

I will venture the opinion that you will yet have many a round with these cold-blooded, constantly calculating, squatters. Up till now the Mexican armies have fought only against city dwellers, all volunteers, who had to attribute their demise to their own internal discord. No one was willing to take orders from anyone else, and each one fought on his own account. Even in such circumstances the little groups have shown you what determination of the will can do. Be free! was their motto, but Texas or Death! is that of the militia."

This conversation was conducted in English and had to be partly translated by the adjutant. As I ended, the general smiled, tapped me on the shoulder and said in questioning tone:

"Still rebellious?"

"General," I replied, "as long as I have a breath left in me, all this shall happen only for the sake of freedom. And if new blossoms will some day appear on the tree that is called the Rio Grande, General Urrea can depend on it that his prisoner, (who was fighting for the broken-off leaf that had been planted individually) will as readily fight for the new buds and blossoms on the old plant."

"This is very good. A praiseworthy zeal," said Urrea. "However, we have dispatches from the commander-in-chief that leave us to infer that we will depart soon for Durango." He turned to Martiny and directed him to translate the main sentence of a dispatch from Santa Anna, which he did as follows:

"Much to our dismay, the old Tennessean [Sam Houston] is avoiding us everywhere, so that not even our cavalry can catch him. Soon he will be beyond the Sabine and all of his rabble with him. Then our brave officers may enjoy a period of rest or follow me across the Sabine. Our national honor demands from me that I most severely punish that town of shopkeepers [New Orleans] that dared to recruit troops against Mexico. Once more I remind you that the congress of the nation has ordered to shoot to death everyone. Keep this in mind—"

He stopped.

I laughed over this boasting and thought it was advanta-geous for my country to support the enemy's boasting. The question was on my tongue to ask what kind of a congress this had been that had passed that order. Was it composed of repre-sentatives elected by the people? If this was the case, was the law passed through the house of representatives with the bayo-nets of Santa Anna or with the *pesos* of the Catholic priests? But I chose the wisest; I held my tongue and left the tent in order to get some fresh air.

---

[39] Cottonseed - which can be found in large amounts on the plantations.

[40] All Jews in Mexico are called *non-Catholics*.

[41] A lizard in Texas. [chameleon]

CHAPTER TWENTY-THREE

Old Sam

THE GUADALUPE ROARED DOWN between its banks past the little town of Gonzales, where the Texas militia under Sam Houston was making its quarters. A strange stillness prevailed in the camp. With dark and moody expressions the tanned planters stared into the fires, and barely a word passed their lips except an occasional criticism of Fannin. Even the whittling had ended. Instead, the men played with their shiny Bowie knives. They threw them alternately into the ground and drew them forth again. One could easily see that a bloody, frightful catastrophe was playing before their imaginations since from time to time they would make fierce gestures.

The fall of the Alamo [March 6, 1836] and the death of the heroes who so gallantly died there put the whole camp in this mood. Since the sixth of March the signal cannon that [William B.] Travis fired regularly every morning had not been heard, and the worst was feared. And today the worst had been substantiated as the exact news of the battle and the death of the unfortunate ones became known. Imagine the mood of the little army of slightly less than six hundred men!

Several were sitting around a large fire and were reading the letters that Travis had written to the national assembly shortly before. In a soft voice the reader, an old, brave planter dressed from head to foot in Indian attire—he was our old acquaintance[42] from San Augustine—continued:

"I am besieged by a thousand men or more under Santa Anna. I have sustained an incessant bombardment for the last twenty-four hours without the loss of a man. The enemy has demanded my surrender at discretion, or to expect no mercy if the fort be taken. My answer was a cannon shot."

"Hear it, boys, did you hear it? It was a cannon thunder, boys. That was the proper way to answer those bloodhounds," the old man interrupted himself and then continued:

"Our flag still floats on the walls. I will never surrender or retreat: Victory or Death!"

"Victory or Death! Yes, you brave Travis, Bowie, Crockett, Evans, Paw and all you heroes are no more. But boys, boys, I swear to you these old bones will never find rest if terrible vengeance is not taken for our comrades. Boys, you hear it, you may accuse me in high heaven if old Jack doesn't do it."

A long pause followed. No one spoke until it seemed that the spirits had somewhat quieted down.

"But father," hesitatingly said a slender boy shyly, "let us read the last letter from Travis. I have not yet heard it—just came back today from Mama about whom you have not even inquired."

"Ha, you saucy brat, who would speak of Mama in times like this! Go, you pinfeather hero—help the old woman cook her tea! Who thinks of wife and child when such giants like Crockett and Jack [James] Bowie fall? Who would think of kitchen affairs when the hell-hounds, the Mexicans, aim to bring the red cock into our midst? [burn us to the ground] But we'll give it to them—damn it—we'll fight back. Damn it. Jack Bowie, my old fellow, you died honorably and will be remembered as great forever. All of you, old comrades, are gone—are happy. But old Jack from San Augustine is still here and is weeping bloody tears. Yes, you old comrades, Jack is weeping blood—and Jack is thirsting for blood. Blood is his rallying cry; either the blood of your murderers or mine must flow."

Great tears ran down the brown cheeks of the old fellow as he was staring into the fire. None of his sons nor his listeners dared to try to stop the stream of words that relieved his heart.

Finally, after a while, the old man[43] began to read the second letter, which Travis had written on the third day of March.

"The enemy has continued his incessant cannonading to the present time and surrounded us on all sides with fortified positions. However, thirty-two men from Gonzales have stolen into our camp and my couriers have gone in and out. I fortified this place in such a way that the walls are cannonball proof and continue to reinforce them from inside with earth walls. We have been lucky enough not to lose a man, but have killed many of the enemy. We have now fought for ten days against a fighting force estimated from fifteen hundred to two thousand men. A reinforcement of approximately two thousand men is now moving into town. And judging by the general cheering, Santa Anna himself must have arrived.

"Colonel Fannin is said to be on the way with reinforcements for us. Unfortunately I fear that this is not true, as my several appeals to him for aid have remained unanswered. From the colonies alone I am expecting help, and without its speedy arrival, I will have to fight the enemy regardless of the consequences. I trust that my countrymen will not lose courage in this hour of death. If they themselves should fall victim to the vengeance of a barbaric enemy, this one shall cost the enemy more than a defeat. God and Texas! Victory or Death!

"The Convention must declare our independence. Then we will know for what we are fighting, and the world will understand us. If our independence is not declared soon, my men and I will lay down our arms. But under the flag of independence we are willing to risk our lives daily and to resist the monster, who is fighting us under the red flag and is threatening to murder all prisoners and to convert Texas into a desert. I will have to fight the enemy on his terms and am ready to do so. If my fellow countrymen do not come to my support, my bleaching bones will be an eternal reproach to them. With five hundred reinforcements I could drive the enemy back over the Rio Grande and could throw back the revenge on the enemies of Texas, whether they are its inhabitants or not. All inhabitants who are not for us are against us. The government should declare those detractors to be enemies of the country, and not doing so would amount to suicide."

"Women!" interrupted the mumbled voice of a strong, six-foot tall man. His crumpled, broad brimmed, grey felt hat was pushed deep into his face as he stepped through the rows of fires. Yellow leather trousers and high-water boots dressed the lower part of the gigantic torso, and a Cherokee hunting shirt with fringe hung over his shoulders. A rather long vest, reaching well down to the hips and buttoned half-way up, added to the figure a quiet dignity that not even his enemies could deny. The collar and crumpled front ruffle of his fine linen shirt hung out of his vest, and his white throat and chest formed a sharp contrast with his brown, although friendly, facial features. But now his brow was greatly wrinkled and he had a morose expression. With arms crossed on his back Old Sam—for it was he—walked through the camp. Working out plans, he walked up and down and did not hear the report that the Mexican cavalry had arrived on the other side of the river.

When he returned, the old planter was just reading the last lines of the letter. "What is it, man!" he screamed across to him. "How can you now read so quietly? Have you no feeling, man? Every line, every word cuts and tears and rakes like a dagger in my heart! Man, and you read as if it afforded you pleasure. Speak it with much more emphasis as if you were standing on a stage, man! Ha, must Sam Houston have such men in his army—hadn't expected it. All our healthy young men dead! Their blood cries from heaven for vengeance, and here you sit and don't give a damn!"

In a rage the old planter from San Augustine jumped up before Sam Houston and, gnashing his teeth, broke the silence with the words: "Stop, Stop! Not another word! Not another word! Lies! Infamous lies! Who dares to say even now that Jack has no feelings? Who dares?"

"I! I! Sam Houston said it!"

"'Tis a damn lie![44] I say," answered the planter, out of himself with emotion.

"And who dares to call Sam Houston a liar to his face, who dares it? Who?"

The old general, who had not looked at his opponent in his rage, now fixed his stark, protruding eyes on those of old Jack. Piercing glances shot back and forth. And with arms pulled back and clinched fists, the two gigantic figures stood opposite each other. Neither breathed. Nobody, not even the militia itself that had gathered in a circle about the two, dared to interrupt the pause with even a syllable. But the clinched fists dropped, the stark eyes began to sparkle anew, the rage changed into sorrow and,

"Jack!" said the one.

"General!" the other.

The hands fell into each other, and they shook heartily. Again the tears ran over the cheeks of the old planter. But the old general, as morose as before, walked his usual way through the surprised militia with his hands crossed on his back. After a while the general disappeared into his tent, but his gigantic mind worked as usual with astonishing coolness.

Order after order flew into the colonies, to Fannin, to the National Assembly, to the states and to his own men. Soon the light artillery of the Texans drove the Mexican cavalry far out of reach. It put a spark of life into the militia that had been beaten down but not discouraged.

"Remember the Alamo!" was heard from every direction. The folding of the tents and the packing up of the soldiers' articles of the little army proceeded rapidly in order to break camp speedily for the Colorado [River], to assemble there the whole military force of the republic and then to destroy the enemy.

"Sam Houston is himself again!"[45] cried the troops as they marched away. With the cannon in the lead, they marched off to the Colorado [River] forests, where they arrived late in the evening of March 11.

Here Houston pitched his camp in the hope that the reluctant citizens would rally to his cause after hearing the news. Heretofore people had regarded the Mexicans as too contemptible to be accorded any attention; but after such a deed was committed, everybody could see that only the speediest general cooperation would save the republic.

The Texans threw off their apathy; but in spite of this present revolt, the army did not increase in the least. In fact it had dwindled down to an insignificant mass, as the citizens who composed the army at Gonzales were obliged to leave the colors and take their women and children over the Brazos to safety. Because who could predict the outcome of the first battle?

The general had deluded himself, and his only hope was to block the march of the enemy over the Colorado until the returning citizens and Colonel Fannin, who had received repeated orders for an immediate retreat, united with him. Then he would make a sudden attack on the enemy's main group or corps. The enemy was rushing forward divided into three divisions, and by attacking the main corps, Houston could cut off the remaining two divisions from Mexico.

[42] Scherpf
[43] Scherpf
[44] *Verdammte lüg* [Damned lie]
[45] Similarly, "Richard is himself again" in Shakespeare.

On the Colorado

By the twenty-fifth of March the army had increased to thirteen hundred men, but one dispatch after another with terrible news had brought out a murderous spirit among the men. The murder of Grant and his men, of Johnson's detachment, of Captain King's, the inexplicable disappearance of Ward who was wandering around somewhere in the wild prairie, Horton's final report of the capture for which Fannin himself was to blame, together with the fall of the Alamo, called forth such a rage among the backwoodsmen that only a Sam Houston was able to lead them.

The old general sat on a stack of saddles with several letters and a map of the former province of Texas before him. In a circle surrounding a large fire, the captains sat or stood propped on their rifles. Surrounding this group in dense masses were the complaining backwoodsmen. The captains wore civilian clothing of various kinds. These strong figures were almost without exception six-feet tall. Their dark, fiery eyes flashed first at the glowing coals and then at old Sam, who was the only composed person in the whole group.

Sam Houston.

Archives and
Information Services,
Texas State Library.

Slowly he took a small knife from his vest pocket, opened it, brought forth a huge piece of real Cavendish, cut off a quid, shoved it between his front teeth and his upper lip and passed the remainder to his neighbor, a huge captain whose upper torso was also covered with an Indian hunting shirt. The broad brim of a former extra fine beaver flopped down over his ears, and from the feet to the knees his muscular limbs were wrapped with thick, crimson colored flannel as is the custom among the inhabitants of the western part of America and is a very practical protection in Texas against the thorns of the mesquite trees. The ammunition pocket was made from the scalp of a pretty leopard skin. The eyes, being finished with red cloth, considerably enhanced the beauty of the pelt. It hung from the brown, untanned deerskin belt that fitted close around the strong figure on account of the weight of the pocket. With a bitter expression, the one described passed the black tobacco from hand to hand but no one served himself, which was evidence of a very unusual mental agitation.

After the tobacco had made the rounds, the old general put it back into his pocket and, whittling, continued the conference. He was as cool and composed as one would be in the company of a person whom one meets for the first time in his life.

"I tell you," proceeded the general, "our situation is somewhat precarious—cannot deny it—but it is the only thing that will bring our people to reason—Santa Anna will destroy the colonies, but it is not Sam Houston's fault—instead of coming together hastily, the militia remains nicely at home with the women—very comfortably at the chimney fire—thinking a few volunteers can fight it out with ten thousand of these half-breeds—false conclusion, gentlemen, you see—the brave boys are gone—a shame for us—and the enemy is on our heels. Instead of four thousand to five thousand of our men being here, there are thirteen hundred, gentlemen—the others are packing up—taking long pleasure rides to the Sabine.

General Sam Houston, with knife, is shown whittling while giving orders to his adjutant.

Cannot help it, comrades—will have to retreat again—into the timbers of the Brazos—must move on—on, even today."

"Stop, General, those are idle words," cried one with a cap made of a wildcat skin, "not a step from here—the enemy must soon be here—and then we will give him such a glorious whipping that it will be a pleasure for every right-thinking person to dish it out to those miserable vampires."

"To Battle! To Battle!" cried the crowd surrounding the conference. "Here for Texas or never!"

"Sam Houston is not of this opinion, my braves," answered the general, "nor is it his will. Sam will not risk the fate of the entire republic on the basis of one daring encounter here. The mile-wide forests of the Brazos shall render us splendid service. Even if you are brave and are willing to risk your lives, the interests of our country are not served if you are killed. No, my boys—we will give it to the grasshoppers as surely as Sam Houston is standing in his own boots."

"It is impossible for us to retreat further, General," said another, "Will not do—it will not do—we must fight. Why, General, our richest settlements lie between the Colorado and the Brazos. The old Austin [Moses Austin] would turn in his grave if he could hear the footsteps of these murderous bands across the prairie. No, General, we must fight. We must either win or die."

"Must either win or die!" came the muffled refrain from the two circles, but the old general whittled quietly on and seemed determined to win a victory in his own camp first.

"Boys," he addressed himself to the crowd, stood up, took another quid, closed his knife and began: "Boys, you want to fight—very praiseworthy. Your courage is in fact very praiseworthy. But suppose the enemy with his large amount of artillery should win, can you, will you assume the responsibility? Can you assume the responsibility for having wanted a battle before our somewhat tardy fellow citizens were in position to hasten to our

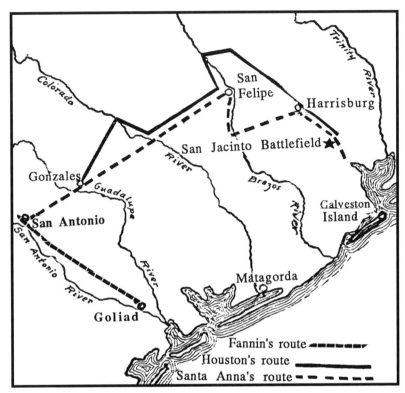

Route of Sam Houston's retreat over the Brazos to Buffalo Bayou near present-day city of Houston, and Santa Anna's pursuit. Ehrenberg's escape route took him from Goliad to Matagorda.

reinforcement? Would you take it on your conscience if the republic fell again under the Mexican yoke because an undisciplined crowd would not wait for a favorable moment for the battle? No, no, citizens, we must move back to the Brazos where our men can give good service with their rifles without risking much themselves. If we attack the five-times stronger enemy here, we will have to storm him in the open prairie.

"I assuredly do not doubt what you call your courage, which, however, is pure foolhardiness. I am accountable to the republic, to the whole people, for what I do. I can never consent to fight here. Again I call on you to follow me to San Felipe, and he who wants the best for the republic, let him be ready in an hour. We may expect the main force of the enemy any moment on the opposite bank, while a significant detachment of cavalry already has reached the Colorado above us. And General Urrea with practically two thousand men cannot be far from here, further down near the sea [Gulf] coast. So once more, let's head to the densely wooded banks of the Brazos!"

The old general walked off to his tent, and the crowd, ill-tempered and mumbling discontent, went back to the fires and began polishing the guns. But in only one and one-half hours the Texan army vacated the camp on the Colorado. Sam Houston had won, and the next evening he arrived at San Felipe. However, he did not stop here but marched up the river.

On March 30th the first enemy cavalry appeared near San Felipe, which lies directly on the Brazos. The residents set fire to their rich stores and warehouses and fled across the river. Barely had they departed when the enemy moved in, flying into a rage to encounter only brightly burning buildings instead of rich booty.

Houston now disappeared and his enemies could not determine his location, until he appeared suddenly like the messenger of Nemesis on the arena of war and refuted the false and low-down accusations of the enemies of Texas that he was fleeing because of cowardice. This had been done only by those who did not have the slightest idea of the general's character or, as has been mentioned, by the armed, two-faced enemies of the republic. But from both sides it sounded as convincing as when one would say that the Bengal tiger was fleeing from a dozen barking dogs.

It is still a puzzle to me how the general succeeded again in persuading those independent spirits to retreat over the Brazos to Buffalo Bayou. I am fully convinced that only a Sam Houston could do so—no other man in the republic could do it.

CHAPTER TWENTY-FIVE

The Amnesty

URREA SAT MUSING IN HIS TENT, great plans crossing through his mind. Didn't Santa Anna rise so high? Why should not Urrea, who needed to take one more step to grasp the helm of the government by force, also be in position to bring under his banner the Mexicans? After all, hadn't they for centuries been used to being governed by the rod and the sword, just like another great body-politic of this kind comfortably holds its masses together with the whip? But he had done a stupid deed. The *señor* saw that now. He should have protected Fannin's men against Santa Anna, and he would have won the sympathy of the Texans to the highest degree by such humane procedure. But everything was not lost yet; there was still something he could do in order—as he calculated—to redeem himself with the Texans. Santa Anna had so often changed his color that he should be called the Mexican chameleon rather than the Napoleon of the West. Urrea, therefore, suddenly decided to become exceedingly humane and began to treat very well the Texan prisoners—approximately twenty-eight men, all carpenters who had been saved from death—to build bridges. Their

304

rations were larger and better than those of the soldiers. I later became quartermaster at Matagorda.

But a big, tall Yankee submitted a special plan to him incognito. Doctor Harrison was a narrow-shouldered figure whose oblong, Lord's-prayer face showed the colossal and ever-active spirit of the Yankee nation. Notwithstanding that, the incognito Yankee stated that a truer Buckeye[46] never traveled through the states than the Doctor Harrison standing before us. He said that his father was the old General Harrison who soon expected to become president of the Union; that his party aimed to take the field with the catchy slogan of Log Cabin and Hard Cider[47]against the metallic silver system of [Andrew] Jackson, [Martin] Van Buren, and company.

Urrea also was on the side of the apple-cider drinkers and log cabiners, at least so long as he was a public servant. He pledged himself, as long as Harrison, Clay and Company would do so, to drink nothing but hard cider and, like the most menial son of Mexico, to live in a block house and to wear trousers and jackets of ordinary linen.

But after the victory he expected, just like the above named firm, namely the rag factory of Harrison, Clay and Company,[48]to consign the hard cider and log cabins to the workmen and country folks, the so-called democrats, who are characterized as *locofocos* in the territory of Uncle Sam.

In other words, we noticed that General Urrea had plans that were to be exhausted, if not at the present, at some time in the future. We will also see how the would-be son of the old would-be president showed the would-be-no-telling-what Urrea a Yankee trick by which the disguised doctor aimed to use both parties.

This hero was found by the Mexican cavalry in the valley of the Guadalupe river and was at first cuffed about in regular Mexican custom, but after a little while, he succeeded in winning the favor of Urrea. He was in fact a very peculiar individual, and up to the present time,[49] his appearance on the prairies had been a riddle. That he was not the son of the old General Harrison has long been proven. But why he wandered around alone in the wild west and who he was is yet to be solved. We know that it was he who persuaded Urrea to issue a proclamation to the citizens of Texas promising a general amnesty. We also know that Urrea expected attractive results, notwithstanding the promise made by Santa Anna for this purpose that had been contemptuously rejected by the colonists. We learned later on that the Yankee doctor was finally sent with a large bundle of Mexican magnanimity and love to the rebels to whom he actually presented many of the promises, showing them the hand-signed authorizing seal of Urrea.

The Yankee speculated in every direction: If things would not go one way, they would probably go another, and words as sweet as honey flowed from the lips of the doctor.

"Yes, gentlemen," he continued, addressing a large group of young colonists who were the first ones that he met with his message, "this Urrea is a big-hearted soul." He paused a moment to take a breath.

"Surely! I think he is," said a colonist.

"Fine pretenses that you parade before us," added another.

"I have a desire to swear allegiance to his flag," contributed a third.

"I think Jonathan Harrison must be making good profits— good business this—isn't it, Harrison?" asked another.

"Is not our honored friend one of those fellows that deal in wooden nutmegs?" asked a deep bass voice.

"Or a cypress-ham manufacturer?" joked another.

"Or does the gentleman come from the clock-makers craft, who make such elegant clocks that they can be hung on the wall only for ornamental purposes, those that we need not to wind up as they indicate the time as well when they are run down as when they are wound up?"

"Yes!" interrupted a Mississippian, "Old Dan, our neighbor, had one of these would-be clocks. It told the time only when the hand was moved to the proper figure on the dial."

"Or, Jonathan Harrison, do you possibly belong to the factory that sells these shoes? Strange footwear—peculiar manu-
facturers, these Yankees—did not walk an hour—gone are the
heels—completely gone, Jack," said a young Kentuckian, who
stood nearly seven-feet tall, not counting the heels, in the shoes
that were so easily damaged.

Harrison was surprised that the wind now suddenly blew
against him, while his well-thought-out speech seemed to have
such good effect on the simple backwoodsmen at the beginning.
A few times he tried to interrupt them and give the situation a
different turn, but the strong voices of his former listeners
would not give him the opportunity.

"What do you think?" said one in the meeting, "Suppose,
boys, we let our honored friend here ride off in triumph?"

"Ride, Jack? Oh, I understand—ride on a rail."[50]

"Hurrah for the rail!" they all cried. "Let's see how the Yan-
kee-delegate from Mexico can ride."

The doctor made a very miserable face. Riding had never
been his hobby, and now he experienced a distinct repulsion for
this art—because it was usually followed with a tar and feather
operation or at least with frequent gentle dips in the next best
river or pond. He pleaded with his executioners and promised
he would disappear at once if they would let him off this time.
But to no avail. A strong eighteen-feet long rail was brought up
by two young athletes, while several hacked off with their
Bowie knives the cross rods on which the rail was to rest. The
doctor, who now saw that no amount of pleading would save
him from his ride, stepped up boldly and said that he would
just as soon ride on a wooden horse as on one of flesh and
bones.

"Damn it, I don't give a damn for it—but you are low-
down dogs to bunch up on a well-meaning person like this. You
want to fight for right and freedom, and yet you blame me for

nothing but reading to you something from the enemy, something I was never serious about, damn you! The doctor will fix you all yet—remember this." With every explosion of the doctor the backwoodsmen would say, "Go it, Jonathan Harrison."

"That fellow has more spunk than I thought," said one in the laughing crowd. "Suppose we let him run—he may move off with his proclamation, boys, run this off-breed Yankee across the Brazos; he will not proclaim any more. You can depend on it. Do it to please me, boys; I am a Yankee myself, y' know, I have never dealt in hams and clocks nor in wooden nutmegs."

During this time the doctor had pushed himself off to the side, and now walked off with long strides through the tall grass, pondering deeply over the depravity of the human race and declaring that less business could be done with this rabble of miserable Texans than with the ragged Mexicans. He was big for a Yankee, but if, as he pretended, he was no Yankee, he nevertheless possessed a genius to carry out tricks like this, that would have done honor to a "downeasterner."[51] Through one of his tricks he got out of Urrea's imprisonment and by another trick he evaded the unpleasantness of a lynch operation, by playing the bold and unfrightened role when his pleadings would not help. By his boldness, he knew how to deal with the weakness of the backwoodsmen, who respect everywhere the courageous and daring.

The Doctor X, as we may call him, disappeared and no one ever heard who he was, what he was, where he went, or from whence he came.

[46] The inhabitants of Ohio are jokingly given this nickname.
[47] Log cabins and pure apple wine.
[48] The bank party.
[49] 1842
[50] A punishment from the lynching laws.
[51] Yankee

The March to Matagorda

WHEN IT CAME TO CULTIVATING THE SOIL, the Mexicans could not deny that the *carajo Americanos* were entirely different creatures from the Mexican planters. The plantation of the average Mexican (provided that he had one, which is only seldom the case) consisted of a few hundred corn stalks among which a forest of weeds nestle, and only seldom does one see the yellow face of a pumpkin shimmer through. The entire field for the family is so small it usually can be covered with their blankets. It is mainly the occupation of the wife to cultivate the field, to sow and to harvest. This is an old custom of the Mexicans that goes back to their Indian ancestry. With their conversion to Catholicism they threw away the noble customs of the ancient Indians and took on the worst and most sensuous habits of civilization.

The officers had not seen so much land in cultivation during a whole day on their great journeys in Mexico as practically each planter here in Texas owned and had fenced in.

The cotton fields of a few plantations on the left side of the Navidad stretched practically for miles among the jungle that borders the stream. In this splendid region, the plantation of

309

Colonel Southerland, where the army camped for the night, is especially favorably located in the bend of the river, whose course one can only surmise by the dark forests that enclose it. The residence of Colonel Southerland, like all others that I had seen since my flight, was deserted, and on the arrival of Urrea's troops the poultry fled frightened into the forest or into the immense cotton fields, which was lucky for the feathered friends for otherwise not a trace of them would have remained in evidence very long.

On the second evening after we had left the Navidad, we arrived at the Colorado, whose swollen and red-colored waters pressed their way down to Matagorda Bay. The colonists here also, as on the Guadalupe, either had destroyed all boats or concealed them in the forest, and after innumerable planning and trying, they succeeded with the aid of the Texan prisoners to get the army across the river in four or five days, which the unnerved half-Indians would never have succeeded in doing with the river then at high water. An officer, who had ordered a giant cypress tree of approximately two square feet to be debarked, carved for two days on it to indicate that Urrea's division had crossed the red waves of the Colorado triumphantly as of this date.

We prisoners had expected to meet at least a few hundred Texans here to obstruct Urrea's passage, a job one hundred men could have done. But we didn't know then that the Mexican armies had already crossed the Colorado fifty miles up and were on their way to the Brazos. Consequently it would have been foolhardy to venture that far among enemies. Meanwhile Urrea was much concerned.

After we had left the river behind us, our way went through the lush edges of the forest toward the coast for a period of two days. We constantly paralleled the river, only a few miles away on our right. It ran through a jungle more than a mile wide. From the jungle great arms ran out in right angles and acute points into the immense prairie that extended on our left to the forests of Cany Creek and the San Bernard.

The further we penetrated into the colonies the scarcer the herds of cattle became, because the planters here had had more time to take at least that part of their property to safety, although an immense number was still to be found in this immeasurable maze of nature.

We stopped a mile this side of Matagorda, and General Urrea, who was usually the last one in breaking camp in the morning, galloped by us with his bodyguard of dragoons to determine the cause of the sudden stop. As he rushed by me, he called out laughingly: "The Texans, my little Prussian!"

Actually, I had hopes that the ironic call would be true. At least I expected that the citizens, before they would leave town, would give the enemy a fight. But I was mistaken. After a halt for hours, the spies returned and reported that everything was safe. Later I learned that the Texans had placed a scarecrow with a musket in its arms on the flat top of a house, and this had the impudence to halt Urrea's whole glorious division.

Since it was now known that not a person was in town, everybody went boldly and hurriedly forward, as large quantities of food and drink probably awaited them. The officers were already rejoicing over the booty that was to be carried off to the Rio Grande.

CHAPTER TWENTY-SEVEN

Matagorda

MATAGORDA IS A LITTLE TOWN of several hundred very lovely houses that are usually one-story and painted white. The dull blue or even flat red roofs and pretty green window frames of the generally new and elegant buildings present an appearance of neatness and give the town an atmosphere of friendliness that can be found only in the new world. The surrounding country is extraordinarily pretty. An immense green, treeless undulating plain rolls away from behind the town toward the northwest, until in the far distance it reaches to the horizon, whose majestic arch seems to rest upon it. Great herds of deer graze here on the luscious meadows. Wolves and jackals chase about in daylight without disturbing the other wild creatures. Before us waved and roared the mighty waters of Matagorda Bay. As far as the eye could see, the water moved in the wind, and we could hear the muffled tumbling of the surf. A foggy forty-two-mile-long peninsula on the south protects from the Gulf of Mexico the body of water here known as Matagorda Bay. Countless buffalofish, redfish, sheepshead, and other fish could be seen in the waters. Even the jumping porpoise showed himself, and not

infrequently one could see the fins of the greedy shark projecting out of the water. Oyster banks of the finest kinds sprawled
for miles in these waters, and flocks of pelicans, snipes, ducks,
swans, coots and other varieties of the feathered species would
sing and cry wildly along the coast as the wanderer walked
along the sandy beach. To the rear and west of the town flowed
the Colorado, which was alive with fish, alligators, and turtles. A
mile further down it mixed with the salt waters of the bay. Its
dark forests extend up the valley in a northwesterly direction
and project about six miles out into the great breathing prairie.
The woods follow the stream that rushes down from the west
out of the—albeit distant—mountains and block the view of the
city completely for the inhabitants on this side, toward the
Lavaca. The first bend of the river forms a sharp angle of about
50° with the bay. Less than a mile from the point lies the town,
whose outer edge is bordered with a bayou that cuts off a part of
the corner near the point. It empties into the bay only a few hundred yards from the Colorado.

The detached piece of land is low and swampy and is a
favorite camping ground of the Carancahuas, who frequently
pitch their camps here, as the fish and game offer them food in
abundance. But at the arrival of Urrea's troops the redskins had
disappeared. They had aided this general in the battle against
Fannin and they could ask for a part of the booty. Instead of
giving them their just dues, he had six of the best warriors of
their tribe hanged; and only after the hangmen had marched
away were they permitted to rescue the bodies of their brothers
and friends from the vultures and to bring them safely to the
hunting grounds of their fathers.

It was an hour before midnight when I made this round
with Holsinger, who was the officer in charge that night. The
pale, silver moon floated over the dark forest from which the
melancholy calls of the whippoorwill could be heard. Muffled
thunder, the hollow mumbling of the armored alligators, rolled

over to us from the Colorado River. Not a human voice was heard except the *¿quién vives?* that the sentinels called out to us.

The quiet night in a camp during war times always calls forth sentimental thoughts when one considers that any moment may be the end of the course of one's life. This, combined with the beauty of nature about us, the muffled murmuring of the distant bay, the magic moon hanging in the blue sky, had made Holsinger first pensive and then talkative. The fine large plantations, the neat, pleasing houses that indicated a never resting people in this splendid luxury, the budding industry of a young land, such as the people of the most densely populated part of Mexico could not imagine, made the inside of Holsinger a rebel against his own principles. He knew that he could boldly trust me, that I was still for the independence of Texas with my whole soul, that I cherished sanguine hopes for our army that were so active in me that Holsinger himself began to believe in the ultimate victory of the Texans in spite of the latest dispatches from Santa Anna, which really were not very comforting to us men of freedom. He reports: "that the Old Tennessean [Houston] with his small group had disappeared and that he had probably escaped to the area of the States. He had, therefore, dispatched six hundred men to Nacogdoches to build up the garrison there."

The colonel admitted that Texas deserved the name of *El Dorado* [the golden], as it is called in Mexico, and was delighted with everything he saw. He considered Texas much more charming than the state of Vera Cruz, where his large, but unimproved landed estates were, and said frankly, but in suppressed tones, that he would just as willingly serve the Texans instead of Santa Anna if they would give him the same rank that he held in the Mexican army and would give him reasonable compensation for his thirty leagues of land that he would naturally lose.

Hastily I seized the idea of depriving Santa Anna of a follower and began to explain to him conditions in my country. My description caused him to change his mind. He believed in aristocracy and said he would rather continue to serve Santa Anna than to live among a people who did not esteem him more highly than any other carpenter. Since he had now become very talkative, which, by the way, was one of his weaknesses, he honored me with his confidence. He related to me the story of his whole life, and I did find that he had had much misfortune, especially in romantic love affairs. When his wife arrived from Europe, she had hardly stayed an hour on Mexican soil when she and the entire family, except the eldest son, departed again on a ship just then leaving for Germany. Another woman in the city of Mexico who was running a large millinery business and whom he fervently loved, ran off with the intermediary messenger whom he had sent to take her to the wedding, and nothing else was ever heard of them. Consequently the colonel had to seek his happiness in other places, but he was completely rejected in all of his amours. But, as he said, it was for his own benefit, as he now had prospects of becoming really happy. A high mining official, a nobleman from the Harz mountains, had promised to him his foster-daughter, a real angel. At our dwelling, he read to me her entire correspondence since she had already written him several letters. Only a girl of highest education and finest feelings could have written such letters. The letters also of the foster-mother of this angel indicated a splendid person, such a refined spirit, that I inwardly regretted to see her thrown into the arms of a person of such questionable character.

I knew his whole life now, and I stood a tremendous step closer to him than before. For an hour I had been only a listener because I did not wish to tear him out of his fantasy world; but as I was very sleepy I had to inform him that I was human too and needed sleep. He might have wondered that I could feel like sleeping as he was presenting to me these fantasy paintings.

The next day was a noisy one. Long trains of loaded pack-mules carried the booty of the general and the officers away to Matamoras in order to safeguard their share in case of a bad turn, as they did not trust the quietness. The most valuable of the large storehouses of my republican fellow citizens of Matagorda were plundered by the officer corps of the enemy, one rank after another had permission to do so. One circle after another received that permission and great quantities of wares were removed to the Rio Grande.

Two days later Urrea moved with his division to the Brazos. However, since four hundred men remained with Holsinger at Matagorda to construct a fort, I decided to remain there also. Practically all the Texan prisoners remained there to work on the fortification. The next morning we witnessed a fight among the noble defenders of the fatherland because some of the men had tried to steal sugar. But in order to avoid a misunderstanding, I must observe that they were not beaten up because of the theft, an offense not taken seriously if the thief is not so simple as to put his hands on the belongings of officers or Catholic priests, which was the case. Sugar was a very rare article in Matagorda. And what would become of the officer corps if this article should give out? This offense required an exemplary punishment, and its infliction took place in the usual interesting manner "for the spectators": the hands of the offender were well tied together and the circle thus formed with his arms was hung over an amazing creation of the Mexican nation, namely, a beanstalk-like, six-foot tall sergeant. Half Negro and half Indian, this righteous citizen of Mexico, who, in spite of his height, had an indescribable aversion to the work of war, had one day been lassoed like a buffalo and brought to Texas, where henceforth he occupied this honorable position. It was, in fact, really amusing to see the little hero wiggle on the back of the muscular man while a dignitary strained his arms to whip half a dozen sticks to pieces on the back of the top man.

Another group of people were caught stealing half a dozen bottles of wine. The contents were being thoroughly enjoyed by the thieves when Holsinger and several lieutenants came by and almost fainted when they discovered the merry revelry. Even the guard, who was supposed to protect the contents in the house, was drinking mightily with his buddies. A crashing thunder of *carajos* [curses] tore the surprised drinkers from their blessed state, and a horrible vengeance was to be taken on the thieves who had the temerity to drink wine. After all, the Lord did not let this heavenly gift grow for the ordinary people.

It soon turned out that fate had again protected these noble people for soon the poor devils began to stoop far over and to make very unpleasant faces. A frightful vomiting set in, and suddenly awful cursing followed in all parts of the camp. Many provisions were thrown away as it was generally said that the damn Yankees had poisoned the food, and only with fear were small particles eaten.

As I examined the emptied bottles, it evidently was wine that they had drunk; and I could barely suppress my laughter when I read the words, *Antimony Wine*.[52] I, however, kept quiet, as I figured it would be a great advantage to the Texans, since people would now eat minimally and what was absolutely necessary.

Next morning the chaps were out of danger but very weak, and they swore never to touch another drop. However, they had not kept their vow. I discovered five days later one of the patriots was so thoroughly befogged that he could not dance the fandango but tumbled to the floor probably five times in a few minutes.

[52] Vomiting wine

CHAPTER TWENTY-EIGHT

San Jacinto

SANTA ANNA, who as already mentioned, thought the war was over, marched without a worry through this country that was completely unknown to him. Fire and plundering accompanied him as he went through the colonies. Hardly had he pillaged and burned Harrisburg, a little town on Buffalo Bayou, when the Texans under General Houston marched unseen on the opposite bank of the bayou determined to finally put a stop to the doings of this monster.

Houston's hope to assemble a large army around him were not realized, because the more plantations the army left behind, the more healthy bodies were called upon to take their families to safety over the border. The streets of the republic were alive with caravans of women and children who were fleeing from the blood-thirsty enemy toward the Sabine [River].

The Napoleon of the West did not know that the troops of Old Sam swarmed all around him. Neither did he suspect that a backwoodsman had captured his courier who had been sent to General Filisola, who was standing on the Brazos with approximately thirty-five hundred men. This courier was led into

Houston's camp with his messages. The captured messages contained Santa Anna's campaign plans and indicated the route that he expected to take in order to destroy the last traces of the heretics.

Hardly were the messages read, when the plan of the Texans was completed. "Now is the time or never!" cried all the men as with one voice, "The usurper or Texas must now fall. Not another step backward. Forward! We are strong enough. We are men. We know what we are fighting for. Our God will be with us," and the like was heard throughout the volunteer army.

No man could have stemmed this tide, not even a Houston. But fortunately the Texas Oak this time agreed with the colonial army.

"Forward!" the loud call thundered through the troops. On the 19th of April he crossed Buffalo Bayou to occupy a firm position near the little town of Lynchburg to which Santa Anna, according to his dispatches, intended to march. The troops lay in a well protected position in the forest near the Bayou and behind an elevation in the ground. They were not noticed by the enemy on their arrival on the 20th until they greeted him with a discharge of grapeshot from two six-pounders [likely the "Twin Sisters," two cannon given by the citizens of Cincinnati to the Texans]; whereupon Santa Anna hastily retreated in order—as our people learned only later—to wait for the arrival of General [Martín Perfecto de] Cos with five hundred men and a twelve-pounder. To the surprise of the Texans, it arrived the next morning.

For some time, Deaf Smith had vexed and greatly annoyed Urrea's division at the Brazos River, especially during the arrival of the Mexicans in [the town of] Brazoria. Standing on the opposite side of the river, he held off the entire division for several hours and kept the men from fetching water or watering their horses. He did that with his rifle, in that he shot anybody that he could reach.

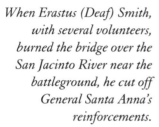

When Erastus (Deaf) Smith, with several volunteers, burned the bridge over the San Jacinto River near the battleground, he cut off General Santa Anna's reinforcements.

This unforgettable, courageous patriot, with several volunteers, surrounded Santa Anna's troops through the prairie. Eight miles from the place where the fate of the young republic was to be decided, he had, on orders from Houston, demolished the bridge [Vince's Bridge]. It was the only bridge available to the Mexicans to re-cross a river [San Jacinto River] that was winding here through the prairie, in the event they were beaten by Houston and wanted to return to the Brazos.

The retreat was cut off without the enemy even knowing it. Santa Anna had taken up a position several hundred yards from Houston. His right wing with the artillery remained on a prairie island, and the rest of his troops stretched in a straight line down to the San Jacinto River, which a short distance above the battleground takes up the waters of Buffalo Bayou.

The army of the Napoleon of the West was just cooking its afternoon *caldo* and roasting beef on the fires when suddenly Old Sam and his men dashed upon them, running over the hill that had concealed him and his troops so far. Then Mirabeau B. Lamar and some sixty men of his cavalry attacked the left wing, and the advancing artillery sent its angry grapeshot against the artillery of the enemy on the right wing. Simultaneously with these movements, the entire front of the backwoodsmen marched in double-quick-time toward the astonished Mexicans who, however, shot off their copper bullets in spite of this. But the advancing troops were not to be confused. Without firing a single shot they advanced through the open prairie toward their goal. And at a distance of about twenty yards in front of it, when they could see the white of the enemies' eyes, then did they all fire their rifles. They turned their guns around with the rifle butts high in the air, and holding the glistening Bowie knives, they dashed forward with the battle cry, "Remember the Alamo!"

"Revenge, terrible revenge!" thundered from all sides, and the wild chaos of shouting names: father—brother—friends—fellow countrymen—rejoiced the destroying masses. As the tiger thrusts his fangs into the lion killed in battle and tears him to pieces, so the raging backwoodsmen now cut the enemy to pieces with their dripping, almost two-feet-long Bowie knives that were as wide as a hand. Their pistols smashed the brain and the heart of the Mexicans that were on their knees begging for pardon. "No mercy—no mercy—death—remember the Alamo—Fannin's blood is crying to heaven!" shouted the raging ones to them, and stroke after stroke, shot after shot crashed down the enemy who now was fleeing in every direction. In vain Santa Anna shouted curses at his fleeing forces—in vain did he strike down the first ones who were fleeing—it did not help anything. The entire stream of fleeing soldiers thundered away—bloody death on their heels. There was no halting, no reflecting. All of the people were running as if crazy—out onto the infinite plains. And the fleeing cowards fell individually under the hands of the

The battle at San Jacinto on April 21, 1836,
impacted Texas and American history.

almost dehumanized backwoodsmen. A few officers fled in
full speed from the grim reaper and Santa Anna also seized his
splendid warhorse and swept like a hurricane through the
prairie toward the Brazos River.

The chaos and murderous action moved toward the place
where the bridge over the shining stream (rather an arm of
the Gulf nearby) had been demolished. An adjutant becomes
the first to dash into the high flood that crashes back to
Galveston Bay—his noble animal struggles and breathes hard.
It is about to sink. The rider throws himself into the water. A
good swimmer, he and the horse swim forward a distance.
Again the horse staggers—it breathes heavily—it snorts—the
eyes begin to pop out—it lets its limbs drop limply—and suddenly the dagger of the rider goes into the neck of the sinking

horse—the almost dead noble racehorse one more time rises up wildly with new life—then the blood rushes from the wound. Again it frantically tries to reach the shore and again it is about to sink. But solid bottom is reached—and trembling and panting it walks slowly to the shore. A minute of rest— and the rider mounts the still-panting horse and rides off slowly to the forests in the southwest. Several other officers stand on the bank and shudder—and hesitate. Nobody is willing to risk such a terrible battle again. Now they see a single rider about a mile behind speeding toward them, and still further in the distance one can see the dark masses of the fleeing infantry and their pursuers. The officers forget the terrible struggle with the waves and plunge into it. They move forward—but only for a short distance. The floods push them out into the bay—their horses become tired—the riders jump off similar to the adjutant—they stab the already dying horses, but to no avail—nothing. And on and on it goes, outward and into the waves—In vain they fight against the wet, foaming death—The noble horses disappear—behind them the riders still calling out for help or cursing them—both victims for the shark.

The lone rider speeds up—it is our Napoleon himself—he wants to dive into the waters—but then he sees the demise of his officers—shudders—and turns his horse—He jumps down—lets his horse escape—and he himself disappears from the banks of the river—into the prairie.

Only a short time had the floods roared over those who had just disappeared, when the black cloud of the puffing infantry stormed in horror toward the wet grave. No shot could be heard any more, but a miserable, confused call for help could be heard from the decimated, weaponless infantry. They jumped into the water in order to escape the still thirsty Bowie knife. Many looked to the opposite shore and tried to reach it—even those who had never swam before trusted themselves to the waves, but the waves closed in over them and carried them out into the bay to their companions.

The remainder soon stood in water up to their necks, clinging to one another to keep the current from carrying them away; but from time to time those on the outer rim would disappear, taking some of their comrades with them to their death.

A few of the backwoodsmen stood on the banks and fired into the despairing masses with their pistols. Others went into the water with swinging rifle butts, and still others rushed forward with their horrible, dripping knives in order to utterly destroy all who had any part in the horrible and dishonorable murder of their fathers, brothers, and friends in the West.

But enough blood had been spilled, a higher power wanted to save the miserable ones so that they could tell their brown brothers on the other side of the Rio Grande this horror story of the Battle of San Jacinto.

Orders were issued to put an end to the slaughter, but it was difficult to console the raging colonists since they had made up their minds to stop only after the last Mexican soldier had been killed. But several Texan officers, rushing forward, brought them back to their senses, and the word "Pardon!" came out of the mouths of all people. The Mexicans, more dead than alive, came out on the river bank and fell trembling on their knees. They were, however, immediately dragged from this position so repulsive to a free man and sent to the camp under a light guard.

But imagine the disappointment of Houston's troops the next morning—the arch-enemy, the evil murderer, Santa Anna was missing. The troops raged about angrily, and as the thought that he had probably escaped passed through their angry minds, the stress increased and the lives of the prisoners hung on a thread.

During this general excitement, a small troop rode into the camp with a prisoner who seemed to be a common soldier. But he had hardly entered the camp before the Mexican prisoners noticed him, and from the lips of all sounded a lamenting and whining "Santa Anna!" They clasped their hands together and fell on their knees in front of their idol. It was Santa Anna indeed, the master himself, and those who brought him in were astonished at their precious catch. They had found him in the high prairie grass where he had hidden; and he assured them on the way to the camp that he did not know anything about the flight of Santa Anna. He did, however, work to bribe them with a gold watch, with his purse, and other valuable articles, which were refused with typical Texan-American contempt.

The jubilation was now as unrestrained as had been the noisy confusion before. The delighted backwoodsmen vowed not only to keep their promise to pardon the prisoners but also to treat them in real Yankee manner—that is, humanely.

The prisoner, who was quivering on all limbs, was now taken to General Houston, who had been wounded in battle and who, as one might understand, was not in the best of moods. But he received the prisoner in such a way as to instill courage in him.

The general listened to the insipid, miserable flattery of the Mexican without appearing to be much elated, as his wound was causing him great pain. Santa Anna, who had meanwhile gotten new courage by taking a powerful dose of opium, continued with what he was doing, and he asked what was to be done with him.

"What to do with you? What to do with you?" said Houston grumbling, "No discussion about you now—First let's drive all Mexicans over the Rio Grande—then we will consider what kind of fate the murderer of our people, especially the murderer of Fannin, deserves."

A terrible confusion indicated excitement outside of the tent. The troops unanimously demanded the death of the prisoner and then to hasten forward immediately to destroy the remainder of the enemy on the Brazos. Santa Anna, although

Houston and Santa Anna.

he did not know what the raging meant, suspicioned the true
state of affairs and his opium courage left him again. This evil
murderer, who had caused the death of thousands, who, instead
of fostering the welfare of his fatherland when he reached the
highest position of honor, hurled it into an abyss with the help
of his accomplices, the Jesuits, to put the shackles of slavery
anew on the splendid land. This characterless criminal trembled as he now realized that his miserable life was the cause of
the tumult outside. He denied that Fannin concluded a capitulation but rather he maintained that Fannin had surrendered on
discretion, by individual choice. "Discretion? Ha! I would
almost like to laugh when I hear of Mexican discretion, but
instead the memory of my butchered comrades would cause
tears to flow from my eyes."

The fallen Napoleon spent the night jumping up restlessly and in constant fear of being murdered—only the firmness of Houston, whose only concern was the welfare of the republic, saved his life for now.

Since the captured president was anxious to know soon whether he would ever set foot on Mexican soil again or die here, he asked for pen and ink with which he wrote several dispatches to General Urrea (at Brazoria) and General Filisola, who was stationed also on the Brazos River but higher up. He instructed these two generals to leave Texas speedily without risking another fight with the raging backwoodsmen.

The dispatches were sent out to the place of their destination with Houston's consent, but with the Texan's greatest anger. The discontented troops felt that only their rifles had brought about freedom for their country, and feared that an agreement would be made with the murderer that would justify his claims for his life which, in their opinion, should no longer be saved.

Thomas J. Rusk.

But at the same time that Santa Anna's dispatches were sent, General [Thomas Jefferson] Rusk,[53] a young [age 33], lively, and popular officer, advanced onward with the liberation army. Sam Houston had given him temporarily the direct command of the army, since Houston's wounds did not allow him to accompany the advancing troops.

The loss of the enemy was: 630 dead including one general, four colonels, two majors, seven captains, and twelve lieutenants;[54] 280 wounded, among them eight high officers; 730 men captured, including General Santa Anna, General Cos for the second time, four colonels, six majors, and Santa Anna's private secretary.

Also, 1,600 muskets, 300 sabres, 200 pistols, several hundred horses and mules and 1,200 *piasters* [Spanish coins] were taken, which sum was renounced by the army in favor of the small navy of the Texas Republic. [The Texas Navy helped win the war by blocking shipments of supplies to Santa Anna's army.]

Independence, war vessel of the Texas Navy.
Port of Galveston print.

David Burnet, the president of the provisional government established by the national convention, arrived several days after the battle in order to talk with Houston about the fate of Santa Anna.

Mirabeau B. Lamar, who led the cavalry at San Jacinto, was president of the Republic after Burnet and Houston.

[53] In earlier times and again later, a lawyer in Nacogdoches County.
[54] This list is by Scherpf, page 45, and, I testify this strictly corresponds to the truth.

The Retreat

HOLSINGER'S DETACHMENT IN MATAGORDA during this important epoch continued to busy itself in devouring and devastating
supplies and provisions stored there, and in moving easily trans-
portable and more valuable articles up to the Guadalupe River.
Everyone was of the firm opinion that the existence of the
Republic of Texas had been only a mere dream. Conversely, the
happy dream for the dictator of Mexico and his instruments was
to put the Federation of Mexico into shackles. Their wishes to
drive the colonists out of their new fatherland—something they
had brooded about for a long time—had all at once been fulfilled; and now they, seemingly with good justification, could
take possession of the beautiful, cultivated plantations. In their
imaginations they already were selecting the houses and plantations where they decided to live later on.

Even don Juan Holsinger had his little place. On the 19th of
April, two days before the Battle of San Jacinto, a small sloop
approached the harbor. However, it didn't quite seem to fully
dare trust to enter the harbor and crossed the Bayou in respectful distance in order to reconnoiter the city.

When the Mexicans saw that this vessel could not venture closer, they decided to entice it in by trickery and ruse, by hoisting a white flag since they did not have a Texas flag, and this seemed to work. The sloop came closer, the men looked the situation over, and the boat turned as if it had to cross the sand bars, and then with the rather strong wind coming from the land, moved out to sea again. The officers had not expected this and had failed to direct their cannon on to the sailboat. Therefore, the single cannonball that they fired toward the ship fell short and into the waves.

Soon the sails disappeared on the distant southern horizon and nothing remained for us except the sullen faces and the *carajos* [curses] of the officers.

Holsinger now had the Texan prisoners work quickly on the construction of a boat with which he expected to investigate soon the long peninsula that was separated from the mainland by a strip of boggy land. He promised himself much booty and aimed to use this boat for taking the booty into safety from Matagorda [Texas] to Matamoras [Mexico].

Every afternoon at six o'clock the numerous bugles of the Mexicans sounded for roll call and thereupon for prayer when all troops were required to uncover their renowned heads and to fall gracefully on their knees. Here they prayed for the annihilation of the heretics in which, as I believe, we accursed Texans were especially mentioned as appropriate subjects to be taken off by the devil.

Meanwhile the officers, who seemed to think that since so many voices were being strained in fervent prayer theirs would really not be necessary, during this time went about their usual business, that is, they did nothing except they smoked *cigaritos*.

It was just at this time on the 24th of April—as the troops as usual were lying on their knees and praying devotedly for our destruction, although a little intoxicated as Santa Anna had just issued them ten percent of their wages, or who knows if they were not just kneeling down—when a long individual on a little Indian pony rushed wildly into the camp. According to his uniform, the tall fellow was an honorable sergeant of the central government. His feet were hanging down deep into the grass, and it looked as if a six-footed animal had come galloping, all of which was all the more deceptive since the motion of his feet paddled along with those of the horse in perfect harmony. Even his hands were in constant motion and the whip moved incessantly around the feet of the panting Indian pony. But this instrument did not seem to have enough effect, as he shouted and cursed terribly as he sat on the almost sinking animal. The rider's fear-inspiring beard hung in long braids from his lips, and his burning black eyes through the drawn-together eyebrows expressed a true picture of fear.

"*Presidente* dead—*Presidente* dead!" he shouted to the frightened lines of soldiers, and they stared after him as if he were a delegate from hell. This messenger with frightful news now trotted, spreading consternation to the house where Holsinger's headquarters were and hastily reported that an adjutant and his own tall self had been the only ones to have escaped the claws of the cannibals. At the same time he said he had orders from Urrea to retreat immediately, which that officer, the same one who had been forced to shoot Fannin, did at once. In half an hour this officer whipped away in full speed all by himself to escape the vengeance of the backwoodsmen, leaving behind soldiers, booty, and everything else.

Holsinger, who had no less fear, now took the command, but only to bring his rich, extensively accumulated plunder to safety. On the following morning, when the boat was rolled from its scaffolding and found fit for service, he had his belongings, his booty, provisions and an excellent eighteen-pounder brought onto it. He then advised the troops that he would retreat by sea, and directed them to take their former route back over the Colorado River [of Texas] and admonished them to discipline. Soon we had the pleasure of seeing the whole detachment hastily leave in unorganized little groups as if the *diablos* (Texans) were already on their heels.

At sundown we also left under full sail in our twenty-feet-long and twelve-feet-wide flat-bottomed frigate. At the mouth of the bayou we found a flat-bottomed boat about fourteen feet long and eight feet wide, which we took in tow. We freighted it with part of our cargo and crew—Holsinger with eight Mexicans and six of the captured Texans. On the small boat there was a kitchen, namely, a large iron cooking stove plundered at Matagorda.

Because of the poor construction of our vessels, we did well to sail close to the shore, and moved forward by pushing or rowing. For several days we went along a low dreary coast where not a single tree broke the monotony. But millions of sea birds and countless herds of deer enlivened this desolate region, many parts of which are flooded by the bay when the high spring tide presses in from the main body of the Gulf of Mexico. The trip from Matagorda to Matamoras can be made by shallow draft vessels between lands because a chain of long narrow islands form a channel about one hundred miles long composed of bays and lagoons. A pilot acquainted with these waters can land within a few miles of the Rio Grande in a few days, whereas a stranger to these waters would require weeks or even months to reach the same destination.

According to Holsinger's map[55] and calculation, we could not be far away from Matamoras, notwithstanding the fact that we seldom hoisted our sails since we usually had side winds that we could not use with our flat-bottom boats. On the third afternoon we arrived at a peninsula projecting far out into the bay, and on whose other side we reached a tremendous area of water that extended at a right angle from our direction and from the bay into the land. Not a trace of land was to be seen ahead of us and neither to the right nor to the left. Nothing but endless masses of water. If we should get out of the lagoons and out into the open Gulf, we would be lost, because a single strong wave of the Gulf would smash our boats and send us to destruction. With the seemingly endless stretches of water ahead of us and with equally immense steppes [prairie] behind us, we were in a very precarious position. If we could have had a seagoing vessel, we could have rocked with the greatest pleasure on the raging waves of the Gulf. But as it was, we could not risk it. Nothing but a slightly indented coast line was on Holsinger's map, and he could not explain from whence came the immense masses of water ahead and to the right of us.

For our part, we Texans were very glad and estimated correctly that we were still between land and, at that, not very far from Matagorda. As the land rose only from ten to fifteen feet above sea level, a person could see only a few miles. However, as we headed toward these Southwestern ports, we kept silent and hoped that the Texan army would reach these ports faster than our boats. Thus, plan after plan to attain freedom rolled through the heads of four of the prisoners.

I and a young Yankee, my confidential friend, were quietly working to get free, but we wanted to do it intelligently and only then when we had come to more beautiful regions. I had enjoyed myself enough wandering around in the wilderness alone and did not wish to risk it another time, at least not on this prairie [steppes]. We decided to spend the night on the point of land and had just prepared supper, when one of the prisoners came to me and told me confidentially that they aimed to take possession of one of the boats during the night and return to Matagorda, and furthermore, that they had decided to kill the Mexicans if they should offer resistance. At the same time he earnestly requested me not to tell our young Yankee friend anything about it. I shook my head, went to the others and told them that I would be willing to make the trip with them by land, but that under no conditions would I agree that either the Mexicans or Holsinger be murdered. Regardless of how cruel the enemy had been toward us, they should at least consider that Holsinger, even if only through selfish motives, had saved the lives of twenty-eight Texans, that the Mexicans had been very friendly toward them and that, even though they had been beguiled by their priests [*padres*], they were still citizens of Texas. There were actually several from the San Antonio area and one from Nacogdoches in the group, and I felt sorry for the miserable chaps who had been incited or forced to go to war against us.

The prisoners shook their heads disapprovingly, and I suspected nothing good. Consequently I decided on a plan as the night set in and informed my friend, the Yankee.

John Adams, I have to remark in his honor, had nothing to do with the "anti-slavery, anti rum-drinking, and I would like to be president"[56] movements, but was a genuine Yankee, a perfectly independent sort of a fellow; and although he could not help from following his Easterner nature at times, his tricks were usually harmless. He had seen much of the world and knew a little about every trade. He could ride, hunt, and fish. He had taught school and had learned the carpenter's trade. He was an excellent housepainter. He had sold matches and medicine in the backwoods. At one time he also dealt in jewelry and who knows what else, until he finally, while serving as a supervisor in a tobacco factory in New York and selling tickets at the Bowery Theater at night, came to the decision to enter the war in Texas with Colonel Miller.

Holsinger and his men usually slept in the little boats while we quartered ourselves on the coast, but this evening Adams and I went unnoticed into the big boat and raised the anchor that held the two boats. The anchor was nothing more than an anvil that anchored both boats, and we drifted from shore unnoticed in the darkness; but we were afloat only a short time when the foaming waves began to beat severely against the sides of our boat. In vain our anvil floated in the deep trying to anchor again; the chain did not reach bottom. The boat rocked back and forth and the breaking waves threw spray into our faces.

Black clouds were hurrying across the sky; the already strong wind howled stronger and more furiously every minute over the spraying sea, and we rowed with all our might to return to the shore we had just left, but in vain.

Holsinger jumped up and, frightened by the storm that howled about us, stared outward. He was looking for the land but it had disappeared. In despair he cried, "Up, up, you sleepy-heads! Treason! We are lost!" Everybody jumped up immediately and howled in competition with the wind.

Then my companion yelled, "Shut up, you cowardly tramps, take hold of the cars, you dogs, if you do not want to swallow salt water in half an hour." He then continued in a more friendly tone to the despairing ones, "Must row hard, boys—the coast is not far away—see that black cloud in the west—that is a squall—If it hits us, you might as well pray to your Ave Maria—damn us once more as you often have done before, because tomorrow the thorny Jack[57] will have a splendid breakfast on your smoked skeleton that is long overdue for the henchmen."

The firm voice of the Yankee, who was rowing for life and death, somewhat quieted the discouraged ones, since before they had been of the opinion that we had allowed them to drift out into the bay without oars.

"Over here, Colonel Holsinger, with your people—every one an oar in his hand—pull courageously—quickly—quickly, if your life is dear to you—only a short time and it may be too late forever. Look—you understand just as much about life on the water as John Adams understands your politics."

The Mexicans and even Holsinger tremblingly obeyed the orders that thundered from the lips of the Yankee so coldly, so piercingly in such a superior manner.

336   THE FIGHT FOR FREEDOM

"Hello, you mud turtles, strike in well with your oars!—time, boys, keep time—mixed up too much—as if thrashing peas—time, time—reckon we won't get to land if it keeps up like this—what, damn your bottoms! Why do you wiggle your fannies about in your seats when a little water spatters into your faces—don't look that way—don't give a damn—it's a little refreshment. Hey there, Pulaski,"[58] he shouted out to me. [General Pulaski (1747–1779) was a Polish soldier who joined George Washington's forces.] "Take the helm away from that miserable Apache,[59] or I will take it myself—reckon he fits better to a fandango than to the helm of a boat in a storm—must worry myself to death with these—Stop! Stop! boys," he cried suddenly, interrupting himself—"only the devil knows where the land is—oars up, Mexicans—I have to listen for the breakers."

Everybody instantly obeyed the Yankee dictator, and he listened intently and stared with protruding eyes into the impenetrable darkness. But the raging squall that began to whistle in its approach drowned the sound of the surf, and vainly we tried to get some sign of directions. The storm whistled and hissed about us, which caused us to be tossed back and forth. Two Mexicans were busy dipping out the water that was dashed in by the waves of the ocean, and our chances to be saved became increasingly hopeless.

"Sir," said Holsinger real submissively, "wouldn't you consider it wise to throw the stove, the cannon and other heavy articles overboard?"

"Sir," the dictator replied, "sir, I say, I figure I would not think it wise—I figure it would be better to be perfectly still. Figure that I, John Adams, knows what he has to do." A pause set in and again the present pilot appeared to listen with head stretched forward.

"Oars up—up with your oars!" he called again, and everybody obeyed and was quiet.

"I reckon—I reckon—land is behind us," mumbled Adams to himself, but then he continued louder: "Hello, I say—Pulaski, my boy—we must turn around—the wind has changed. It's turned around. It's favorable toward the land—I hear the breakers."

He brought the rudder into the proper position for the turn and continued with his preemptory orders:

"Sails up! up *Mexicanos*—quickly! quickly!—will soon have a calm—and then we may row until tomorrow morning and then not get to the land."

The Mexicans didn't need to be told for the second time, and in a few minutes the mast bowed under the pressure of the sails. The frigate now glided firm and straight over the bay; the storm died by degrees; the sky began to brighten up; only a few single clouds now hastened along the horizon, but in front of us the wind roared like the continuous dull thunder of an earthquake. Something dark like land appeared before us, and between it and our boats boiled the whirling, foaming waves.

"Sir," cried the colonel in greatest fear—"land—land!—the breakers—we must cast anchor."

"Damn you and the surf, I say," the Yankee exploded, "keep yourself cool—entirely cool, Colonel Holsinger—not a word—I reckon I know how to look after my post—calculate, you see."

A fearful grinding jolt, a trembling of both boats—all masts were bent similar to the bows of the Comanches. A confused scream from the Mexicans and a loud, uncanny laugh by the Yankee followed. The latter now composedly opened his blankets and went to the sandy beach in order to sleep.

It was really solid ground. The boat lay high and dry and the Mexicans took down the sails, during which time I also left to find a place to sleep.

When I awoke the sun was high above the bay. The same desolate prairie and the same masses of water lay about us, but we discovered a dark streak inland that we thought was a forest.

And above the mass of water lying before us we also discovered dark, cloud-like figures that also revealed the presence of land.

Holsinger still could not comprehend how he had gotten out on the bay during the night and what had become of the other four Texans. Neither could he explain to himself the dictatorial language of the Yankee the previous night, and he confronted us about it.

"Well, sir,—reckon, I was right—reckon so, Colonel—saw that the whole bunch did not understand a bit about seafaring—and I reckon I understood a little bit—took, therefore, the rudder—had no particular desire to swallow salt water—did better, sir, reckon, than if I had stood up and howled along with the chorus—reckon the sharks would have had a good breakfast of us."

The colonel shuddered.

"Yes, sir—absolutism is necessary in such a ticklish predicament—reckon sir, last night, I wanted to knock every one down who would not work—did not want to make any distinction, Colonel—It was very good, sir, you did exactly that—very well—last night I was captain, and, sir, today I am again your prisoner—do whatever you think is right."

After we had told him everything, the colonel was quite satisfied with our precaution and praised John Adams quite a bit.

The weather was beautiful, the bay was quiet, and a favorable east wind was blowing toward the land on the opposite side. Consequently we immediately floated the boat, set sail, and sped pleasantly through the small waves. On this trip we caught astonishingly many fish, and after eating we sailed into a shady cove about thirty feet wide. The evergreen magnolias on both banks of the sparkling canal had overlapped in the middle, and the closely interlapping tops were closely interwoven with air plants and vines. The silvery festoons six to eight feet long of Spanish moss in places hung down to the surface of the water; and only in a few places could a ray of the burning sun come through or a speck of the blue sky appear. Scattered, penetrating rays illuminated the cool, evergreen arcade and with the mossy festoons added bewitching beauty. Often we were obliged to bend the waving moss to the side. We liked it so well here that we decided to spend the night and determined to reconnoiter the surrounding regions the next morning to find out, if possible, where we were. Holsinger did not doubt that we were nearer to his Matamoras [Mexico] than to Matagorda [Texas]; we Texans, however, hoped for the contrary.

After night had set in and our fire had practically died down, Adams the Yankee and I walked off with quiet but long strides, leaving Holsinger and his men in the wilderness, and directed our steps north toward the colonies that, according to our opinion, could not be far away. We were convinced that the peacefully sounding blow of the axe and its echo would soon resound in the forests, and that rich growth would soon shoot up from the plowed earth, and we felt that with the coming of splendid spring, also the spring of the republic had been born.

We traveled all night, and at the break of day we arrived at a plantation on the Tres Palacios [Bay]. Flocks of fowls and grunting herds of hogs were the only inhabitants of the deserted buildings that were full of implements and furniture and provided a few articles of food. Since we did not consider ourselves safe here from Holsinger, who would surely follow us, we resumed our journey after several hours of rest. As the boats here had been concealed and the bridge broken down, we swam across the little stream. Before sundown we arrived at several plantations on the left bank of the stream. They were located on a little prairie about two miles wide that ran toward the southeast between two densely forested little streams. Toward the north, however, we could discover nothing but endless blue sky, and toward the remoter outlines of the rising western prairie, the sun, bloody as the murdered men of Goliad, quietly sank into the water.

We spent the night in a house in which we found an abundance of corn and a mill. As usual the trees around the house were alive with poultry. A barrel of salt pork stood in the pantry. Consequently we proceeded at once to get some of the chickens out of the trees, a process my friend understood very well how to do. He held under their bills a bit of burning sulphur fastened to a stick. Although several fluttered away shaking their heads, two hens and an old rooster fell down. Although we had cut the rooster into small pieces, the more we fried it the tougher the meat became.

We had spent several very comfortable days here, when we decided one beautiful morning, as practically all mornings are in Texas, to go out into the neighborhood on an expedition of discovery and to find out, if possible, where the retreating Mexicans had left the Colorado [River] and our area behind them. That they would have to cross the Rio Grande was positive in our conviction, although we knew nothing outside of the defeat of Santa Anna. We knew the spirit of our people. "Victory or Death" was their watchword. And because they fought for a just cause, like their fathers, they were always successful since a higher power watched protectingly over the Anglo-Americans.

We had visited several very pretty plantations where provisions were present in abundance, while the greatest order prevailed in the dwellings themselves,

The San Jacinto Flag, bearing the Goddess of Liberty, was the only flag carried by the Texans in the Battle of San Jacinto. It was brought to Texas by a volunteer company from Kentucky.

from which we concluded that no plundering enemy had entered this part of the republic. But what part of Texas this really was still remained a puzzle for us, although we cared little. We believed that the Texans would be back as soon as circumstances would permit. Until then we would be masters of the plantations.

When we came around a bend in the forest, we discovered a majestic grove of live oak trees and the little home of a settler who likely from appearances had only recently moved in. No field surrounded the house; but the neat improvements around gave an impression of wealth; and the large herds grazing in the distance could belong only to a man who would be among the richer class of people.

We stole up carefully like Indians through the bushes along the edge of the forest, but we neither saw nor heard anything more than that the house, like others, had been deserted. Therefore, after a short while we proceeded a little more boldly yet still with caution toward the door, when suddenly we heard the tenor voice of a man sing the lines:

> In Mexico none shall be free,
> The people is too blind to see,
> They cannot cheer the liberty,
> O Yankee doodle dandy.

"Hello, John Hitchcock, old soul, where do you come from?" shouted my visibly surprised Yankee friend to an approximately twenty-two year-old slender Georgian, who sat on the floor among piles of books.

"Hello!" exclaimed the kid from old Georgia, who jumped to the side to grasp an axe standing nearby, looked at us, and then rushed recklessly out to us and related to us between protracted questions and answers how he had come out here.

"Boys—you know—twelve of us from Matagorda—were

obliged to go to the Colorado—had to build a boat for Urrea's division to cross over the stream—Well, we did it—but the copper faces, the Mexicans, my boys, wanted to take us along to Mexico. But John Hitchcock had no desire to go along—took a long shot—came here yesterday—found everything comfortable, well suited to amuse this kid for a while—so I decided, boys, to remain here at least a week—to enjoy the happiness of freedom. Then I will trot to Matagorda."

So the Mexicans already had the Colorado River behind them; they must be in a hurry.

That evening I shot a little, fat, two-year-old steer with my pistol, and for the first time in quite a while we enjoyed a tender steak. The remainder of the meat was cut in Mexican fashion, in strips possibly twenty feet long and hung up under the live oak trees to be dried by the air and not by the sun.

During the night the great herds frightened us a lot when they stampeded up to the building. The house and earth trembled, and we thought at first that the whole enemy cavalry was sweeping across the prairie.

---

[55] All maps of Texas except the one in Scherpf's works are incorrect.

[56] John Quincy Adams. [Ehrenberg points out here that his friend was not the statesman.]

[57] The Shark

[58] Because of the difficult pronunciation of my name, I was usually called that way. [Possibly comparing him to a young Polish soldier who fought in the American Revolution with George Washington and became a general by act of Congress.]

[59] A hunting tribe in the northern part of Mexico.

CHAPTER THIRTY

Away from the Free, Sovereign Prairie!

∼

BOOKS, BEEFSTEAKS, WARM CORNBREAD, large bottles full of milk, maps, and well-cooked hominy were on the table the next day, around which we three were seated quite comfortably.

My friend Adams had just helped my friend Hitchcock to a piece of ox-heart fried chestnut-brown.

"Well, John Hitchcock, here is as fine a piece as is barely to be had at Bishop's[60] in New Orleans," said the Yankee who was playing the host, "and I must confess, John—you have improved yourself considerably in the noble art of cooking."

"Why, who would not?" answered John, "I have had to cook enough for the brown bums, and the worst of it was that I generally did not get any of it myself."

"Your own fault, Johnny, your own fault, must look out for yourself—satisfy yourself—then the others," answered Adams, cutting the heart of the ox to pieces and taking a large gulp of milk from the gourd cup.

"A long life to the old blind cow that furnishes us with milk evening and morning!" he continued. Whereupon John Hitch-cock brought to the milk-delivering Adams and his worthiness another milk toast, which we gallantly and merrily drank and then gave our attention to the other things again.

"Perfectly at home, gentlemen? Perfectly comfortable, I hope?" called a small person from a Comanche pony. A grey felt hat shaded the sun-tanned features, and the dangerous rifle lying across the saddle betrayed the backwoodsmen.

We looked up in surprise and discovered the gentleman in front of the door who had just addressed us. Adams, who recovered from his surprise first, stood up to examine the rider. But he still did not know what to say, and consequently he began as follows:

"Pretty weather, stranger!"

"Very pretty weather, sir," was the reply of the smiling felt-hat man.

"Reckon you come from the army, stranger?"

"Guessed it, sir, I come from General Rusk's camp."

"General Rusk, stranger? What kind of a general is that?" said friend Adams in astonishment.

"Well, I must confess, Adams," interrupted Hitchcock, "Rusk! Rusk! You don't know who Rusk is, the gallant Rusk! the attorney from Nacogdoches?—very ignorant, Adams, don't even know our leading men."

"Rusk, sir, is a gallant young lawyer who, since Houston is wounded, is driving the enemy out of the country in his stead," explained the stranger.

"Thank you, sir," said Adams, "reckon you could tell us much about our friends—provided, you get off—come in—this house is an asylum for every Texan."

"I noticed it, gentlemen," smiled the stranger again, dis-mounting from his horse, and Hitchcock immediately unsad-dled the horse and took it to the river for water.

"Now, stranger, be seated and help yourself to our modest meal," I wanted to say, but the gentleman seemed not to need an invitation and without formalities moved his chair to the table, cut off a considerable piece of the heart, and asked for a gourd of milk.

"Thunder," mumbled Adams, looking at me, "what kind of a fellow is that?"

"Thunder," I replied, "a real Texan, I suppose." Adams shook his head, brought the requested milk and placed it beside the stranger.

"Now, sir," said the inquisitive Yankee, "what is the name of our guest, if we may ask?"

"Thomas Kelly, gentlemen, who is enjoying your steak very much," was the answer of the continually smiling backwoodsman.

"Reckon Mr. Kelly is correct—excellent beefsteaks—splendid boy this John!" Adams interrupted in praise. "The best Guinee[61]-Negro could not deliver a better one; but by the way, stranger, ah Mr. Kelly, I wanted to say," corrected my friend, "reckon you are one of the colonists of Texas."

"Reckon, sir, you are correct," was the answer.

"And, Mr. Kelly, I am very curious," apologized my friend who indeed revealed more than American inquisitiveness, "do you live in this region when you are at home?"

"At one time this was my home. Now it is yours; but in about eight days, gentlemen, I would be glad to have you give it back to me again." Again his uncanny smile followed as we looked at him in astonishment. "Yes," he continued, "Mrs. Kelly will soon be here and will be surprised at the good order of everything. But especially will she enjoy the books. But, gentlemen," he asked now, "I have had to tell you everything about me. Now you will not consider it impolite if I ask for the names of the inhabitants of my property, who have evidently remained here during the whole of our retreat."

"Missed it, Mr. Thomas Kelly," replied Adams, "have been here only a few days—are prisoners—escaped from the Mexican camp—Here, sir," pointing to me, "is one of Fannin's men, and there," indicating the entering Hitchcock, "is someone from Major Ward's division, and here, the speaker, sir, I am John Adams, one of Colonel Miller's hundred Yankees who completely lost their common sense and good judgement when they landed on the coast of Texas."

"So," said Mr. Kelly, vigorously shaking hands with us another time. "Welcome! welcome to within my walls, you, who fortunately escaped from the bloody catastrophe where your—and also my—brothers were so shamefully murdered, be welcome one more time; and Thomas Kelly will always gladly remember that he waited on one of Fannin's men on his flight from the Mexican hyenas." Once again we shook hands, and he continued to speak to us: "But, my boys, do you know too that soon not a Mexican copper-skin will be on this side of the Rio Grande? They are running home with all their might to their women who cook their tortillas."

"We really do not know," interrupted Adams, "but we reckon, sir, that you would do us a great favor if you would tell us what has happened since the splendid Battle of San Jacinto, after which the Texans immediately advanced."

"Indeed! Indeed! my brave boys, with the greatest pleasure for you as well as for myself I will repeat the miserable scenes that followed the twenty-first and the twenty-second [of March]. But a little more milk—I am very thirsty."

Adams filled the gourd again, and after the gentleman had drunk he began: "You probably know, my boys, that, after we had painted the grass of the San Jacinto prairie red with blood for vengeance and had captured Santa Anna, this characterless monstrosity sent off dispatches to General Filisola to flatter us and directed him to evacuate Texas. But almost simultaneously with the dispatches, the troops from San Jacinto were at the Brazos with their rifles. Rusk was, as already indicated, our leader. The opposite bank was clear of enemy troops and we crossed the Brazos to observe the movements of the enemy.

Even before Santa Anna's orders reached the headquarters of General Filisola, he had sent couriers to all of the other detachments, ordering them to immediately unite with the main army and to retreat beyond the Colorado River.

"There were approximately six thousand of the enemy in the land, and we felt obliged to know something definite of their intentions before they united. Consequently Rusk with three hundred cavalry rushed ahead and reached the enemy just as Filisola united with Urrea between two prongs of the Bernard.

"Now, boys, two days in succession whole clouds fell from the skies. Possibly you know how it rains here when it once begins, and you may also know the rich black soil of the Bernard where the upper soil is over twenty-eight feet thick and not a stone is to be found in the whole region. Every inch of it is just as rich as—and healthier than—the dense chills-and-fever-forests of Illinois. Now in just this region Filisola was sitting in a most highly unpleasant predicament—the cannon—over the axles in the mud—and the soldiers knee deep in water. Sleeping was impossible. And the squatters and Deaf Smith and his companions on their large American horses, for whom it is a small matter to travel through country like this, drove all the cattle away from around them. A famine broke out among the Mexicans, and practically the whole army got the shivers,[62] especially when three hundred of our cavalrymen moved along as if it were the most beautiful weather in the world. To try a defense was out of the question, but it was a matter of surrender. But General Rusk would not consider the matter as he did not want to have these five thousand eaters on his hands. On the contrary, 'forward' was the command, forward over the Rio Grande. 'You get out of here the way you came in here. Forward, or we will fire on you,' was the word of the Texans.

"It finally touched our hearts to see these miserable people in such a condition, but we could do nothing for them as we did not have anything for ourselves except the cattle that had been driven some distance away. When they saw that we did not want

any prisoners, another [Mexican] delegate came and agreed with
General Rusk that they should be permitted to have sufficient
time to retreat without being disturbed, whereupon they
promised to vacate the republic as quickly as possible. The
march forward continued. All bonds of order were severed, and
not an army of soldiers but a starving mass, a whirlwind of
sneaking shadows, approached the Colorado River. They had
expected supplies and provisions to be landed at the various
Texas ports, but our little fleet [the Texas Navy] destroyed their
hopes. On their glorious march through the colonies they need-
lessly destroyed the herds of cattle and unpardonably offended
their confederates, the Indians. These wild hunters of the
prairie, these never forgiving redskins, now scalped the single
stragglers who fell out behind the main army and those who
dared to search through the country for herds of cattle. Even in
broad daylight they would rush out of the woods in the river
valleys, strike the rider from his horse with the tomahawk and,
in the presence of the frightened army, rush off with the captured horse. Barely a gun was fired as the load had gotten wet
and practically all ammunition had spoiled. Consequently the
redskins could carry on their work almost unhindered.

"Every night our three hundred cavalry riders camped in
their vicinity so that they could survey the whole Mexican
camp. Our guards and scouts roamed clear around, and under
constant fear that our people would repeat the San Jacinto
scene, the glorious army finally reached the Colorado. The
crossing of this stream took them three days and cost them
much of their baggage, which we found partly ruined when
shortly thereafter we crossed the stream with all our belongings
in three-quarters of an hour."

"Thunder and lightning, stranger! How did you do that?"
asked Adams.

"Well, sir, how did we proceed? We all swam across, and the
few who could not swim crossed over on horses or in the boat
that our people had built for Urrea; then we fastened long cables

to the cannon and dragged them without difficulty—as if we had steam engines—through the muddy bed of the red water. At the other bank of the river I departed from the army to look after my house and my farm. But Rusk is continuing to follow the sombre army, in whose ranks things are getting worse every day.

"We had already left behind us several living skeletons who had laid themselves behind a bush or under a live oak tree with death before their eyes, to be possibly eaten alive by the wolves. But it is too horrible, boys, to describe all of these scenes that will be a great—a frightful—warning to the Mexicans; and I venture to say boldly that never, never will a Mexican army rob and defile our colonies again."

"It will be well for the enemy if they do not," answered Hitchcock, "we will not proceed so kindly the next time."

"Reckon not, sir, in spite of the fact that our people in the face of hellish slaughter by the enemy have done honor as descendants from the great nation beyond the Mississippi. Santa Anna was their objective, they wanted the murderer, and the fear of his escape made them angry. But as soon as he was safely in their hands, the cruel demeanor, so unsuitable to North Americans, was cast off. They pursued their enemy with the humanity characteristic of Uncle Sam.

"I have probably described the conduct of our people as too cruel, but the misery of the enemy was so great that we could not help them. Many a one of our fellows gave a miserable starving wretch the last bit of food that he had, although he had possibly murdered a brother or a friend on the western prairie. And they obligated the enemy through humanitarian acts to bless those whom they had been taught all of their lives to curse.

"It is great, sir, even noble, and I'm proud to belong to this nation," said Adams, and a pause set in.

Hitchcock now asked the stranger how far it was to Matagorda and which road to take to get there.

"Gentlemen," answered the planter, "this road here winding off toward the east will take you directly to the lower

Colorado ferry. The stream is ten miles from here, and then there are just as many miles to the town."

"Sir, only twenty miles! Sir, that is impossible," interrupted Adams, "I figure, sir, that it is at least forty-five miles."

"You are completely off, sir," said the planter, "I am well acquainted here—completely at home in this region. Formerly when I still lived on the other side of the river, I chased about for days after the red thieves, the Indians. At that time they were still rather bold and practically every week they stole an ox or a horse from me or one of my neighbors. But that time is past, and the countryman in Texas can now wear his scalp[63] in safety." The table was cleared.

A half hour after this scene we three defenders of liberal principles, loaded with a few provisions, were walking over the great, somewhat rising, prairie toward the Colorado River, where we aimed to spend the night. The few tree tops that we

Ferry.

could at first see projecting over the distant low elevations grew from minute to minute, and soon the primitive forest extending off toward the northwest lay before us. Even a few miles from the stream itself we walked in the densely wooded valley where we could not see for ten steps into the dense forests. The whole forest was alive. Flocks of wild turkeys were crying in every direction, and the splendid wilderness resounded with the many varieties of beautiful woodpeckers, whose little axe could be heard from almost every tree. The whippoorwill was already calling from the dark interior, although the sun had just hidden its fiery face. And the mockingbird[64] was twittering his variations, composed of the melodies of all the other charming songsters of the forest. A herd of stately deer walked across the road and looked curiously but not fearfully at the wandering trio. Many rabbits darted across our path and whole bunches of black

Ehrenberg wrote, "Many rabbits darted across our path." Drawn from nature by J. W. Audubon and titled "Texian Hare."

Natalie Ornish Collection.

and grey squirrels danced along the road in front of us or merrily chased one another through the highest tips of the oak and
pecan trees, or flew from one limb to another, or shot like lightning down the stately trunks, whose species one could barely
determine on account of the many air plants and vines that covered them. Everywhere gigantic grapevines hung down from
the trees. And when one comes to the stream itself and looks up
and down over the surface of the water, one sees nothing but a
dense growth of plants that rise obliquely from the water. The
banks themselves are bordered by weeping willows whose tender branches droop sadly into the constantly moving waters.

Not a boat was to be seen, but that was no obstruction to us.
Without hesitation we swam across and landed on the other
bank only slightly fatigued.

The first things that we saw on the other side were a few
unrecognizable and decomposed corpses; we hurried past.

About half a mile from the stream we came to the edge of
the forest and a devastated plantation lay before us. The
dwelling had been burned down by the enemy and only a black
spot indicated where it had stood.

We gathered some half-burned fence rails and started two
large fires between which we arranged our beds. The flames shot
probably fifteen feet up into the raven black sky. The glow of the
fire extended high above the two fiery pyramids, and millions of
insects, bugs, moths, and butterflies swarmed out of the forest
toward our camp and—with singed wings—fell like rain upon
us. Instead of protecting us, our fires worked to the contrary
and we were obliged to retreat. A clear place in the open prairie
exposed to the wind offered us a better place to sleep.

60 In earlier times, the best hotel in the city.
61 Instead *Guinea*
62 The cold fever [chills and fever].
63 The headskin which the Indian pulls off the head of his killed enemy.
64 A ridiculing bird, giving imitations.

The Capture of the Rhenish-Prussian

HARDLY HAD THE SUN RISEN before we were in our shoes and jumped joyfully along the edge of the woods to the little town of Matagorda, where we shouted for delight:

"Joy, joy, finally we are free; Today we'll see our countrymen again; the prairie is ours—the young republic has been victorious—the new star rising on the western horizon is radiating freedom—and the magnificent park, the El Dorado, our Texas, our new, eternally dear, precious fatherland, is finally opened to the work-loving inhabitants of the north—of the new and the old world. The welcome immigrants will stream in, and the wild flower garden, the colorful savannas, will soon disappear under the plows that are guided by a strong arm. But large fields of snowy cotton, the juicy sugarcane and the noble tobacco will in a short time equally enchant the eye just as pleasantly. The orange, the lemon, the peach, the papaw, the magnificent magnolia, everything beautiful that the South produces will adorn the home of the countryman, and a king in his own house, on his own land, he would not exchange his lot with the rulers of Europe."

We could hardly speak because of joy when we entered the nice little bay city for the second time. We could still see on the roof of the one-story house the scarecrow that put Urrea's division into halt, and the inhabitants, who had returned only a few days before, looked with pain upon their devastated property. They received us with warm empathy and did their best to make us forget our former suffering. Those four volunteers whom we had left on the beach when the storm almost delivered us over to the raging sea were also here and raved and chanted toward us. But we laughed and received the applause of the inhabitants of Matagorda.

Hardly had we been an hour in the city when, after we related the story of our escape and indicated the place where we had left Holsinger, an expedition on horseback under the leadership of the Yankee went off to Lavaca. This was in order to cut off the colonel who, according to the reports of some old planters, still had to circumnavigate two mighty bays before he was to be some forty miles from Matagorda. It was to bring back him and the eighteen-pounder and the booty. I, however, remained in town.

Holsinger and his people, who could not sleep for fear, had discovered our escape; but instead of following us, they put out to sea as they feared that we would pursue them with the aid of the Texans. They worked with more than usual Mexican strength. Under considerable worry and not without danger they finally worked themselves out of the first bay. They thought that they were now finally in the Laguna del Madre [near South Padre Island] that reaches down nearly to Matamoras. But, Oh horrors! On the fourth day they discovered another endless mass of water. Since they did not dare to sail straight across, they were obliged as before to shove the boats around in the shallow water near the shore. As they were lying in a bayou a few days later, the red Carancahuas paid them a visit, which was not at all agreeable to the colonel and the half-Indians as they remembered that they had hanged several warriors of this tribe near the Guadalupe River. The redskins received many presents, and while they were sleeping off the effects of the whiskey, the crew of the boat sneaked off to find another endless bay after several days of wearisome labor. They believed it to be the Gulf and would not venture out in it.

But they could neither stay here nor turn back unless they wanted to be captured and, as they believed, shot. Their food supply also was running short. Consequently they were obliged to go forward.

Slowly and wearily they moved forward. Day passed after day without an important discovery being made. Completely exhausted, they were camping during the noon hour under several small groups of mesquite trees when suddenly a thundering: "Surrender or I'll shoot!" frightened them. It was a single backwoodsman who had stopped at a distance of forty yards with hammer cocked and gun in position. His voice was so positive and his rifle so threatening that the whole troop didn't hesitate a moment and surrendered unconditionally. The next minute the remainder of our Matagorda expedition rushed up, which was composed of five men. Three of them took charge of the boats and the prisoners with the exception of Holsinger. The colonel was required to mount one of the horses. And after each of the colonists had tied with the lasso one of the other horses to his saddle, they went off in a full gallop over the prairie to Matagorda.

On the third day after departure, our land expedition returned; on the fourth day the boats with the recaptured booty and the excellent cannon appeared.

Our oarsmen had made the journey that had taken the Mexicans some ten days in a little more than two days and had caught a lot of fish besides.

Adams and I had considerable trouble in protecting Holsinger against mistreatment from several of the inhabitants of Matagorda, whose left behind property he had appropriated for himself and put on his boat. Undoubtedly he would have been shot if we had not preached peace from morning until night among the embittered people. We brought forward his virtues: He had saved the lives of about twenty-eight men and it was due to him alone that they did not find ash piles in place of their houses on their return.[65] But the four prisoners left behind contradicted our first reason, although it really was their rescue also. They argued, and rightly so, that he saved their lives only because he needed their help in building bridges and boats, which his unnerved soldiers would never have been able to accomplish, and that he intended to take them as slaves to his estates, which indeed, was the case. They were to build for him several houses and a steamboat. The robbed citizens contradicted the second reason in that they contended that this was no act of virtue on his part. On the contrary, they claimed, he had protected the buildings because if destroyed he would have to fear a catastrophe like the present one. And what would the owners then undoubtedly have demanded? "His death!" cried one, and "his death!" shouted another. "He is the scoundrel who made Fannin so many sweet promises in order to induce him to surrender—His death!"

The prisoner seemed to be lost. But suddenly a brilliant idea passed through the head of the Yankee. He stepped to the front, asking for attention, which was given him. He made an eloquent speech that I will here try to reproduce in short outline:

"Citizens of a free republic!

"John Adams is no Cicero, to be sure, but he cannot avoid speaking. Yes, he feels compelled to thunder away when justice, the honor of the state, and the laws are at stake, if they will be defiled and stepped on." He took a breath—the crowd mumbled. "Yes, gentlemen, I reckon you want to shoot this fellow[66]—you are right—he deserves it—Adams thinks so also, but—there is another nut to crack; citizens, is it just?—are we allowed to? Reckon not"—he shook his head seriously.

"Reckon no one can forbid us to do it, John Adams. We are a free nation," cried the crowd somewhat dubiously.

"Reckon our principles," continued Adams, "forbid us to do so—reckon, gentlemen, you know General Rusk's agreement with Filisola—reckon, one article reads like this: free departure over the Rio Grande—isn't it so?"

A deathly stillness followed this question, and for a considerable time not a one of the reflecting crowd answered. They knew that he had spoken correctly. At last one called out: "Let him live, the rascal!"

"Let him live!" several more called out.

"Well, people," continued the Yankee, "I see that you are reasonable—you say, he shall live—must turn him over to the government—he will be treated honorably—he is our prisoner—has surrendered on our honor, our humanity."

"Stop, gentlemen," cried one from the crowd. With the characteristic propensity of Americans to dispute things when matters of politics and laws are concerned, he announced, "That fellow is free—can't keep him—it's against the law— Firm treaty with Filisola."

"Hey, sir, you're going too far," interrupted John Adams, "the prisoner will be turned over to the government—the president can decide—he has violated the agreement—has plundered—that is against the article where it says: All the property belonging to Texas citizens shall be turned over to our people intact, and payment shall be made for that which has been taken away. By the way, people, we cannot abandon the beautifully glistening cannon before we know whether Filisola has completely fulfilled the treaty."

"John Adams is right," shouted the crowd. "Liberty and Law forever!" was the cry, and Holsinger was saved. The next morning he was led to [a port west of Galveston called] Quintana, then the seat of the government.

---

[65] It was after Santa Anna's defeat that Filisola issued a command not to do harm to the Texans any more.

[66] Rogue

CHAPTER THIRTY-TWO

Santa Anna

WHEN THE BRAZOS RIVER HAS PENETRATED the high plateaus where it takes its rise and has worked its way through the densely forested lower regions, it suddenly enters a broad area about six miles from its mouth. The area extends all along the shore line of the republic from the Gulf or the lagunas and often extends twenty miles inland. Only in the southwest beyond the Guadalupe River does one see occasional cactus groups and mesquite trees and now and then an aloe; but eastward of this stream, the eye wanders always over immense treeless meadows. Only off in the far west appears a faint, dark streak, the forests, and to the south flow the waters.

The basin here into which the Brazos River rushes, thunders its mighty and highly dangerous waves against the sandy beach. Most of the time it splashes and froths its silken spray over the clay banks that enclose both sides of the stream at its entrance into this whirl. Not without danger and only guided by the skilled hand does the pilot boat shoot safely through this endless rushing together and whirling of the raging Gulf. But not only here but also the whole solitary beach, both upward and downward, trembles and groans under the approaching waves that break almost everywhere, as at the mouth of the river, in roaring surf. Woe to the wanderer who is seized by this wild surf. In no time does he disappear under the snowy sea and far, far out in the quiet Gulf his corpse may appear on the quiet waters again. Seldom does this restless sea lie still before us, for the surf is thundering practically constantly. The only time when the traveler can find this coast practically quiet is when a strong land wind is battling directly against the foaming waves. But this is rarely the case. Then the Gulf is roaring instead of the surf, and the storm blows the merchantman far out onto the bosom of the Gulf.

At the mouth of the Brazos are two small villages, Velasco together with a little tree-trunk fort on the left side, and Quintana, then the seat of the government on the right, exactly opposite each other. Both are competing for pre-eminence in trade. I would probably prefer the latter one on account of its safer harbor. The shores here are bordered with layers of immense tree-trunks for width of a hundred yards or more that were brought down by the Mississippi from its primitive forests thousands of miles away and thrust out into the bosom of the sea, which then deposited them along the low shores toward the left. In this respect is Texas especially favored, as not only good fire wood can be found here but also excellent building timber.

It was this Quintana where we arrived after a three day's journey with our prisoner, Holsinger, toward the end of the month of May. The colonel was charmed with the beautiful landed estates that we passed, but he was also in constant fear of being murdered, although not a single incident had occurred that could have given him cause for this fear.

We rode to the residence of the president, Mr. David Burnet, who was living in the large storehouse of the firm of McKinney and Williams, and delivered the colonel to the highest officer of the land. He received him in a friendly manner;

and after we had made our report, a man of middle size, approximately five feet six inches tall, with bowed head, stepped in. He appeared to be a Mexican of a very common type, but his pale features led us to assume that he had some Indian blood in his veins. His rather long, shiny black hair lay flat on his well proportioned head, and his sparkling black eyes rested humbly on the floor. But the hyena might as well be as flattering as a hunting

General Antonio López de Santa Anna, Mexican dictator.

dog, as this man with the sinister expression could pretend to be humble. But he stepped rather reservedly through the door. His hands hung folded and limp before him, and he gazed constantly at the floor as if he feared the glances of the Texans.

"Presidente, Señor Presidente, mi General Santa Anna!" cried Holsinger to the fallen idol-of-blood, and he rushed toward him. No doubt he would have dropped to his knees before the fallen general had not he grasped him by the hands and greeted him with a duplicitous look. The features of Santa Anna seemed inclined to take on a more friendly expression when he saw before him such a willing tool of his former splendor and despotism, a thoroughgoing aristocrat, or was it possibly a consolation to him not to suffer alone.

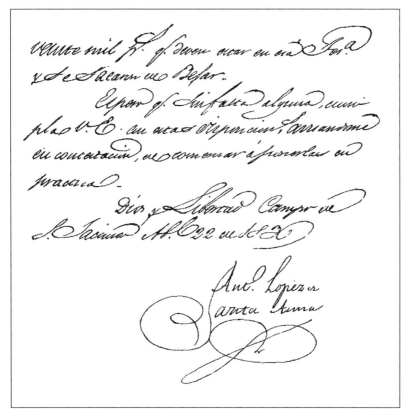

Letter and signature of General Santa Anna.

After the first greeting was over, questions and answers in Mexican [Spanish] proceeded rapidly of which I could understand very little since my conversation 'til now had only dealt with the army, mustangs, the noble art of cooking and baking, and other sentences from prosaic life. Consequently I cannot give an account of the emotional language that took place between the hero and his subject. After a modest meal I went over the river to Velasco.

"The war has ended," was the report from the West, "and although the enemy has not fulfilled all the terms of the agreement, his tattered columns have recrossed the Rio Grande after the Comanches robbed and almost destroyed them on their way across the Tamaulipas Prairie between the Nueces and the Rio Grande. Many are lying scalped in the road and in the tall grass. The redskins have moved off to the mountains with all the horses and mules."

That was also the end of the famous expedition that intended to chastise the congress of the United States and that probably was intended to subjugate all of the damned *Americanos*. O Gloria! Even the majestic old tree trunk on the shores of the Colorado River bears in large letters the triumphant crossing of Urrea's division, but a small cut underneath it informs the traveler at the same time of the re-crossing and retreat of the General. Although there is plenty of space on the high tree trunk, no other sign of this kind will ever decorate it again.

The next day I asked for my discharge, which Mirabeau B. Lamar, then the minister of war, immediately granted. [Copy of discharge to Ehrenberg signed by Mirabeau B. Lamar is reproduced in this volume's Book I.]

Volunteers from the States streamed in great numbers into the new republic. Although they came too late for the fighting, the government accepted their services for a definite time. The following day, one of the last in May, Mr. Burnet sent Santa Anna to one of the little warships that was anchored outside in deep water. The ship was to take Santa Anna to Vera Cruz.

Mr. Burnet's course of action certainly would not have been bad if one could have trusted Santa Anna. The captured Mexican president still had power if he should be set free, as his term of office did not expire until the fall, but if we kept him in prison until the expiration of this time, we would not need to expect anything from him on the treaty of independence that Mr. Burnet had entered into with him. The people of the two towns, General [Thomas] Green's volunteer brigade that had just arrived from the States and the minister of war with his elegant power of speech as leader, were determined to prevent his departure. Even the Texas Navy sailors made assurances that they would under no circumstances take him to Vera Cruz. All of Texas at this moment demanded his death with the possible exception of a few politicians, who thought more of the welfare of their country than the gratification of the passions of their hearts. But the latter were obliged to yield to the general voice. Santa Anna, who was already cherishing the wish soon to be free, was brought back. When this order was disclosed to him, he requested, battling with despair, to be shot on the ship as he feared that he would be hanged on the land. But the officers assured him that he was under the sacred protection of the laws and that the next congress would decide his case.

After the long boat in which the prisoner sat had made its way from the fleet through the surf, it cut over to the Velasco side where all the inhabitants, militia, and travelers had assembled. The trembling *presidente*, who accidentally sat under the flying colors of the Republic, drew his hat far down as he sat crumpled up in the boat; he bowed constantly to the spectators on the shore—a revolting spectacle. A deathly fear stood on his features, and he dropped exhausted into the stern of the boat after it had passed the Texans.

But this picture of humiliation did more to save the fallen one than all the speeches of Houston or Burnet could have done. It reminded the extremely offended ones that he was now their prisoner, the prisoner of a civilized people. Without asking for it, he was not prevented from moving again into the rooms near our president that he had formerly occupied, and under the noble treatment of Mr. Burnet he finally gave in to his fate.

Holsinger received his freedom, and at the same time an order was sent to Matagorda to deliver to him on his arrival his entire private property. But the colonel did not dare to go near the town. And ignoring our encouragement, he forfeited his several hundred dollars worth of effects among which, especially, were several very splendid uniforms. A few days later he sailed on the *Pennsylvania* to New Orleans. He had orders from Santa Anna for the Mexican consul in that town to purchase for Santa Anna a silver coffee service and all the other necessary accessories to fit up an elegant table, a number of delicacies and, finally, a Negro cook, as the plain manner of living and art of cooking of the backwoodsmen did not appeal to the taste of this fine gentleman. But the very respectable consul conducted himself entirely without propriety and would not advance the crushed president a single dollar. Consequently Holsinger had to travel on without completing his mission. Meanwhile he did not go to Mexico but pursued romantic matters pertaining to affairs of the heart. New York was his destination. But here also he found the doors to his happiness closed. His ideas of marriage were "blown up," as our people say, and with a raging hatred against the Yankees and their breed such as had never burned in his breast before, he returned to his own dear Mexico. Mexico—Santa Anna—and the priests eternally—that is now the motto of don John Holsinger, as it had been before.

CHAPTER THIRTY-THREE

Santa Anna's Attempted Escape

"ISN'T THIS AN AGREEABLE COUNTRY, this Texas, stranger?"
asked a slender young backwoodsman to his companion as they
rode along the road.

"Excellent, sir, enchanting, although I have traveled a great
deal, such a paradise as yours, sir, I have never seen," responded
the other, apparently a gentleman from the old world. "To be
sure," he continued, "it was worth fighting for such a country.
What man would not dare the utmost for such a homeland?
No, this strip from Bastrop up to Waterloo is incomparable.
[The town was called Waterloo until designated as the capitol
site, when Congress re-named it Austin.] I only wish that my
poor countrymen could have a single look at this heavenly park,
and I am convinced that they would have a different opinion of
the magnificent countries on the other side of the Atlantic
Ocean. Letters of praise are of no value, sir, as they do not want
to believe us. Everyone prefers to rely on the newspapers. There

it is written—it says—see—'famine in America—revolution—
fire—murder, etc.—Stay in the old country, here you have your
bread—what else do you want?' If one reads the article, he sees
at once that it usually is a fabrication from the *New York Herald*,
but all contradictions are in vain—They will not help—We on
this side are all barbarians, sir—you know sir, what kind of
articles usually fill the political newspapers of the United States
before the elections, and that sentences such as: 'Dissolution of
the Union is certain when H....'s party gains power'—'Revolution if van Buren follows Jackson's principles'—'Destruction of
the Southern States, when X.....'s tariff bill passes the house,'
and others are misleading. I do not want to talk about the
countless articles that are written only because of envy between
cities and between states, not to speak of the many senseless
witty articles with which the editors fill their columns or allude
to local affairs. No, sir, all talk is useless, and the only remedy is
to print the defense also. Then, sir, it may work better—it is
then in print. That is the only thing that shakes up the firm,
educated ideas, at least a little bit."

   "Well, stranger," interrupted the backwoodsman, "it is not
necessary for you to tell me that—I reckon I know what the
Northerner says of the Southerner—I am something of a
Northerner myself, sir,—I am a Hoosier[67] and proud of it, sir.
But I had to laugh, sir, when I made a little trip to the City of
Brotherly Love[68] a few years ago. Sir, you should have seen the
old venerable Quakers when they warned me of the hell that is
New Orleans. But you would have also enjoyed, sir, seeing the
old cunning, pious shopkeepers in their stores, compete with
the down Easterner in trying to sell their cloth to the simple
backwoodsman. But, sir, we Hoosiers have a little wit also. The
Quakers could not get the best of this kid. But I must admit
that I was a little afraid of New Orleans, sir. Not really afraid,
but I thought, sir, a little precaution is better than a calculation
too late as to how I should have done it. The old foxes had told

me how the Spaniards in New Orleans fought with long knives
during broad daylight in the open streets and in the market
place; how the French *parlevoos* relieved every honest Northerner or Westerner of his money; how people would disappear
in the mud in the streets; how two hundred people died daily of
yellow fever, and no telling what else. I figured, therefore, sir,
what I should do. First I went over to Chestnut Street and
bought me a twelve-inch long Spaniard[69] from a respectable
Quaker, which this pious shopkeeper kept on sale for the benefit of those who were traveling in the South. In regard to my
money, sir, I did not need to be afraid. I had left behind in the
City of Brotherly Love almost everything except the goods that
I sent back to father in Indiana. In order to prevent yellow
fever, I bought thirty boxes of Dr. Brantreth's Universal Pills.
Now I seated myself on the *Eliza*, a real Baltimore clipper.[70]
You may judge for yourself: in eleven days we were in the
mouth of the Mississippi—and sailed up that mighty stream.
The banks on each side, sir, for the first forty or forty-five miles
consist of immense drift logs, alligators, reeds, marshes, mosquitoes, and snake colonies, and a little further up bears, pan-
thers, and wolves appear. But on the next day, sir, we passed an
altogether different strip of land. Sugar plantations miles long
lay like a chain on both sides of the mammoth stream, compared to which our Ohio is only a small brook. The land, sire, at
this time lay below sea level and was held in its bed by levees
from twenty to thirty feet wide. But, sir, when a man has had
nothing under him for ten or twelve days but the rolling waves
and has seen nothing over him but the endless blue, he would
like to jump overboard for joy and swim ashore to a plantation.
Next to the beautiful residence of the plantation owner are
joined, like a little town, the group of Negro huts, each with a
little garden, together with the storehouse and the refinery."

The stranger interrupted the speaker, asking why a small
garden was with each little house.

"Why, sir," continued the backwoodsman, "do you not know that each black man has his little piece of ground—raises sweet potatoes, corn, cabbage, red pepper, cauliflower, turnips, and no telling what else. You know, we Americans are satisfied with good beefsteak, ham and eggs, cornbread together with tea, coffee, or milk; but the French in New Orleans mix together everything that can be found in the house and make their excellent gumbos, kickshaws [a fancy dish or delicacy], and other dishes from them. The Spaniards will not be outdone and throw in a few handfuls of fiery red pepper besides. Those, sir, are dishes that no honest man of our type can eat."

"But what do the Negroes do with all the vegetables?" asked the wanderer.

"Why," said the Hoosier, reflecting a little, "I reckon they take them to New Orleans—sell them—It's their grog money, sir. But," he continued, "one night the captain who towed us up the river[71] cried through his megaphone, 'Look out on the *Eliza*—look out—I let you go'—and before we had time to do anything we crashed into a brig from Havana and splintered up its back-board, or star-board, or lay-board side, as they call it, for which our captain had to pay every pic[72] of damages. The next day, as I wandered from the landing with my big knife always handy, I saw no Spaniards who wanted to fight. On the contrary they cried in competition with their parrots and monkeys, 'Here the best oranges—here the best pineapple, gentlemen—here the best of everything, sir!' and so forth, and then in French, and then in Spanish and Italian. Those black and brown and yellow people make a real hellish noise. Even the filthy Choctaws,[73] who bring weeds and roots of the forest to the town for sale, were there; but one sees no knives, daggers, or pistols.

"After I had wandered about for a while, I came to the American quarters, called a municipality, and met a large number of my countrymen, who were carrying long knives like mine. We soon, however, discovered that the many frightful stories that we had heard were absolutely untrue, and we had no other use for our knives than to pitch for quarters[74] with them on the large sugar and tobacco barrels.

"About yellow fever—no one had heard anything for two years, and my Brantreth pills were money thrown out—couldn't sell them—could not even induce one of my countrymen to take them for nothing. You see, sir, every false rumor has its good side; if it isn't for one person, it is for another. The rumors are speculations, sir—idle speculations. In order to keep me as a good customer, because I annually bought many wares for my father, the old Quaker shopkeeper warned me against New Orleans—he feared I would buy there in the future, which, in fact, I did, sir, and—"

"Hey there, gentlemen! Hey there! Good morning to you— Suppose you are freighting for Waterloo? Take me along—the best way to idle away the time is in good company, and it is also safer and more relaxing for a trip in the country where the red-skins still roam about at times."

The two travelers looked around and beheld a rider with narrow shoulders about five feet and eight inches tall. White and blue striped trousers, a short-sleeved shirt, half boots, and a sagging Kentucky felt hat from which the good rain had washed all the starch adorned the figure of the stranger. After the customary salutations of which, I must admit, there were only a few, and a few trivial remarks, "male talk," the stranger asked in English, sounding somewhat through the nose, "I reckon, gentlemen, this is the Waterloo Road [the road to present-day Austin, Texas] on which we are now traveling?"

"Perfectly correct, sir," was the reply of the backwoodsman.

"I suppose, gentlemen, that it isn't very far to town?" asked the apparently very talkative stranger again.

"A few miles, sir," was the laconic answer.

"Well, sir, you have a different kind of miles in Texas—are they horse-miles or ordinary miles that you mean?"

"Certainly, they are our horse-miles, mister—but you need not be afraid—we will soon be in sight of the Colorado chain of hills and at its foot lies the little hill-town."

In fact, the forest now became open and several miles to the northwest gradually appeared the dark mountains out of which the Colorado flowed onto the plains. In the forest, both sides of the road were bordered with gigantic pecan trees, oaks, cypress, and other varieties of trees. Little of their mature trunks could be seen as immense masses of interwoven grapevines rose from near the road and reached to the tops of the gigantic trees. Often garlands of the same growth thirty to forty feet long hung down over the center of the road so that the traveler was frequently obliged to cut off these and other vine growths. A cover of large black grapes concealed the green color of the underbrush from the traveler, and the European, enjoying the view, rode on in delight through the natural alley.

"I suppose, gentlemen, you know of Santa Anna's trick?" asked the stranger after a pause.

"What, sir? What kind of a trick?" asked the two together, starting up out of their musings. "We don't know anything of Santa Anna, stranger, except that the fellow is being treated altogether too well and that he is causing us a lot of unnecessary cost."

"That fellow should be treated differently," added the backwoodsman, "or they should run him home to the *padres*, so that we would at last be rid of him—he lives like the Pope in Rome—"

"Don't reckon that's so, sir," said the stranger, "the gentleman—decorated with ribbons of medals—is presently sitting shackled in irons."

"Shoot, is it true, stranger," asked the backwoodsman, "How come? What has happened to David Burnet? Has he gone crazy or had he been stung by the sun?"

"None of all that, gentlemen, but Santa Anna has again acted in Santa Anna style. I will tell you about it if you want to hear it. You no doubt know, gentlemen, that this fellow was taken to Columbia[75] last June because the government was transferred there. To make it short, I must tell you that this gentleman some time ago had devised a plan to poison his guards and run away—had gotten some poison from some free Mexicans that were standing around, and last week it was to be used. However, his secretary, gentlemen, a very clever fellow who probably suspected that nothing good would come from it, betrayed the matter to the last detail. You can imagine how raging Burnet was—had him placed in irons at once and liberated the secretary. This will probably be the end of him—according to my opinion he is a dead man—the congress will soon act on him, gentlemen—must admit that I would not like to be in his shoes."

The European could not speak for astonishment, but the backwoodsman was perfectly cool and swore that it would have made little difference to him if the prisoner had escaped. He added that David was responsible to the nation for him, and if he let him escape he [Burnet] would have to decide how to deal with the rage of the people.

The stranger was on the point of entering his objections to the indifference of the backwoodsman, when he was distracted by the appearance of the charmingly situated little town.

The conversation now turned to the army of the republic which, as the stranger stated, consisted of almost three thousand volunteers from the States, adding that should the Mexicans ever step over the Rio Grande again, the people could easily raise an army of ten thousand men. Also the presidential election that was soon to take place, was discussed, and it turned out that the three travelers were fans of Houston through and through and did not want to have anything to do with the hypocritical David Burnet, who otherwise was a real gentleman.

Old Sam had the votes of the traveling cloverleaf [trio] and he also had those of the nation.

67 Nickname for the inhabitants of Indiana.

68 Philadelphia, called this way because of its Quaker inhabitants.

69 A knife in which a spring, when it is opened, prevents the blade from clicking back.

70 Excellent, very fast, sailing schooners that are built in Baltimore.

71 The ships that are loaded to and from New Orleans are towed by steamboats the 120 miles that this place is located up on the Mississippi, because it is quicker.

72 The smallest coin in New Orleans, approximately two sgr. [Pic refers to picayune, a Spanish-American half-real piece formerly used in parts of the southern United States; a five-cent coin.]

73 An Indian tribe that supplies New Orleans with Venison and various herbs and forest roots.

74 quarter dollars

75 A little city at the Brazos River, twenty-five miles from its mouth. [It served as official capital of Texas from September to December, 1836. There the first congress of the republic convened and Sam Houston was inaugurated president on October 22, 1836.]

CHAPTER THIRTY-FOUR

Conclusion

THE MIGHTY NORTHWEST STORM howls again down over the treeless plains of the Rocky Mountains, and again the redskins and the buffalos are fleeing ahead of it down toward the mild climate of the free young Republic of Texas.

The star of the hopeful West glistens joyfully from the lofty tip of the liberty pole.[76] And just as boldly does the flag of freedom defy the northwest storm as it defied the political storms, the confusion of the elections has passed; Old Sam [Houston] is standing at the helm. And he—the sensible pilot who had led the frail craft safely through the foaming, thundering, breaking surf; he whom the voice of the people had made also their pilot after the brig had passed over dangerous cliffs and banks—is now cutting through the gently rocking waves.

The old general or the new president, as one likes, has immediately applied the holy power entrusted to him and sent Santa Anna home. And that gentleman [Santa Anna], because he still had power, obligated himself to recognize the independence of Texas and to bring Mexico to the same recognition. Is he going to honor his obligations?

[76] Freedom tree [Flagpole flying the Lone Star flag?]

"I suppose, never," the backwoodsman mumbled, "Old Sam acted damned arbitrarily."

But the general took his own course; he knew what should be done. He understood the backwoodsmen and they understood him.

The old oak therefore was mistaken; because when the Mexican had escaped the trap and had ended a journey through the United States in order to make a similar concession in Washington [D.C.], he sailed home. His presidential term had expired and he was in no mood to take a seat in the decaying chair again. He rather declared to the world that his power had passed, that he could not be active any more and therefore he could not fulfill his pledges.

Old Sam laughs and says that he had half-way known this in advance, but that he did not want to shed any more blood, but wanted to build the state on a more noble foundation.

Sam Houston, general of the army of volunteers, president of the Republic of Texas, and United States senator. His fourteen years in the senate were used to defend the rights of native American Indians.

Photograph by Brady. Line engraving published March 30, 1861 in Harper's Weekly. *Natalie Ornish Collection from Laurel Ornish.*

The citizens have forgotten all this and the streets make a living from caravans of immigrants. The woods groan under blows of the axe, and felled forests are cleared on all sides. Sunlight is finally penetrating into the regions of the jungle-like forests, numerous houses of the working, industrious settlers spring up on the edge of the prairies, and everything points to an enormous harvest in the next few years. Never, never ever, has Texas seen such life.

Since there is no enemy to be feared, three thousand volunteers have been discharged, and the old worn out Mexican wheel-work trembles when the deaf patriot Smith with his rangers undertakes an excursion toward the Rio Grande. This gentleman, I must remark here, is now captain of a ranger corps that is guarding the desolate region between the Nueces and the Rio Grande. It is very dangerous to get within range of his always well-loaded rifle, as he shoots without making many formalities about it if he does not get a satisfactory reply to his three-worded "Who goes there?" Not everyone knows that it's necessary to speak very loud to communicate with him.

As already stated, Mexico has not recognized our independence, but what is better, the most powerful, liberal, and enlightened nations have done so. Even that holy cornerstone, the vicar of Christ that sends out his bulls [papal letters], (the Pope) has from his seven hills graciously granted us his protection. O lucky Texas! Isn't all this proof that Texas can defend itself against its miserable enemy?

Yes, the sons of Uncle Sam proved to the world again that they possess common sense and that they also know how to defend themselves. They have also proven that to gain freedom, all special interests must step into the background; furthermore, that for this highest gift of the World Spirit, wealth and blood must be risked; in one word, they have proven that the people must have patriotism, but a real patriotism, not an evaporating one. It must be felt deeply, deeply, in the heart, and it must discuss clearly and truly the shortcomings of the fatherland. Fatherland doesn't mean the soil on which we saw the sun for the first time, if we are arbitrarily pushed about like grain on it. Only in the country where I myself am a cog in the wheel, can I say this is my fatherland.

For this, my life!

Only this fatherland, will the patriot defend with the sword. When dark rascals, heartless, and unscrupulous characters are trying to rob the nation of its consciousness by attempting to bring back the "good old days" with its hypocrisy and inequalities, then this divine and godly inner feeling will not remain idle with empty words and useless protestations, but rather, it progresses forward to become a mighty deed.

The farmer as well as the merchant, the worker as well as the factory owner, the soldier and the bureaucrat, all are servants of the people. All of them are citizens of the state. Each one is part of this vast machine; and everyone must help bear the burdens of the country; and everyone must, therefore, have equal rights before the law. No monopolies, no favors, no class system, no meaningless formalities, no arbitrary action in anything that concerns the whole, and no restrictions on the press! No restrictions for the brilliant idea!! No restrictions for the tongue that speaks the truth!!!

These are the principles of the Texans. For these, we are willing to give our lives, and once more I cry out:

Liberty! Law! and Texas forever!

PETER MOLLENHAUER
ABOUT THE TRANSLATOR

Personal: Born 12 August 1929, in Königsberg, Germany. U.S. Citizen, veteran, married.

Department: Foreign Languages and Literatures.

Academic Position: Associate Professor of German, 1967-present.

Education: B.A., *cum laude*, German, Spanish, French, Philosophy; The University of Texas at Austin, 1962. Ph.D., German Literature; The University of Texas at Austin, 1965.

Academic and Administrative Experience:

1965-67: Assistant Professor of German; University of Wisconsin at Madison.

1967-72: Associate Professor and Chairman, Department of Foreign Languages and Literatures; Southern Methodist University, Dallas.

1972-73: Academic Dean of Schiller College; Germany, England, France, Spain (leave of absence from SMU).

1973: Resumed teaching duties at SMU. Director of undergraduate studies, German (to 1982).

1976-: Director, *SMU-in-Austria* summer program.

Publications:

Books

John E. Crean and Peter Mollenhauer, *Briefe aus Deutschland*, Harcourt, Brace and World, 1968. 236 pp.

Die Satiren Friedrich Nicolais. Ein Beitrag zur Kulturgeschichte des 18. Jahrhunderts. German Language and Literature Monographs, No. 2, Amsterdam, 1977. 267 pp.

Rudolf Steiner: *Christ in Relation to Lucifer and Ahriman: The Threefold Configuration of Being*, edited, introduced, and translated from the German by Peter Mollenhauer. The Anthroposophic Press: Spring Valley, NY, 1978. 40 pp.

Rudolf Steiner: *The Karma of Vocation (Das Karma des Berufes* in Anknüpfung an Goethes Leben), edited and translated from the German by Peter Mollenhauer. The Anthroposophic Press: Spring Valley, NY, 1986. 164 pp.

Rudolf Steiner: *The Principle of Spiritual Economy in Relation to Questions of Reincarnation*, edited, introduced, and translated from the German by Peter Mollenhauer. The Anthroposophic Press: Hudson, NY, 1986. 184 pp.

Articles and Scholarly Translations

"Dissertations in Progress." *MfdU*, Vol. LVIII, No. 3, 1966, pp. 258-267.

"C. Lottner: Exceptions to the First sound Shift," translated from German by Peter Mollenhauer, in *A Reader in Nineteenth-Century Historical Linguistics*, Winfred P. Lehmann, ed., Indiana University Press, 1967, pp. 97-108.

"Dissertations in Progress." *MfdU*, Vol. LIXc, No. 3, 967, pp. 255-267.

"A Thematic Approach to Multi-disciplinary German Studies." *Schatzkammer*, Vol. II, No. L, 1976, pp. 18-25.

"Wahrnehmung und Wirklichkeitsbewusstsein in Hofmannsthals *Reitergeschichte*." *The German Quarterly*, Vol. L, No. 3, 1977, pp. 283-297.

"Friedrich Nicolai: Catalyst of the Prussian Enlightenment." *Schatzkammer*, Vol. X, No. 2, Fall 1984, pp. 19-25.

"The Way the Cookie Didn't Crumble: An Essay on the Liberalization of Cultural Content in FL Classes." *Schatzkammer*, Vol. XII, No. 1, Spring 1986, pp. 68-78.

"Alfred Kubin's *The Other Side*: An Artist's Nightmare of Utopia." *West Virginia University Philological Papers*, Vol. XXXII, 1986/87, pp. 49-53.

"Nicolai, Friedrich, 1733-1811." *Dictionary of Literary Biography: German Literary Figures of the Age of Goethe*, Bruccoli Clark Layman: New York, NY, 1990.

English translation of "Uber Sprache und worte" by Arthur Schopenhauer, as published in *Parerga und Parlipomena* (1800); and an English translation of "Zum Problem des Ubersetzens" by Friedrich Nietzsche, as published in *Die frohliche Wissenschaft (1882)*; in *Theories of Translation: An Anthology of Essays from Dryden to Derrida*, edited by John Biguenet and Rainer Schulte, University of Chicago Press, 1991.

BOOK REVIEWS

Karl Wilhelm Ramler. *Lieder der Deutschen*, Stuttgart, 1965, *MfdU*, Vol. LVIII, No. 2, 1966.

Friedrich von Blanckenburg. *Versuch "uber den Roman*, Stuttgart, 1965, *MfdU*, Vol. LVIII, No. 2, 1966.

George K"uhlewind, *Vom Normalen zum Gesunden*, Verlag Freies Geistesleben, Stuttgart, 1983, *Anthroposophic Journal*, Spring, 1984.

Some Papers Read and Seminars Given:

Three week Seminar at the 1976 Rudolf Steiner Institute in Natick, MA. Topic: "The Perception of Knowledge by Rudolf Steiner and Goethe."

Paper read at the 1976 annual meeting of the SCMLA: "Uber die Grenzen der deutschen Aufklarungssatire."

Paper read at the 1978 annual meeting of SCMLA: "200 Years — Werther: Entwertung or Entwerdung."

"Das amerikanische und das "osterreichische Demokratieverst"andnis," Univ. of Graz Colloquium, Graz, Austria, June 26, 1981.

Paper read at the 1981 meeting of the ANE Modern Language Association, Quebec, Canada: "On the Satire of the German Enlightenment."

Moderator of Section 5: Eighth Annual Colloquium on Modern Literature and Film, University of West Virginia, Sept. 22-25, 1983.

Paper read at the 1983 annual meeting of SCMLA: "The Prophecies of Lessing and Kleist: Journies through Time and Revealed History."

Paper read at annual meeting of S.C. Society for Eighteenth Century Studies (Colorado Springs, March 2, 1984): "Friedrich Nicolai, Catalyst of the German Enlightenment."

Paper read at the Ninth Annual Colloquium on Modern Literature of the University of West Virginia (Sept. 27-29, 1986). "Alfred Kubin's *The Other Side*: An Artist's Nightmare of Utopia."

Seminars held at the Walden Institute in January 1991: "An Introduction to Rudolf Steiner's Anthroposophy," and "The Philosophy of Spiritual Activity."

Some International Seminars and Conferences Attended:

"International Academic Conference for Germanists." Weimar, German Democratic Republic, July 2-7, 1977.

"The Imperfect Reason." Alpbach European Forum, Alpbach, Austria, August 3-21, 1979.

"Seminar for Business German." Carl Duisberg Society, Cologne, Germany, July 5-28, 1982.

"Applied Language Study Conference." Oklahoma State University, Stillwater, OK, February 18-19, 1983.

Departmental Expertise:

Advanced Composition and Stylistics; Commercial German, the Enlightenment, Goethe, Klassik; Cultural, Intellectual, and Literary History; Satire and Comedy; Perception as a Philosophical and Literary Problem. Recently taught advanced literature courses: 5310: Goethezeit (Klassik), 5340: Laughter and comedy, 5350: The Perception of Self in German Literature

Humanties Courses taught:

LS 1309 (Freshman seminar) *Satire and the Satiric Mood*

LS 3368 (Junior elective) *Search for Identity in Modern German Literature*

FL 3371 SMU-in-Austria *Trends in Austrian Literature and Culture*

FL 3369 (Junior elective and area study course) *Perspectives on Modern Germany*

FL 3375 (Inter-disciplinary) *The Young Man's Perspective in Literature: Images and Modes of Experience*

LS 3351 Humanities III: *Rationalism, Romanticism, Revolution* (Discussion groups, evening classes, superior studies sections. Eight years.)

CORE *Religious and Philosophical Thought III.* (Member of pilor group, 1981; taught the course three years.)

CAPSTONE

    CAPS 3318 *Perspectives on Modern Germany* (Spring 1983, 1984, and 1986).

    CAPS 3352 *The Europeans* (Spring 1985, 1986, 1987, 1988)

MASTER OF LIBERAL ARTS

Search for Identity in Modern German Literature

Problems of a Divided Country

The Germans: Their Heritage and Culture (MLA 6388, 1986 and 1987)

Modes of Being in World Literature and Thought (MLA 6350, 1986)

New Humanities Courses Proposed:

CAPS — *The Young Person's Perspective in World Literature* (1988/89)

Major Offices and Memberships at SMU:

President of AAUP Chapter, 1969.

Member, University College Council, 1971.

Member, Faculty Senate, 1970; 1982-1984.

Chair, Department of Foreign Languages and Literature, 1967-1972.

Area Chair, German, 1973-1982 and 1988-1990.

Director, SMU-in-Austria, 1976-.

National Honors and Offices:

SCMLA, Chair of Committee on Honorary Membership, 1971.

Dallas Goethe Center, Vice-President, 1969.

One of seven U.S. professors invited by West German Foreign Office to study educational institutions, two weeks in 1971.

Junior Year in Freiburg/München, Member of Advisory Board, 1971-1976.

Schatzkammer für deutsche Sprachlehre und Dichtung, Consulting Editor, 1973-.

Community Service and Consulting:

Translator and certified court interpreter, 1974-.

POSTON POETRY ON EHRENBERG

Twelve years after Ehrenberg's death, his close friend Charles D. Poston wrote a book called *Apache-Land*.[1] More than a hundred years later, historian Ornish researched and learned that Otaheite was an early name for Tahiti, bringing to light Ehrenberg's connection to the South Pacific.

Poston wrote *Apache-Land* in verse form. The excerpt on Ehrenberg follows:

> The Tubac[2] chief brought in his band
> The natives of most every land,[3]
> But not for him these sketches made;
> For what is he, to Sonora maid?
> But for their own intrinsic worth,
> I must in duty set them forth:
>
> First, Ehrenberg, a Saxon mild,
> Who had in youth been very wild,
> And ranged in Texas border wars
> Until his face was full of scars.
>
> Thence wandering far to Oregon,
> He earned his way with trap and gun.
> From thence he sailed to Sandwich Isles[4]
> Where he was employed by Minister Wiles
> To make survey of Honolulu,
> And paint eruption of Tululu,
> Whence he sailed to island Otaheite,
> Where, 'tis said, he was Queen Pomare's deity;
> How this may be we must not scan—
> He was an interesting man.

1 San Francisco: A.L. Bancroft & Company, 1878, pp. 51-52.
2 Tubac refers to the town in present day Arizona where the Sonora Mining Company was located.
3 "Natives of most every land" likely refers to the eclectic group of ethnic peoples who worked in the mining towns.
4 Sandwich Islands was the early name for the Hawaiian Islands.

EHRENBERG'S TEXAS LAND AND HIS ORIGIN

The State of Texas granted Herman Ehrenberg's 1600 acres of land near Liberty, Texas, to his three-years-older brother Emil Ehrenberg, sole surviving heir. Emil, a resident of Teplitz, Bohemia, drew up an agreement with a Bohemian merchant, Heinrich Cohn. If Cohn would pay Emil's expenses for a trip to America, he would receive half of Herman's estate, 800 of the 1600 acres. (T. L. Miller, *Bounty and Donation Land Grants of Texas 1835-1888*, pp. 247, 248, and 763, states the heirs received on 13 May 1880, 960 acres under Bounty Warrant 93, and 640 acres under Donation Certificate 36.)

Emil and his backer Cohn came in 1884 to Houston, where Emil — then age 71 — transferred the entire 1600 acres to Cohn for $1,415, only 88 cents per acre. In 1885 Cohn conveyed 400 acres to Stanley Epstein of San Antonio and used his other 1200 acres to pay off debt to the Steiner brothers of New York, who on March 19, 1912 sold their 1200 acres to W.H.H. Miller of Harris County, Texas, who in two weeks sold the land to the Old River Rice and Irrigation Co. of Jefferson, Texas. This company eventually sold it, including mineral rights, to the Kirby Lumber Company of Houston.

Regarding Herman Ehrenberg's background, Senator Barry Goldwater said, "My uncle always referred to him as Jewish [and] there has never been any question in my mind but that Ehrenberg was a Jew."

Professor Carlos E. Castañeda of The University of Texas at Austin's history department listed Ehrenberg as a Jew in his series *Our Catholic Heritage in Texas 1519-1936*. Castañeda wrote, "The brave messenger who chose to share the fate of his companions was Herman Ehrenberg, a volunteer German-Jew. . . Herman Ehrenberg, the German-Jew who chose to remain with Fannin at Coleto when his two companions galloped away, lived many years after the massacre." (vol. 6, pp. 297, 299) Dr. Benjamin Sacks, an Arizona physician who spent years researching Ehrenberg, sent a query to Castañeda. In answer to Sack's query, Castañeda wrote him on January 21, 1955:

"As far as I know, the first to make a public statement about Ehrenberg being a Jew was Clarence Wharton. Wharton was a prominent lawyer and historian of Texas, who gathered a respectable library of Texana and wrote extensively on various topics connected with the Texas Revolution." Wharton wrote in his book *Remember Goliad*, "Herman Ehrenberg, a young German-Jew, halted and dismounted and took his place with his comrades" (p. 43). "One of the most interesting of these refugees was a young German-Jew named Herman Ehrenberg" (p. 52); "the restless wandering Jew" (p. 55).

Frank C. Brophy asserted in his *Arizona Sketch Book*, "Some of the best and earliest cartography, after the Guadalupe-Hidalgo Treaty in 1848, was done by that scholarly Jew, Herman Ehrenberg."

It has been speculated by some writers the possibility Ehrenberg was Lutheran and was descended from German nobility. One of the reasons the author of this book takes the position that Ehrenberg was a Jew is the fact that his best friend, Michel Goldwater, who knew him personally, considered him a Jew.

There is a document that indicates the birth of Ehrenberg children in the early 1800s was recorded by the parish priest in the church records of their little village. According to these records, Herman's parents were Johann Friedrich Vollrath Ehrenberg and Johanne Sophie Juliane Hesse Ehrenberg. Children from this marriage were Friedrich Ludwig Ehrenberg, Emil Constantin Vollrath Ehrenberg, and Herman Vollrath Ehrenberg, who were born in Steuden. Although it would appear to the casual reader that this documents that they were members of this church, this is not necessarily so. An internationally renowned scholar said, "During the Napoleonic era, for census purposes, it was not uncommon for the birth of Jewish children to be entered in the local parish records, especially if it was in a small town." The Ehrenberg children were born in Steuden, a tiny village. Dr. Abraham Peck, whose credentials follow, wrote the following to this author:

"I think your question regarding children born in Germany to Jewish parents in the early 1800s is a most interesting one. It seems to me that because Germany was such a broken community in terms of the various states that made up the German territories, it is quite possible that records of Jewish children were deposited in the local church record storage facility in one of the ecclesiastical states, especially where there was not a large Jewish community. I know of cases where records survived because they were housed in the local parish archives."

ABRAHAM J. PECK, CURRICULUM VITAE

Abraham J. Peck did his doctoral work at the University of East Anglia, Norwich, England, and at the University of Hamburg, West Germany.

From 1976 to 1997, Dr. Peck served as administrative director of the American Jewish Archives of Hebrew Union College-Jewish Institute of Religion in Cincinnati and lecturer in Judaic studies at the University of Cincinnati. He was also managing editor of *American Jewish Archives*, a scholarly journal of history published since 1948.

Dr. Peck, in the spring of 1997, was appointed executive director of Holocaust Museum Houston.

He is the author or editor of twelve published volumes: *Radicals and Reactionaries: The Crisis of Conservatism in Wilhelmine Germany* (1978); co-editor (with Jacob Rader Marcus) of *Studies in the American Jewish Experience* (1981); editor of *Jews and Christians After the Holocaust* (1982); *Studies in the American Jewish Experience II* (1984); co-editor (with Jacob R. Marcus) of *The American Rabbinate: A Century of Continuity and Change, 1883-1983* (1985); co-editor (with Uri D. Herscher) of *Queen City Refuge: An Oral History of Cincinnati's Jewish Refugees from Nazism* (1989); editor of *The German-Jewish Legacy in America: From Bildung to the Bill of Rights* (1989); and editor of *The Papers of World Jewish Congress,*

1939-1950 (2 vols., 1990). Co-editor (with Martin A. Cohen) of *Sephardim in the Americas: Studies in Culture and History* (1992). He co-edited (with Michael Berenbaum) *The Holocaust and History*, the most comprehensive collection of scholarship on all aspects of the Holocaust (1997).

Articles include "Vom Monolog zum Dialog," *Aufbau*; "Germans and Jews in Dialogue: Is there Anything to Discuss?" *German Life*, April-May, 1995; "Notes of a Native Landsberg Son" in *Ein Ort wie jedes Andere: Landsberg, 1932-1958* (Rowohlt Verlag, 1995); "A Continent in Chaos: Europe's Displaced Persons," in *Liberation 1945* (United States Holocaust Memorial Museum, 1995); "Europe's Displaced Millions," in *Dimensions* magazine; "The Contradictions Still Remain: Jews and Germans Fifty Years After the Holocaust" (Hebrew) in *Gesher*, fall/winter 1993; "The Town Where the Holocaust Was Born" (German) in *Semit*, Fall, 1992; "Sharing the Burden: Post Holocaust Jews and Germans and a Search for a New Beginning" (Hebrew) in *Gesher*, Summer 1992; "She'erith Hapletah: The Purpose of the Legacy" in *Midstream*, 1991; "The Jewish DP Experience in Germany, 1945-1951" (German) in Julius H. Schoeps and Andreas Nachama (eds.) *Aufbau nach dem Untergang*. Deutsch-juedische Geschichte nach '45; "The Agony of the Lodz Ghetto" in the *Simon Weisenthal Center Holocaust Annual*; "The Brother's Keepers: Isaac Mayer Wise, Stephen S. Wise and Dilemma of American Jewish Responsibility" (Hebrew) in *Gesher*, Fall 1989; "Jewish Survivors of the Holocaust in Germany: Revolutionary Vanguard or Remnants of a Destroyed People?" in *The Tel Aviv Yearbook for German History* (1990); "That Other Peculiar Institution: Jews and Judaism in the Nineteenth Century South" in *Modern Judaism*; and "The Contradictions Still Remain: Jews and Germans Fifty Years After the Holocaust" (Hebrew) in *Gesher*, fall/winter 1993. Author of "Our Eyes Have Seen Eternity: Memory and Self-Identity Among the She'erith Hapletah" in *Modern Judaism* (Spring 1997). Author of "Voices for Change: Chapters in the Post-Holocaust Dialogue" in *From the Unthinkable to the Unavoidable: American Christian and Jewish Scholars Encountered the Holocaust* (1997).

Later writings include a history of the Jewish DP Camps from 1945-1957 and also a history of the Southern Jewish experience.

Dr. Peck is a special consultant to the United States Holocaust Memorial Museum; a member of the International Advisory Board of the International Center for Holocaust Studies of the Anti-Defamation League of B'nai B'rith; a member of the Advisory Board of the Museum of the Southern Jewish Experience; a member of the Ohio Council on Holocaust Education; a founding member of the Cincinnati Interfaith Holocaust Foundation; and a member of International P.E.N., Center of German-speaking Writers Abroad.

He is listed in *Who's Who in the Midwest*, *Who's Who of Emerging Leaders in America*, *Men of Achievement*, *Men and Women of Distinction*, *Who's Who in World Jewry*, *Who's Who in American Jewry*, *Who's Who in the the World*, and *Who's Who in America*.

BIBLIOGRAPHY

SOURCE BOOKS

Alessio Robles, Vito. *Coahuila y Texas en la época Colonial.* Mexico City: Editorial Cultura, 1938.

————. *Coahuila y Texas desde la consumación de la independencia hasta el tratado de paz de Guadalupe Hidalgo.* 2 vols. Mexico City: Antigua Libreria Robredo, 1945-1946.

Alonso de León, Capitán, with General Fernando Sanchez de Zamora. *Historia de Nuevo León con noticias sobre Coahuila, Tamaulipos, Tejas, y Nuevo Mexico.* Mexico: 1649. Reprinted in *Documentos Ineditos o Muy Raros para la Historia de Mexico* edited by Genaro Garcia, 25: 75-77, 90-95; Mexico: 1909. Translated with commentary by Carl L. Duaine in *Caverns of Oblivion,* Corpus Christi, Texas: privately published, 1971.

Baker, DeWitt Clinton, ed. *A Texas Scrap-Book: Made Up of the History, Biography, and Miscellany of Texas and Its People.* New York: A. S. Barnes, 1875, p. 573. Reprint, Austin: Steck, 1935. Index by Richard Morrison. Austin: W. M. Morrison Books, 1984.

Bancroft, Hubert Howe. *Encyclopedia of Frontier Biography.* Vol. 2: *History of California.* San Francisco: A. L. Bancroft, 1886. Vol. 5: *History of Mexico.* 1887. Vol. 15: *History of the North Mexican States and Texas.* 1889. Vol. 17: *History of Arizona and New Mexico.* 1889.

Barker, Eugene C. *Mexico and Texas 1821-1835.* Dallas: P.L. Turner, 1928; reprint, New York: Russell & Russell, 1965.

———— ed. *The Life of Stephen F. Austin, Founder of Texas, 1793-1836: A Chapter in the Westward Movement of the Anglo-American People.* Nashville: Cokesbury, 1926; reprint, Austin: Texas State Historical Society, 1949.

Barker, Eugene C. and Amelia Williams, eds. *The Writings of Sam Houston.* 8 vols. Austin: University of Texas Press, 1938-1943.

Barnard, Joseph H. *Dr. J. H. Barnard's Journal.* Hobart Huson, ed. Refugio (or Goliad): 1949.

Barnes, Will C. *Arizona Place Names.* Tucson: University of Arizona Press, 1935; reprint, 1960, 1988.

Bartlett, John R. *Personal Narrative of Explorations and Incidents in Texas, New Mexico, California, Sonora, and Chihuahua Connected with the United States and Mexican Boundary Commission During the Years 1850, 1851, 1852, and 1853.* 2 vols. New York: 1854.

Bedichek, Roy. *Karánkaway Country.* New York: Doubleday, 1950.

Brown, John Henry. *History of Texas 1685-1892.* 2 vols. St. Louis: L. E. Daniell, 1892.

Browne, J. Ross. *Adventures in the Apache Country.* New York: Harper & Brothers, 1869.

Brownell, Elizabeth. *They Lived in Tubac.* Tucson, Arizona: Westernlore Press, 1986.

Caillot, E. *Histoire de la Polynesie Orientale.* 1910.

Carvajal, Luís de [the Younger]. *The Enlightened: The Writings of Luis de Carvajal, el Mozo.* Edited and translated by Seymour B. Liebman. Coral Gables: University of Miami Press, 1967.

Castañeda, Carlos Eduardo. *Our Catholic Heritage in Texas 1519-1936.* Vol. 6: "The Fight for Freedom 1810-1836." Austin: Von Boeckmann-Jones, 1936-1950; reprint, New York: Arno Press, 1976. Chicano Heritage Series.

————, ed. and trans. *The Mexican Side of the Texas Revolution, by the Chief Mexican Participants.* Dallas: P. L. Turner, 1928 and 1956; 2nd edition, Austin: Graphic Ideas, 1970.

Chabot, Frederick C. *With the Makers of San Antonio: Genealogies of the Early Latin, Anglo-American and German Families, With Occasional Biographies.* San Antonio: Artes Graficas, 1937.

Chanin, Abe and Mildred, comps. *This Land, These Voices: A Different View of Arizona History in the Words of Those Who Lived It.* Flagstaff: Northland Press, 1977; reprint, Tucson: Midbar Press, 1988.

Cohen, Martin A. *The Martyr: The Story of a Secret Jew and the Mexican Inquisition in the Sixteenth Century.* Philadelphia: Jewish Publication Society of America, 1973.

Day, James M., Richard G. Santos and others. *Battles of Texas.* Waco: Texian Press, 1967.

DeCordova, Jacob. *Texas, Her Resources and Her Public Men.* Philadelphia: J. B. Lippincott, 1858.

De la Peña, José Enrique. *With Santa Anna in Texas.* College Station: Texas A&M University Press, 1975.

Dillon, Richard, ed. *Texas Argonauts: Isaac Duval and the California Gold Rush.* San Francisco: Book Club of California, 1987.

Dobie, J. Frank. *Coronado's Children: Tales of Lost Mines and Buried Treasures of the Southwest.* New York: Grosset and Dunlap, 1930.

Duaine, Carl L. *Caverns of Oblivion.* See Alonso de León, *Historia*, 1649.

Duval, John Crittenden. *Early Times in Texas.* Austin: H. P. N. Gammel & Co., 1892. Reprints: *The Story of an Escape from the Massacre at Goliad.* Houston: Union National Bank, 1927; Austin: Steck, 1935; Dallas: Tardy, 1936, edited by Mabel Major and Rebecca W. Smith; Lincoln: University of Nebraska Press, 1986.

Ehrenberg, Herman. *Texas Und Seine Revolution* [Texas and its Revolution]. Leipzig: Otto Wigand, 1843.

Other editions:

————. *Der Freiheitskampf in Texas im Jahre 1836* [The Fight for Freedom in Texas in the year 1836]. Leipzig: Otto Wigand, 1844.

————. *Fahrten und Schicksale Eines Deutschen in Texas* [Travels and Ordeals of a German in Texas]. Leipzig: Otto Wigand, 1845.

————. *With Milam and Fannin: Adventures of a German Boy in Texas' Revolution.* Translated by Charlotte Churchill. Edited by Henry Nash Smith. Illustrated by Jerry Bywaters. Dallas: Tardy, 1935; reprint, Austin: Pemberton Press, 1968.

Emory, William H. *Report on the United States and Mexican Boundary Survey*. 2 vols. Washington, D.C.: A. O. P. Nicholson, printer, 1857-1859; reprint, Austin: Texas State Historical Association, 1987.

Farish, Thomas Edwin. *History of Arizona*. Vol. 2. Phoenix: Thomas E. Farish, 1915.

Farquhar, Francis. *Books of the Colorado River and Grand Canyon: A Selective Bibliography*. Austin: W. M. Morrison Books, 1991.

Field, Joseph E. [Dr.]. *Three Years in Texas*. Greenfield, Mass.: Justin Jones, 1836.

Frémont, John C. *Exploring Expedition of the Rocky Mountains, Oregon and California*. Buffalo: Derby, Orton and Mulligan, 1853.

Friedrichs, Irene Homann. *History of Goliad*. Victoria, Texas: Regal Printers, 1961.

Friend, Llerena Beaufort. *Sam Houston, The Great Designer*. Austin: University of Texas Press, 1954.

Garber, Paul Neff. *The Gadsden Treaty*. Philadelphia: University of Pennsylvania Press, 1923; reprint, Gloucester, Mass.: Peter Smith, 1959.

Garrett, Julia Kathryn. *Green Flag Over Texas: A Story of the Last Years of Spain in Texas*. New York: Cordova, 1939.

Gleizal, Christian. *Dictionnaire Illustré de la Polynésie, Vol. 3: Tahiti*. Edited by F. Merceron. Tahiti: Editions de L'Alizé, 1988.

Goetzmann, William H. *Army Exploration in the American West*. New Haven: Yale University Press, 1959; reprint, Lincoln: University of Nebraska Press, 1979.

————. *Exploration and Empire: The Explorer and the Scientist in the Winning of the American West*. New York: Alfred A. Knopf, 1966.

Goff, John S. *Arizona Territorial Officials, III: The Delegates to Congress 1863-1912*. Cave Creek, Arizona: Black Mountain Press, 1985.

Goldwater, Barry. *Delightful Journey Down the Green and Colorado Rivers*. Tempe: Arizona Historical Foundation, 1970.

———— *Arizona*. Deerfield: Trade Winds Publishers, 1988.

Grand Canyon of Arizona, Being a Book of Words from Many Pens About the Grand Canyon of the Colorado River in Arizona. Santa Fe Railway Co., 1902.

Greene, A. C. *900 Miles on the Butterfield Trail*. Denton: University of North Texas Press, 1994.

Gulick, Charles Adams, Jr., Harriet Smither, et al., eds. *The Papers of Mirabeau Buonaparte Lamar*. 6 vols. Austin: Texas State Library, 1920-27; reprint, Austin: Pemberton Press, 1968.

Henry, Teuira. *Ancient Tahiti*. Honolulu: 1928; reprint, Paris, France: *Tahiti Aux Temps Anciens*, 1951.

Hinton, R.J. *Handbook to Arizona*. San Francisco: 1878; reprint, Glorieta, N.M.: Rio Grande Press, 1970.

Holley, Mary Austin. *Texas: Observations historical, geographical and descriptive, in a series of letters, written during a visit to Austin's Colony, With a view to a permanent settlement in that colony in the autumn of 1831*. Baltimore: Armstrong & Plaskitt, 1833.

Huson, Hobart. *El Copano: Ancient Port of Bexar and La Bahía*. Refugio, Texas: Refugio Timely Remarks, 1935.

————. *Refugio: A Comprehensive History of Refugio County from Aboriginal Times to 1953.* 2 vols. Woodsboro, Texas: Rooke Foundation, 1953, 1955.

————. *Captain Phillip Dimmitt's Commandancy of Goliad, 1833-1836: An Episode of the Mexican Federalist War in Texas, Usually Referred to as the Texian Revolution.* Austin: Von Boeckmann-Jones, 1974.

James, Marquis. *The Raven: A Biography of Sam Houston.* Indianapolis: Bobbs-Merrill, 1929.

Jenkins, John H. *Basic Texas Books: An Annotated Bibliography of Selected Works for a Research Library.* Austin: Texas State Historical Association, 1983.

Johnson, Charles G. *A History of the Territory of Arizona and the Great Colorado of the Pacific.* San Francisco: Privately published, 1868.

Kemp, Louis Wiltz. *Signers of the Texas Declaration of Independence.* Houston: Anson Jones Press, 1944.

Korn, Bertram Wallace. *The Early Jews of New Orleans.* Waltham, Mass.: American Jewish Historical Society, 1969.

Kurutz, Gary F. *Western Americana in the California State Library.* Sacramento: California State Library Foundation, 1985.

Lack, Paul D. *The Texas Revolutionary Experience: A Political and Social History 1835-1836.* College Station: Texas A&M University Press, 1992.

Lamar, Howard Roberts. *The Far Southwest 1846-1912: A Territorial History.* New Haven: Yale University Press, 1966.

Liebman, Seymour B. *A Guide to Jewish References in the Mexican Colonial Era 1521-1821.* Philadelphia: University of Pennsylvania Press, 1964.

Lockwood, Frank C. *Pioneer Days in Arizona, from the Spanish Occupation to Statehood.* New York: Macmillan, 1932.

McDonald, Archie P. See Sterne, Nicholas Adolphus. *Diary.*

————. *Travis.* Austin: Pemberton Press, 1976.

Miller, Thomas Lloyd. *Bounty and Donation Land Grants of Texas 1835-1888.* Austin: University of Texas Press, 1967.

Mitchell, Mary Agnes. *The First Flag of Texas Independence.* Refugio, Texas: 1937.

Monagham, Jay, ed. *The Book of the American West.* New York: Julian Messner, 1963.

Morgan, Abel. *An Account of the Battle of Goliad and Fanning's [sic] Massacre: And the Capture and Imprisonment of Abel Morgan, Written by Himself.* 1847. Reprint in Kathryn O'Connor, *Presidio La Bahía.*

Murbarger, Nell. *Ghosts of the Adobe Walls.* Los Angeles: Westernlore Press, 1964.

Myers, John M. I, *Jack Swilling: Founder of Phoenix, Arizona.* New York: Hastings House, 1961.

Nevin, David and the Editors of Time-Life Books. *The Old West: The Texans.* New York: Time-Life Books, 1975; reprint, 1982.

Newell, Chester. *History of the Revolution in Texas, Particularly of the War of 1835 & '36; Together with the Latest Geographical, Topographical, and Statistical Accounts of the Country, . . .* New York: Wiley & Putnam, 1838.

North, Diane M. T. See Rose-North, Diane M. T.

O'Connor, Kathryn Stoner. *Presidio La Bahía del Espiritu Santo de Zuñiga 1721-1846.* Austin: Von Boeckmann-Jones, 1966.

O'Reilly, Patrick. Pomare, *Queen of Tahiti*. Paris: Société des Océanistes, 1972.

O'Reilly, Patrick and Raoul Teissier. *Tahitiens: Répertoire biographique de la Polynésie Francaise*. Paris: Société des Océanistes, 1975.

Ornish, Natalie. *Pioneer Jewish Texans: Their Impact on Texas and American History for Four Hundred Years 1590-1990*. Dallas: Texas Heritage Press, 1989.

Paul, Rodman Wilson. *Mining Frontiers of the Far West 1848-1880*. New York: Holt, Rinehart and Winston, 1963.

Pearson, Jim B., Ben Procter, William B. Conroy, Ron Tyler, Annette La Freniere, Jimmye Hays, Larry Hodge, Sharline Lavender, and Richard Sorensen. *Texas, The Land and Its People*. Dallas: Hendrick-Long, 1987.

Petrick, Neila Skinner. *Jane Long 1798-1880*. Austin: Prime Time Press, 1995.

Pennybacker, Anna J. H. *A New History of Texas*. Austin: Privately published, 1900.

Poston, Charles D. *Apache-Land*. San Francisco: A. L. Bancroft, 1878.

Pritchard, George. *Queen Pomare and Her Country*. London: Elliot Stock, 1879.

Pruett, Jackie, ed. *History and Heritage of Goliad County*. Goliad County Historical Commission, 1983.

Pumpelly, Raphael. *Across America and Asia*. New York: Leypoldt & Holt, 1870.

Ratcliffe, Sam DeShong. *Painting Texas History to 1900*. Austin: University of Texas Press, 1992.

Richardson, Thomas Clarence. *East Texas, Its History and Its Makers*. 4 vols. New York: Lewis Historical Publishing Co., 1940.

Riva Palacio, Vicente and Rafael Payno. *El Libro Rojo, 1520-1867*. Mexico City: Diaz de Leon y White, 1870.

Roell, Craig H. *Remember Goliad!* Austin: Texas State Historical Association, publisher, in cooperation with the Center for Studies in Texas History at the University of Texas at Austin, 1994.

Roemer, Ferdinand von. *Texas, with Particular Reference to German Immigration and the Physical Appearance of the Country*. Tr. by Oswald Mueller. San Antonio: Standard Printing, 1935.

Rose, Victor M. *Some Historical Facts in Regard to the Settlement of Victoria, Texas*. Laredo: Daily Times, 1883; reprint, San Antonio: Lone Star, 1961.

Rose-North, Diane M.T. *Samuel Peter Heintzelman and the Sonora Exploring and Mining Company*. Tucson: University of Arizona Press, 1980.

Russell, Robert P. *La Paz County*. Vol. 4: *"History."* Tucson: University of Arizona Press, 1986.

Santa Anna, Antonio López de and General José Urrea. See Castañeda, Carlos E.

Santos, Richard G. *Santa Anna's Campaign Against Texas 1835-1836*. Waco: Texian Press, 1968; reprint, Documentary Publications, 1982.

Schweizer, Niklaus R. *Hawai'i and the German Speaking Peoples*. Honolulu: Topgallant Publishing Ltd.

Seguin, Juan Angel, A. Navarro, and others. ...*Manifestando Los Males Que Aflijen Los Pueblos de Texas...* Brazoria, Texas: D. W. Anthony, 1833. See Weber, David, ed., *Troubles in Texas*.

Soulé, Frank, John H. Gihon and James Nisbet. *The Annals of San Francisco, containing a summary of the first discovery, settlement, progress, and present condition of*

California... New York: D. Appleton and Co., 1855; later edition comp. by Dorothy H. Huggins, Palo Alto: Lewis Osborne, 1966.

Sterne, Nicholas Adolphus. Archie P. McDonald, ed. *Hurrah for Texas! The Diary of Adolphus Sterne.* Waco: Texian Press, 1969.

Streeter, Thomas W. *Bibliography of Texas 1795-1845.* 5 vols. Cambridge: Harvard University Press, 1955-60; 2nd edition, Woodbridge, Conn.: Research Publications, 1983.

Taylor, Bayard. *El Dorado, or, Adventures in the Path of Empire, Comprising a Voyage to California via Panama, Life in San Francisco and Monterey, Pictures of a Gold Region, and Experiences of Mexican Travel.* London: George Routledge, 1850. Many other reprints include New York: G. P. Putnam, 1850; Knopf, 1949; Glorieta, N.M.: Rio Grande Press, 1967.

Thrall, Homer S. *Pictorial History of Texas: From the Earliest Visits of European Adventurers to A.D. 1879.* St. Louis: N. D. Thompson, 1879.

Thrapp, Dan L. *Encyclopedia of Frontier Biography.* Vol. 1. Spokane, Washington: Arthur H. Clark, 1990.

Tyler, Ron, editor-in-chief, Douglas E. Barnett, managing ed., Roy R. Barkley, ed., Penelope C. Anderson and Mark F. Odintz, assoc. eds. *The New Handbook of Texas.* Austin: Texas State Historical Association, 1996.

Urrea, Jose. *Diario de las operaciones militares . . . la campana de Tejas.* Victoria de Durango: Manuel Gonzales, 1838.

Vigness, David M. *The Revolutionary Decades, 1810-1836.* Austin: Steck, 1965.

Wagoner, Jay J. *Early Arizona: Prehistory to Civil War.* Tucson: University of Arizona Press, 1975.

Walker, Henry P. and Don Bufkin. *Historical Atlas of Arizona.* Norman: University of Oklahoma Press, 1979, 1986.

Ward, Henry G., ed. *Brief Description of the Arivaca Estate in the Territory of Arizona, United States of America.* London: Charles Carter.

Webb, Walter Prescott. *The Great Plains.* Boston: Ginn, 1931; reprint, New York: Grosset & Dunlap, 1957.

————. *The Great Frontier.* Boston: Houghton Mifflin, 1952; reprint, Austin: University of Texas Press, 1964.

Weber, David J. *The Mexican Frontier 1821-1846: The American Southwest Under Mexico.* Albuquerque: University of New Mexico Press, 1982.

————. *The Spanish Frontier in North America.* New Haven: Yale University Press, 1992.

————, ed. *Troubles in Texas 1832: A Tejano Viewpoint from San Antonio.* Dallas: Wind River Press for DeGolyer Library, Southern Methodist University, 1983.

Weems, John Edward with Jane Weems. *Dream of Empire: A Human History of the Republic of Texas 1836-1846.* New York: Simon & Schuster, 1971.

Wharton, Clarence R. *Remember Goliad.* Houston: McCurdy-Young, 1931; reprint, Glorieta, N.M.: Rio Grande Press, 1968.

————. *Texas Under Many Flags.* Vol. 1: *The Spanish Goldhunters to the Great Drama of Annexation 1518-1846.* 5 vols. Chicago and New York: American Historical Society, 1930.

Wheat, Carl I. *Maps of the California Gold Region 1848-1857.* San Francisco: Grabhorn, 1942.

Wooten, Dudley G. *A Complete History of Texas*. Dallas: William G. Scarff, 1899.

Wyllys, Rufus K. Arizona: *The History of a Frontier State*. Phoenix: Hobson and Herr, 1950.

Yoakum, Henderson K. *History of Texas, From Its First Settlement in 1685 to Its Annexation to the United States in 1846*. 2 vols. New York: J. S. Redfield, 1855; reprint, Austin: Steck, n.d.

Young, Kevin. *Texas Forgotten Heroes*. Goliad, Texas: Goliad County Historical Commission, 1986.

PERIODICALS, MANUSCRIPTS, ARCHIVAL MATERIALS

Adler, Cyrus. "Trial of Jorge de Almeida by the Inquisition in Mexico," *American Jewish Historical Quarterly* 4 (1896): 29-79.

Alta California, San Francisco. See *Daily Alta California*.

Archives, Comptroller's Military Service Records, Texas State Library, Austin.

"The Arizona Boundary Survey Completed." *San Francisco Weekly Chronicle,* October 6, 1855.

Arizona Citizen, Tucson, August 7, 1875, [p. 3: col. 4].

Arizona Historical Foundation, Goldwater Collection, Hayden Library, Arizona State University, Tempe.

Arizona Historical Review, Phoenix, April 1928.

Arizona Historical Review, Phoenix, January 1930.

Arizona Miner, Prescott, May 9, 1866, [3:1].

Arizona Miner, May 23, 1866, [3:1].

Arizona Miner, October 23, 1866, [2:1].

Arizona Miner, October 24, 1866, [1:2].

Arizona Miner, October 27, 1866, [2:5].

Arizona Miner, October 30, 1866, [4:3].

Arizona Miner, November 10, 1866, [2:6 and 3:1].

Arizona Miner, April 6, 1867 [1:1].

Arizona Miner, August 14, 1869, [2:3].

"Arizona Places Honors Pioneer H. Ehrenberg," *Arizona Republic*, March 8, 1959.

Arizona Sentinel, February 23, 1878, [1:4].

Arizona Sentinel, October 10, 1891, [3:2].

Arizona Silver Belt, August 22, 1907, [2:2].

Arizonian, Tubac, March 3, 1859.

Arizonian, April 14, 1859, [3:3].

Arizonian, July 7, 1859, [3:1].

Barker Texas History Center, Vertical Files, University of Texas at Austin.

Bartholomae, Edgar William. "A Translation of H. Ehrenberg's *Fahrten und Schicksale Eines Deutschen in Texas,* with Introduction and Notes." Master's thesis, University of Texas at Austin, 1925.

Benson, Nettie Lee. "The Provisional Deputation in Mexico." Ph.D. diss., University of Texas at Austin, 1949.

———. "Texas as Viewed from Mexico, 1820-1834," *Southwestern Historical Quarterly* 90 (January 1987).

Nettie Lee Benson Special Collections, University of Texas at Austin.

Bishop Museum Library, Honolulu, Hawaii.

Bisbee Daily Review, May 23, 1907, [2:3].

Bolton, Herbert Eugene. "The Spanish Occupation of Texas 1519-1590," *Texas State Historical Association Quarterly* 16: 11-12.

————. Papers. Item 505, 1582-1602. Documents relating to the exploration of New Mexico which include correspondence of Gaspar Castaño de Sosa. Source: Archivo General de Indias, Sevilla, Spain. Bancroft Library, University of California, Berkeley.

Bolton, W. W. "The Boy-King of Tahiti and his Crowning," *P.I.M.*, June-July 1937, pp. 45-46; April 1938, pp. 17-19.

"The Bridge at Old Ferry Point is Considered," *Arizona Republic*, April 18, 1925.

Brunckow, Frederick. See Ehrenberg "Letter" in *Report*, 1859.

California Academy of Natural Science Proceedings, 3 (1863-1867), p. 50.

Carvajal Collection, Archives of the American Jewish Historical Society, Waltham, Mass.

Carvajal, Luís de [the Younger]. *The Enlightened: The Writings of Luís de Carvajal, el Mozo*. Ed. and tr. by S. B. Liebman. Coral Gables: University of Miami Press, 1967.

————. "Autobiography" and "Letters and Last Will and Testament," in *The Jewish Experience in Latin America* by Martin A. Cohen. New York: KTAV, 1971.

Castañeda, Carlos E. Department of History, University of Texas at Austin. Letter to Dr. B. Sacks, January 21, 1955. Arizona Historical Foundation, Tempe.

Castaño de Sosa, Gaspar. Collection. Bancroft Library, University of California, Berkeley.

Center for American History, Special Collections, University of Texas at Austin.

Cohen, Martin A. "The Religion of Luis Rodriguez Carvajal: Glimpses into the Passion of a Mexican Judaizer." *American Jewish Archives*, April 1968.

Craig, Robert D. "Pomare Family," *Historical Dictionary of Oceania*: 243-244, 281. Westport, Conn. and London, England: Greenwood Press, 1981.

Daily Alta California, San Francisco, February 17, 1854.

Daily Alta California, October 18, 1866, [2:1-2].

Daily Alta California, October 31, 1866, [1:2].

Daily Arizona Miner, Prescott. See Arizona Miner.

Daily Evening Bulletin, San Francisco, June 24, 1859, [3:5].

Davenport, Harbert. "The Men of Goliad," *Southwestern Historical Quarterly* 43 (July, 1939): 1-141.

————. "James W. Fannin's Part in the Texas Revolution." Ms., Harbert Davenport Papers, Center for American History, University of Texas at Austin.

Day, James M., Richard G. Santos and others. "Goliad" in *Battles of Texas,* 25-48. Waco: Texian Press, 1967.

DeGolyer Library, Special Collections, Southern Methodist University, Dallas, Texas.

De Leon, Arnoldo. "Tejanos and the Texas War for Independence: Historiography's Judgment," *New Mexico Historical Review* 61 (April 1986).

Ehrenberg, Emil [Teplitz, Bohemia]. Letter to the "Proprietor of the station 'Dos Pal-mas' between San Bernardino and La Paz and Ehrenberg, on the Colorado, Cali-fornia." Goldwater Collection, Arizona Historical Foundation, Tempe.

Ehrenberg, Herman. "Letter to Ashbel Smith in Paris, *chargé d'affaires*, Republic of Texas," Feb. 9, 1844. Ashbel Smith Papers, Texas State Archives, Austin.

——————. "Exploration of Trinity River," *Placer Times*, May 27, 1850, [4:3].

————. "Letter from Herman Ehrenberg to Col. Charles D. Poston," (pp. 39-47). Appendix in: Brunckow, Frederick. *Report to a Committee of the Stockholders of the Sonora Exploring & Mining Co. upon the History, Resources, and Prospects of the Company in Arizona.* Cincinnati: Railroad Record, 1859.

————. Land document No. 274 in Texas State Library: HR/3 League, Filed Aug. 10, 1838 by T. Girano; Registered March 4, 1859; Withdrawn and approved Feb. 14, 1860 by Jacob DeCordova.

————. Letter to unidentified Los Angeles resident regarding five mining localities, *Los Angeles Star*, November 8, 1862, [2:2].

————. "Report on the 'Colorado' Vein, Arizona," *Los Angeles Star*, January 31, 1863, [2:3].

————. "The Mining Districts in the Colorado Valley," *Daily Alta California*, San Francisco, May 22, 1863, [2:1-2].

————. Letter to the editor, *Daily Alta California*, May 25, 1863, [1:5].

————. "Letter to Governor Goodwin, 1864," *Arizona Historical Review* 7, no. 3 (July, 1936):88-89. University of Arizona, with Arizona Pioneers Historical Society.

————. "Map of the Klamath Gold Region," *New York Historical Society Quarterly* 47, no. 4 (October 1963): 387.

The Friend, Honolulu, Oahu, Sandwich Islands [Hawaii], June 12, 1845.

The Friend, Honolulu, Oahu, Sandwich Islands [Hawaii], October 1, 1845.

Garver, Lois. "Benjamin Rush Milam," *Southwestern Historical Quarterly* 38 (1934-35).

"Good Old Times on the Colorado," *Tucson Post,* May 18, 1907.

Gray, Paul. "A Fight over Liquid Gold: The Colorado, The West's Lifeline is Now Arizona's Most-Endangered River." *Time*, (July 22, 1991), 138, no. 3, 20-26.

Greer, Richard A. "California Gold: Some Reports to Hawaii," *Hawaiian Journal of History*, Hawaiian Historical Society. 4 (1970): 157, 172-173.

Hachette Pacific Library Special Collections, Papeete, Tahiti, French Polynesia.

Hatcher, Mattie Austin. "Letters of Antonio Martinez, the Last Spanish Governor of Texas, 1817-1822," *Southwestern Historical Quarterly* 39 (1935-1936).

Hawaii State Library, Special Collections, Honolulu, Hawaii.

Hayden, Carl [U.S. Senate]. "Herman Ehrenberg." 2-page typescript, California State Library, Sacramento, 1940.

Hull, Dorothy. "Castaño de Sosa's Expedition to New Mexico in 1590," *Old Santa Fe*, 3 (October 1916), 307-32.

Huntington Library; Western American, Manuscript, and Rare Book Collections; San Marino, California.

Huson, Hobart. "Colonel Fannin's Execution of General Houston's Orders to Evacu-ate Goliad." Ms., Center for American History, University of Texas at Austin.

"Inquisition in Mexico, Auto de Fe 1590: Trial of Luís De Carabajal, Governor of the Province of Nuevo León, for Observing the Law of Moses." Original manuscript and tr. from *Inquisition Vol. 1487*, Mexican National Archives, 1927. Tr. by A. J. Baker and A. M. Blake for G.R.G. Conway, Mexico City. Archives of the American Jewish Historical Society, Waltham, Mass.

La Paz, Arizona, Claims and Deeds. Book 1: October 6, 1862 - March 4, 1863. Office of County Recorder, Yuma County, Arizona, January 21, 1863, p. 92.

Liebman, S. B. "The Abecedario and a Check-list of Mexican Inquisition Documents at the Henry E. Huntington Library," *Hispanic American Historical Review* 44 (1964): 554-67.

Lockwood, Frank C. "Native German; Early Leader in Southwest," *Dallas Morning News*, February 11, 1940.

Los Angeles Star, March 19, 1864, [2:5].

Manoa Library Special Collections, University of Hawaii.

"The Mining Districts in the Colorado Valley," *Daily Alta California*, May 22, 1863.

"The Murder of Herman Ehrenberg," *Daily Alta California*, October 13, 1866, [2:1-2].

Musée de Tahiti et des iles Special Collections, Punaauia, Tahiti.

National Archives and Records Administration, Washington, D.C.

National Archives, Southwest Region, Fort Worth, Texas.

"New Route to Walker's Diggings: Expedition led by Ehrenberg accomplished finding a new route from La Paz to Weaver and Walker mines 80 miles shorter," *Mining and Scientific Press,* 8, no. 4, (January 30, 1864), [67:2].

O'Reilly, Patrick. "Iconographie de Pomare, Reine de Tahiti," *Bulletin du vieux paper*, January 1963.

Pacific News, May 1850.

Papers of the Hawaiian Historical Society, no. 20, read before the Society November 18, 1938. Honolulu, March, 1939, pp. 9-10.

Passenger list of the schooner, *General Kearney*, June, 1847. Public Archives of the University of Hawaii, Honolulu.

Phoenix Enterprise, October 21, 1902, [8:4].

The Pioneer, San Jose, California, December 20, 1899.

Poston, Charles Debrille. "Herman Ehrenberg: In Memoriam," *Arizona Daily Star,* Tucson, February 19, 1880; reprinted in *Arizona Historical Review* 2, no. 4 (January, 1930): 25-27, published quarterly by Arizona State Historian, Phoenix.

Quarterly of the California Historical Society, 12, pp. 4, 16-17.

Harry Ransom Humanities Research Center, University of Texas at Austin.

Reports of the Commissioner of Indian Affairs, 1864: 302.

Reports of the Commissioner of Indian Affairs, 1865: 306-307.

Reports of the Commissioner of Indian Affairs, 1866: 108, 110.

Rogers, Lynn J. "Ghost Town of Ehrenberg Once Thriving River Port," *Los Angeles Times*, February 23, 1936.

Rose [North], Diane M. T. "The Maps, Plans, and Sketches of Herman Ehrenberg," *Prologue: The Journal of the National Archives*, 9, no. 3 (Fall 1977): 162-170.

Ryan, Vincent. "The Murder of Ehrenberg," *Daily Alta California*, October 31, 1866, [1:2].

Sacks, B[enjamin], "Be It Enacted: The Creation of the Territory of Arizona." Phoenix: Arizona Historical Foundation, 1964. An expansion of a two-part article originally published in *Arizona and the West*, 5, no. 1 and 2 (1964): 46-54 and 97-109.

———. "Herman Ehrenberg, 1816-1866." Transcript of speech to the Arizona Historical Foundation. Goldwater Special Collection, Hayden Library, Arizona State University, Tempe.

San Francisco City Directory, 1854 Edition.

San Francisco City Directory, 1863 Edition.

San Francisco City Directory, 1864 Edition.

San Francisco City Directory, 1865 Edition.

Schmidt, Louis B. "Manifest Opportunity and the Gadsden Purchase," *Arizona and the West* 3 (Autumn 1961).

Schmitt, R. C. "Some Firsts in Island Business," *Hawaiian Journal of History*, 14 (1980): 99.

Smith, Ruby Cumby. "James W. Fannin, Jr., in the Texas Revolution," *Southwestern Historical Quarterly* 23 (1919-1920).

Smither, Harriet, ed., "Diary of Adolphus Sterne," *Southwestern Historical Quarterly*, 31 (1927-28).

Southwest Review 20 (July 1935): 371.

Telegraph and Texas Register, November 9, 1836.

Texas General Land Office Archives, Austin, Texas.

Texas State Library and Archives, Austin, Texas.

Tucson Post, May 18, 1907.

Von Schweinitz, Helga. "Hermann [sic] Ehrenberg — Fighting for Texas," *True West,* April 1986.

Weber, David. "Mexico's Far Northern Frontier, 1821-1845," *Arizona and the West* 19 (Autumn 1977): 225-66.

———. "Failure of a Frontier Institution: The secular church in the borderlands under independent Mexico, 1821-1846," *Western Historical Quarterly* 12 (April 1981), 125-143.

———. "American Westward Expansion and the Breakdown of Relations Between Pobladores and 'Indios Bárbaros' on Mexico's Far Northern Frontier, 1821-1846," *New Mexico Historical Review* 56 (July 1981): 221-238.

Weekly Arizona Miner. See *Arizona Miner*.

Weekly Arizonian. See *Arizonian*.

White, Nell. "Goliad in the Texas Revolution." M.A. thesis, University of Houston, 1941.

Woodward, Arthur. "Herman Ehrenberg: Seeker of High Adventure," *Desert* magazine, El Centro, California, December 1938, pp. 9-11, 29.

W.P.A. Manuscript and Biography files. Department of Library, Archives, and Public Records; State of Arizona Library; Phoenix.

Zuber, W. P. "Captain Adolphus Sterne," *Quarterly of the Texas State Historical Association,* 2 (1898-99).

TRANSLATOR OF BOOK II

Peter Mollenhauer

Cover design and special pages by Monty Matthews
Book design by Dianne Nelson, Shadow Canyon Graphics
The "Goddess of Liberty" was sculpted by Raoul Jossett.
Printed in U.S.A.

ABOUT THE AUTHOR
OF BOOK I

Born on the island of Galveston, Natalie Ornish at age 14 enrolled in Sam Houston State University, where she received the B.A. degree in English at age 17. At 18, she was the youngest person to receive a Master's degree from Northwestern University.

Ornish then worked for The Associated Press in Chicago and Omaha. She has served as contributing editor for many magazines. In Dallas, she wrote for Rogers and Smith Advertising. She became one of the nation's first female film producers.

Ornish has done extensive lecturing and writing on early Texas history. A previous book by Natalie Ornish received two national awards and merited an illustrated, excellent review in the *New York Times Book Review*. She researched and wrote more than sixty biographies for *The New Handbook of Texas*.

She is listed in *Who's Who of American Women, Who's Who in World Jewry,* and *Foremost Women in Communications.* She has been interviewed widely on radio and television.